"If love is God's primary attribute, why do theologians shun the topic? Perhaps they're embarrassed that discussions of love are often superficial and simplistic, more emotional than reasonable. Not so here. Tom Oord's rigorous survey of the scientific data and philosophical resources breathes new life into the study of theology's central topic. A must read."

—**Philip Clayton**, Ingraham Professor,
Claremont School of Theology

"By focusing on the theme of love, Thomas Oord's impressive book provides a refreshing example of how to connect the insights of science to the visions of religion and theology. This informed and readable work deserves a wide readership. Strongly recommended."

—**John F. Haught**, senior fellow, Woodstock Theological Center,
Georgetown University

"Tom Oord has been on the cutting edge of interdisciplinary research on love for many years. This book represents his most comprehensive contribution to date. Newcomers to the science and religion dialogue on altruism and related themes will appreciate the clarity of his definitions and his overview of the issues. Longtime participants in this dialogue will appreciate the creativity and courage of his controversial proposal for a 'theology of love' informed by the social and natural sciences. Sure to generate discussion in both the church and the academy!"

—**F. LeRon Shults**, professor of theology and philosophy,
University of Agder, Norway

"This book is a thorough-going and wide-ranging effort to place 'love' on the world map by examining cosmology, biology, psychology, social science, interpersonal love, and Christian agape. Oord knows the issues and the sources and is a sure-footed guide in dealing with them. Who are we, and what ought we to do? Oord's vision is that we are placed on Earth with inexhaustible opportunities to love. That makes an examined life worth living. Indeed, that makes life divine."

—**Holmes Rolston III**, University Distinguished Professor,
Colorado State University

Defining
LOVE

A Philosophical, Scientific, and Theological Engagement

THOMAS JAY OORD

BrazosPress
a division of Baker Publishing Group
Grand Rapids, Michigan

© 2010 by Thomas Jay Oord

Published by Brazos Press
a division of Baker Publishing Group
P.O. Box 6287, Grand Rapids, MI 49516-6287
www.brazospress.com

Printed in the United States of America

Library of Congress Cataloging-in-Publication Data
Oord, Thomas Jay.
    Defining love : a philosophical, scientific, and theological engagement /
Thomas Jay Oord.
        p.   cm.
    Includes bibliographical references and indexes.
    ISBN 978-1-58743-257-6 (pbk.)
    1. Love—Religious aspects—Christianity. 2. Religion and science. 3. Love. I.
Title.
BV4639.O628 2010
128'.46—dc22   2009048794

10   11   12   13   14   15   16   7   6   5   4   3   2   1

In Memory of My Father
Eugene H. Oord

Contents

Acknowledgments

Many people encouraged and invested in this project. Here are some who deserve special words of appreciation and acknowledgment.

I thank Stephen Post and the Institute for Research on Unlimited Love for helping with many aspects of this book. Post not only offered encouragement throughout the process but also kindly provided funding for some parts of the writing and research. Stephen and I codirected an Altruism Course Competition, and that experience solidified in me the need for this book. The Flame of Love project that Stephen codirected with Margaret Poloma also deserves my thanks for its inspiration. Stephen has been a supportive friend in many ways, and I extend my deepest appreciation to him.

I thank the John Templeton Foundation for its financial and ideological encouragement. The foundation generously provided funding for research during my sabbatical period. I especially thank Paul Wason and Drew Rick-Miller. I am grateful to the late Sir John Templeton for his belief that studying love from a variety of perspectives is among the most important endeavors of humanity.

My home institution, Northwest Nazarene University, supported me throughout the writing of this book, including providing sabbatical support for some of the research. I thank my friends, colleagues, and assistants at NNU for their support, including Jay Akkerman, David Alexander, Donna Allen, Joe Bankard, Ben Boeckel, Wendell

Bowes, Sharon Bull, Randy Bynum, Rhonda Carrim, Randy Craker, Ed Crawford, Samuel Dunn, Shemia Fagan, Fred Fullerton, Mark Gismondi, Darrin Grinder, Richard Hagood, Dana Hicks, Jeremy Hugus, Jill Jones, Mike Kipp, Diane Leclerc, George Lyons, Brian Mackey, Mark Maddix, April McNeice, Steve Mountjoy, Ralph Neil, Malloree Norris, Brent Peterson, Ron Ponsford, Mark Pitts, Jim Rotz, Astin Salisbury, Gene Schandorff, Andrew Schwartz, LeAnn Stensgaard, Julie and Michael Straight, Libby Tedder, Dick Thompson, Kevin Timpe, Tiffany Triplett, Katie Voelker, Gary Waller, and Seth Waltemyer. I thank the undergraduate students in my classes on theology and love, as well as the graduate students who read parts of the manuscript and made suggestions. I also express my appreciation to the Wesley Center for Applied Theology at NNU.

In addition to the people and institutions noted above, many others have helped through face-to-face discussion, by email exchanges, over the phone, and at conferences. Although, unfortunately, I am likely to forget someone who should be mentioned, here are those from whose contributions I have benefited: Wolfgang Achtner, Amy Ai, Paul Allen, Kathy Armistead, Karen Baker-Fletcher, Ian Barbour, Dave Basinger, Dean Blevins, Craig Boyd, Greg Boyd, John Brasch, Dennis Bratcher, John Brooke, Donna Bowman, Warren Brown, Don Browning, Patricia Bruininks, Barry Callen, John Caputo, Anna Case-Winters, Philip Clayton, John Cobb, Rick Colling, Francis Collins, Robin Collins, C. S. Cowles, Tim Crutcher, John Culp, Scott Daniels, Paul Davies, Hans Deventer, Mark Dibben, Celia Deane Drummond, Ray Dunning, Denis Edwards, George Ellis, Stephen C. Evans, Julie Exline, Roland Faber, Darrel Falk, Andy Flescher, Rebecca Flietstra, Steve Franklin, Todd Frye, Tripp Fuller, Karl Giberson, Bill Greathouse, Yudit Greenberg, Niels Gregersen, David Griffin, Christy Gunter-Leppert, Doug Hardy, Bill Hasker, Jack Haught, Andrea Hollingsworth, Curtis Holtzen, Nancy Howell, Tyron Inbody, Tim Jackson, Max Johnson, Kurian Kachappilly, Catherine Keller, Thomas Kelley, Shelley Dean Kilpatrick, Jeff Koperski, David Larson, Matthew Lee, Michael Lodahl, Randy Maddox, Mark Mann, Robert Mann, Bradford McCall, Steve McCormick, Mike McCullough, Jay McDaniel, Dan Messier, Jim Miller, Ken Miller, Jürgen Moltmann, Brint Montgomery, Simon Conway Morris, Craig Morton, Nancey Murphy,

Sam Oliner, Alan Padgett, Tom Phillips, Margaret Poloma, Clark Pinnock, John Polkinghorne, Stephen Pope, Stephen Post, Sam Powell, John Quiring, Kevin Reimer, Alan Rhoda, Rick Rice, Holmes Rolston, John Sanders, Jeff Schloss, Bill Shea, LeRon Shults, Jamie Smith, Chris Southgate, Atle Sovik, Rob Staples, Ross Stein, Paul Steinhardt, Robert Sternberg, Bryan Stone, Brad Strawn, Brent Strawn, Marjorie Suchocki, Rob Thompson, Don Thorsen, Alan Tjeltveit, Lynn Underwood, Ed Vacek, Wentzel Van Huysteen, James Van Slyke, Howard Van Till, Don Viney, Zhihe Wang, Keith Ward, Wes Wildman, David Wilkinson, John Wilson, Karen Winslow, David Woodruff, Dan Worthen, Ev Worthington, Ron Wright, Don Yerxa, Amos Yong, and Dean Zimmerman.

I thank Brazos Press and its staff for their help, especially Rodney Clapp, Jeremy Wells, Rachel Klompmaker, and Jeffery Wittung. Jeff was involved in a car accident just after completing significant editorial work on this book. His death is tragic. I mourn his loss and pray for his family as they struggle with his absence.

Finally, it would be a major oversight were I to omit thanking family members who profoundly shape my views of love. I thank my siblings, John and Carol; my parents-in-law, Ruth and John; my mother, Louise; my children, Andee, Lexi, and Sydnee; and my wife, Cheryl. This book is dedicated to my father, Gene, who passed on to glory during the writing process. I strive to love with the motivational simplicity exhibited by my father. He was a good man.

Preface

Portions of this book, in different form, have appeared previously in a number of venues. The author is grateful for permission to adapt material for parts of this book from the following:

Chapter 1: "The Love Racket: Defining Love and *Agape* for the Love-and-Science Research Program," *Zygon* 40, no. 4 (2005): 919–38; reproduced in *The Altruism Reader: Selections from Writings on Love, Religion, and Science*, ed. Thomas Jay Oord (Philadelphia: Templeton Foundation Press, 2008), 10–30.

Chapter 3: "Social Science Contributions to the Love-and-Science Symbiosis," in *Applied Process Thought I: Initial Explorations in Theory and Research*, ed. Mark Dibben and Thomas Kelly (Frankfurt: Ontos-Verlag, 2008), 315–28.

Chapter 5: "An Open Doctrine of Creation Ex Amore," in *Creation Made Free: Open Theology Engaging Science* (Eugene, OR: Pickstock Press, 2009), 28–52.

Chapter 6: "A Relational God and Unlimited Love," in *Visions of Agapé: Problems and Possibilities in Human and Divine Love*, ed. Craig Boyd (Burlington, VT: Ashgate, 2008), 135–48.

1

Love and the Science-and-Theology Symbiosis

The Love Racket

In 1974, the National Science Foundation awarded Ellen Berscheid and a colleague eighty-four thousand dollars to better answer the question "What is love?" Berscheid convinced the foundation to award the grant by arguing, "We already understand the mating habits of the stickleback fish. It is time to turn to a new species." The species she had in mind was human.

Berscheid's research might have gone unnoticed if not for the response of Wisconsin senator William Proxmire. "I'm strongly against this," exclaimed Proxmire, "not only because no one—not even the National Science Foundation—can argue that falling in love is a science; not only because I am sure that even if they spend eighty-four million or eighty-four billion they wouldn't get an answer that anyone would believe. I'm also against it because I don't *want* to know the answer!" Apparently, ignorance really is bliss.

Proxmire presented Berscheid the first of his "Golden Fleece" awards. He considered the study of love a supreme example of wasteful government spending. Better to spend money on national defense or other such big-ticket matters. Proxmire's advice to those who funded the grant was simple: "National Science Foundation, get out of the love racket!"

A few came to Berscheid's defense. *New York Times* writer James Reston replied that funding grants to study love "would be the best investment of federal money since Jefferson made the Louisiana Purchase."[1] Apparently, Reston's retort fell on deaf ears. Financial resources for the studies of love like the one Berscheid envisioned remained meager. Few scholars would assume the label "love researcher" after the incident.

The idea that scientists ought to study love—not so much love in its romantic sense, but love in its deepest, ultimate sense— found a strong twentieth-century voice in Pitirim A. Sorokin. In addition to his contributions to love research, Sorokin is considered by many the father of modern sociology. He initially came to his convictions about the importance of studying love when jailed as a Russian political prisoner early in the century. After escaping prison, Sorokin immigrated to the United States and eventually accepted a professorship at Harvard University. In 1949, Sorokin founded the Harvard Research Center in Creative Altruism with financial help from Eli Lilly and the Lilly Endowment.

Sorokin published many books. His major contribution to love research is *The Ways and Power of Love: Types, Factors, and Techniques of Moral Transformation*. In the preface he defends the importance of studying love:

> At the present juncture of human history an increase in our knowledge of the grace of love has become the paramount need of humanity, and an intensive research in this field should take precedence over almost all other studies and research. . . . Considering the immensity of this task, [my] contribution is very modest in comparison with the total sum of the necessary studies. Since, however, the better brains are busy with other problems, including the invention of means of extermination of human beings . . . [and] many a religious leader is absorbed in the intertribal crusades against various enemies—under these conditions somebody, somehow, must devote himself to a study of the miracle of love.[2]

1. James Reston, "Proxmire on Love," *New York Times*, March 14, 1975, 39.
2. Pitirim A. Sorokin, *The Ways and Power of Love: Types, Factors, and Techniques of Moral Transformation* (1954; repr., Philadelphia: Templeton Foundation Press, 2002), xii.

Sorokin offers insights into the power of love, suggestions about how love research might be done, and uncannily accurate predictions about what would occur should society neglect love studies. Sorokin's work continues to inspire, and *The Ways and Power of Love* is now considered a classic.[3]

Unfortunately, however, Sorokin's love research faded by the end of the 1950s. He retired from teaching, and his center ran out of funding. Although his own contribution was exemplary, he inspired no immediate followers to carry his love research mantle.[4] The public was still interested in love, of course, but organized research on love from a perspective that integrated science, religion, and philosophy all but vanished.

At the turn of the twenty-first century, organized research on love reemerged. With funding from the John E. Fetzer Institute and the John Templeton Foundation, biologists, ethicists, sociologists, theologians, psychologists, neurologists, philosophers, and medical caregivers conferred at an MIT conference titled "Empathy, Altruism, and Agape." Of course, a few independent scholars had been doing research on and writing about love in the latter half of the twentieth century. Here for the first time, however, scholars from widely diverse disciplines deliberated together on issues and challenges surrounding the study of love.

One outcome of the conference was the establishment of the Institute for Research on Unlimited Love. Stephen G. Post, professor of bioethics, was named the institute's president, and the John Templeton Foundation provided multimillion dollar funding. President Post set several goals for the fledgling institute. He pledged to fund high-level scientific research on altruism and unlimited love. Post set about to sustain a dialogue between science and religion

---

3. For a brief explanation of the importance that *The Ways and Power of Love* has for the contemporary conversation on love research, see Stephen G. Post's introduction to the Templeton Foundation Press reprint edition.

4. Barry Johnston, in his authoritative biography of Sorokin, tells of an anonymous note found in the records kept by Eli Lilly. The note, apparently written by Lilly, reads: "One of the constantly interesting things about Sorokin is that he is an intellectual genius, who has arrived at truth about love and altruism via this route and has wound up his life a bitter old man with no young disciples. His interpreters are all old men, and as he once told me, 'Sorokin will be rediscovered a 100 years hence'" (*Pitirim A. Sorokin: An Intellectual Biography* [Lawrence: University Press of Kansas, 1995], 268).

on love's meaning and significance. The institute endeavored to disseminate true stories of love as it manifests in the helping behaviors of those whose lives are devoted to serving others. And, finally, Post pledged to enhance the practical manifestations of love across the full spectrum of human experience.[5]

Many find the label "Unlimited Love" in the title of Post's organization odd. Post uses the phrase to refer to three related ideas. First and foremost, unlimited love refers to the promotion of well-being for all others in an enduring, intense, effective, and pure manner. "The ultimate expression of love is love for all humanity," says Post, "and for all that is."[6] Love should be expressed to those who are near and dear and also to those who are enemies. It should also be expressed to the cognitively and physically impaired. No one exists beyond the limits of love.

Unlimited love refers, second, to a hidden reality or energy that underlies all that is good in the universe. Post follows Sorokin in speaking of love as energy, although he sometimes calls this energy the "ultimate environment."[7] This environment provides integration, meaning, and purpose to life. The energy of love, suggests Post, should be studied by science and religion.

Finally, unlimited love refers to divine benevolence. "Unlimited Love is God's love for us all," says Post. It is "the ultimate reality that underlies all that is, and which can transform our limited and broken lives into journeys of remarkable generous service."[8] Given that many consider God both supremely loving and unlimited in many ways, it is natural for believers to connect the phrase "unlimited love" with deity. Some even identify unlimited love with *agape*, an identification that will be explored later in this book.

Research supported by the Institute for Research on Unlimited Love, the Fetzer Institute, and various smaller programs has generated remarkable scholarship in recent years. More than fifty major scientific research projects have been funded. Various conferences on love research and research centers have been sponsored. Several important monographs, anthologies, and handbooks on love have

5. Stephen G. Post, *Unlimited Love: Altruism, Compassion, and Service* (Philadelphia: Templeton Foundation Press, 2003), viii.

6. Ibid., 16.

7. Ibid., 72.

8. Ibid., 11.

been published. And the institutes have funded course competition programs to encourage teaching of love from religious and scientific perspectives.

Post reports on recent social and medical science related to love in his book *Why Good Things Happen to Good People*.[9] He cites research indicating that giving to others can result in good physical and mental health, increase longevity, and reduce the risk of adolescent depression and suicide. Post identifies ten ways that the gift of love promotes well-being: celebration, generativity, forgiveness, courage, humor, respect, compassion, loyalty, listening, and creativity. Drawing from research in the sciences and insights from the humanities, he prescribes love as a course of action for promoting the good life.

I call this newly emergent field of scholarship the "love, science, and theology symbiosis."[10] Exactly how scholars involved in this budding field think that love, science, and theology should relate and/or be integrated varies greatly. What they share in common is the belief that issues of love are of paramount importance. Love really matters. And scholars in the field believe that various research disciplines—whether natural sciences, social sciences, or religion—must be brought to bear upon how best to understand love.

The love research program involves the core belief that the world in general and individuals in particular, all things considered, can become better. A type of progress can be made. Through research and exploration we can come to understand better what love is, what it entails, and which creatures are capable of expressing it. Those who express love consistently will develop the kind of virtues that we associate with saints, sages, and mentors. We should imitate these loving people. Communities and societies that in various ways support love should also be supported and replicated. Religious practices and ideas that promote love should be emphasized. In many and diverse ways, we must pursue research into what love means and how we might best express it.

9. Stephen Post and Jill Neimark, *Why Good Things Happen to Good People: The Exciting New Research That Proves the Link between Doing Good and Living a Longer, Healthier, Happier Life* (New York: Broadway Books, 2006).

10. See Thomas Jay Oord, *Science of Love: The Wisdom of Well-Being* (Radnor, PA: Templeton Foundation Press, 2004).

A great deal of conceptual work must be done at this important stage of the love, science, and theology symbiosis. This work should help both insiders and outsiders conceptualize the issues central to love research programs. Part of that conceptual work has to do with definitions. After all, if one asks a crowd what science is, a variety of answers most likely will be given. Ask that same group what love is, and the variety swells. Before exploring research and proposals in the love, science, and theology symbiosis, we should become clear about what we mean by the key terms, *science* and *love*.

What Is Science?

Defining science is more difficult than most imagine. The field of philosophy of science contains diverse proposals, and scholars disagree about how science should best be understood. In addition, the reaction that many people have when hearing about the scientific study of love is similar to Senator Proxmire's: what does love have to do with science? It is widely assumed that love pertains to values, feelings, and emotions. The popular view is that science limits itself to cold hard facts. Facts and values—like water and oil—do not mix.

A close look at science, however, reveals that values play a significant role in the scientific enterprise. In fact, values shape the interpretation of what counts as good science. Values also shape what we think the proper goals of science might be. Values even shape what scientists regard as the best understanding of research results.

Although there are many ways to speak about and define science, at its bare bones science entails perception and reflection. Scientists perceive an object or objects and subsequently reflect upon what they have perceived. This perceiving and reflecting typically motivates scientists to conduct additional experiments, make predictions about further perceptions, and construct theories or explanations based on predictions fulfilled by or requiring further research.

The perception aspect of science incorporates various techniques and methods for observing the created world. Sometimes what counts as scientific observation arises from fairly random surveys of data; sometimes scientists rely on the observations of others. Most often what counts as rigorous scientific activity is the process of setting up experiments and observing their outcomes. Taking note of the outcomes—commonly called "collecting data"—provides information for the reflection aspect of science.

A number of different factors shape the scientist's perception of observed phenomena. At the most basic level, a scientist's sensory organs—eyes, ears, nose, and so on—are tools by which he or she observes data. Sensory organs are somewhat unique to each scientist. A color blind scientist, for instance, will see somewhat differently from the scientist who is not color blind. A scientist with acute hearing may perceive the unique patterns of birdsong better than a scientist with less-acute hearing.

Perhaps more important, however, is what the scientist expects to perceive. This can influence his or her research. The scientist's emotions, habits, education, personal and communal experiences, and other variables influence the scientist's perceiving activity. In short, factors other than the observed objects significantly shape scientific observation and, therefore, science itself. Additional observations by other scientists can balance the particular perspective that each scientist possesses, but the perspectives that scientists bring to their research inevitably influence their work.[11]

Turning to the reflective aspect of science, we find a number of factors at play. To begin, reflection on what has been perceived involves interpretation. Assorted factors influence the scientist's interpretations, and scientists are not conscious of many of those factors. One of the most important contributions of contemporary philosophy of science is the idea that culture, biology, and other matters shape the scientist's interpretations of the phenomena perceived. Scientists are not wholly objective. Factors other than the objects observed influence the reflective activity of scientists.

It is widely acknowledged that a single scientist cannot ascertain all facts of a given object or collection of objects. He or she can

11. The view that the scientist's own perspective influences the interpretation of scientific work is a view championed by those who research postmodernism and science. Postmodern science challenges the view that scientists are neutral and completely objective. See Stephen Toulmin, *The Return to Cosmology: Postmodern Science and the Theology of Nature* (Berkeley: University of California Press, 1982).

never know all truths, and perhaps not even the most important truths, about a particular phenomenon.[12] Even the collective observations of scientists are unlikely to grasp all that might be true about a particular aspect of existence. No scientist or group of scientists has an unlimited or all-encompassing perspective.

The reflective aspect of science involves analysis, comparison, and systematization. This work typically involves constructing hypotheses or explanations to account for the apprehended phenomena. Explanations involve linguistic or mathematical attempts to construe the world in some way similar to how scientists believe the world to be. Explanations generally are considered good when they are simple, adequate to what is observed, and/or fruitful for future work.

On the basis of a good explanation, scientists can predict with relative accuracy what will happen should a similar set of circumstances arise in the future. We regard as adequate explanations that scientists give when further experimentation and observation verify the explanation's descriptive and predictive power. If an explanation holds up to additional experimentation, the scientist is warranted in believing that he or she generally understands at least some part of the universe.[13] And understanding the universe, at least to some degree, is a major goal of science.[14]

12. In this book I assume that a version of what is commonly called "critical realism" best accounts for the way we relate to the world epistemically. By "critical realism," I mean the view that our knowledge of the world refers in some way to how things really are, but this knowledge is partial and will need to be revised as we accumulate additional data. See Thomas Jay Oord, *The Polkinghorne Reader* (Philadelphia: Templeton Foundation Press, 2010).

13. Answering the question "What is science?" can also be done by simply referring to the practices of scientists. The practice of scientists concerns things such as quantifying outcomes, acting in ways that the scientific community endorses or criticizes, proposing novel theories to account for observations for which standard theories do not account, and, perhaps most commonly, conducting experiments to confirm widely held or one's own pet theories.

14. It has long been customary to divide science by referring to some fields of science as "natural" and others as "social." Natural science has been said to include domains such as chemistry, astronomy, and geology; social sciences typically included fields such as psychology, sociology, and politics. This customary bifurcation is increasingly under criticism, however, as the entities studied in the natural sciences seem more and more analogous to complex organisms studied in the social sciences. And unified theories of evolution have made it more difficult to draw a sharp line between what was once referred to as "animate" and "inanimate"

This brief excursion into the nature of science can help dissolve the skepticism that some express when they hear that love can be studied scientifically. We will explore later in the book some ways that science explores love. At this point, however, we briefly note three ways in particular that understanding science as described helps us appreciate the importance of love and science aspects of the research symbiosis.

First, science is a value-laden enterprise and its practitioners—scientists—are valuing agents. When we say that some scientific practice is good—an explanation is better because it is simple or because it accounts for more data—we are making value judgments. Scientists reveal in their actions (even though they may occasionally deny it verbally) their belief that there are better or worse ways of doing science or arriving at scientific explanations. Philosopher of science and theologian David Ray Griffin says, "We all presuppose in practice that some modes of behavior and intended outcomes are inherently better than others and that some states of affairs, whether internal or external, are more beautiful, pleasing, fitting, tasteful, or what have you, than others. We may differ in our judgments and even our criteria; but *that* a distinction between better and worse exists we all presuppose."[15] If science is value-laden and scientists are valuing agents, research on value-inherent actions, outcomes, or experiences labeled "loving" need not entail inventing a whole new kind of science. Science is already chock-full of value.

Second, science reflects, at least in part, the subjective beliefs and explanatory trends of history. Although some of these explanations have not proven adequate to the research data, the power of these widely known but inadequate explanations continues. For instance, the early notion that the survival of the fittest is the driving force of evolution has been replaced by the notion

---

objects. Added to all of this is the peculiar fact that scientists have very similar views about the composition and nature of objects least like humans (e.g., rocks) and very different views about how best to describe creatures most like themselves. It seems to be a principle that the more complex the phenomena, the less likely any single explanation will sufficiently account for what the scientist observes.

15. David Ray Griffin, *Unsnarling the World-Knot: Consciousness, Freedom, and the Mind-Body Problem* (Berkeley: University of California Press, 1998), 40–41.

that an organism's ultimate goal is the propagation of its genetic heritage. Many sociobiologists today consider the propagation of genetic heritage, rather than survival, a creature's ultimate purpose. Creatures apparently sometimes choose death rather than survival if death better propels their genetic heritage into future generations. The sacrificial death of parents on behalf of their children illustrates this. And yet the commonly held view continues that evolution is primarily a battle for survival among those most fit, not the propagation of genetic heritage.

Even the currently dominant explanation of evolutionary biology—fit organisms propagate their genetic heritage—cannot fully account for the altruistic actions of complex creatures such as prairie dogs, fish, swallows, dolphins, and, especially, humans. The explanations that only the fittest survive or that organisms inevitably act for their genetic self-interest are so powerful that they can blind us to the extensive data suggesting that many animals, both human and nonhuman, act unselfishly. We will explore this line of argumentation more fully in chapters 3 and 4.

When sacrificial love is rejected out of hand as impossible, it becomes difficult for the data to speak for itself. Prejudgments sometimes determine results. In cases like this, it becomes evident that new theories—or new paradigms, to use the language of Thomas Kuhn—with concomitant research programs are needed. The love, science, and theology symbiosis aims, in part, to provide a more adequate explanation of existence. That explanation includes accounting for love and altruism.

Third, the scientific quest to understand the universe through perception and reflection must account for the fact that the beings we know best in that universe—ourselves—are ethical and spiritual beings. Some scientists have attempted to "explain away" this fact. While many in the prescientific age were unjustified in reading complex human ethics and religion onto nonhumans, present-day scholars likewise are unjustified in denying human characteristics presumed absent in nonhumans. Ironically, some of the most widely known scientists (e.g., Charles Darwin) argued that a measure of morality exists among nonhumans.

A good example of the importance of affirming irreducible aspects of human experience is the issue of purposiveness. Some scholars cannot imagine that nonhuman organisms, let alone very small organisms, act with purpose. Consequently, they claim that humans, who have evolved from such small organisms, also do not act with genuine purpose. This claim, however, flies in the face of what we know from experience: we know ourselves to be purposive beings. If understanding the universe is a major goal of science, and if humans are significant organisms in that universe—in fact, the organisms we know best—the study of human existence must at least be part of and shape the scientific enterprise.

As the practice of perceiving phenomena, reflecting on what has been perceived, and conducting experiments in light of this, science has much to offer the study of love. The scientific quest to understand the universe more fully would be woefully stunted if we neglected what many people consider the most important aspect of life: love. In chapters 3 through 5 we will examine recent scientific research on love. These chapters demonstrate not only that good science has a role to play in our understanding of love but also that theories of love, including theologies of love, need science to provide an adequate explanation of the world as we know it. In the final chapter we will turn to integrating the theories and research in the natural and social sciences with theology.

What Is Love?

Important conceptual work must be done before we explore recent scientific research on love. We have seen that part of the work revolves around a more-adequate notion of what science is and what it can do. The greatest amount of conceptual work, however, involves getting a clear idea of what we should mean by *love.*

Virtually all people act, and often talk, as if they have some awareness of love. People talk about loving food, falling in love, loving God, feeling loved, and loving a type of music. They say that love hurts, love waits, love stinks, and love means never having to say you are sorry. Love talk abounds. The fact that people talk of love in such varied ways prompted Sigmund Freud to note that "'love' is employed in language" in an "undifferentiated

11

way."[16] Theologian Mildred Bangs Wynkoop concurs, calling love a "weasel-word" because of its diverse meanings and frequent ambiguity.[17]

Although we often talk about love, few spell out what we really mean by the word. Love goes largely undefined. It may be that resources for love research have been scanty and researchers generally reluctant to pursue love studies in part because so few have given time and energy to provide love an adequate definition. It makes little sense to focus scholarship on or be financially supportive of something deliberately left vague, bewildering, and unspecified. Defining love is crucial.[18]

When we take time to reflect on love, a number of questions typically come to mind:

Is love a decision or a feeling?

Is love blind or universally aware?

Is love sexual, nonsexual, or asexual?

Is love self-sacrificial or self-authenticating?

Is love unconditional or object-specific?

Is love best understood as *agape*, *eros*, *philia*, something else, or all of these and more?

Is love something that only God expresses?

Can we truly comprehend anything about love?

These questions suggest that offering an adequate definition of love can be daunting, and the issues to be addressed are diverse.

Judging by the literature, even scholars find defining love difficult. "Those who write best about love," notes Jules Toner, "devote very little space to considering what love is."[19] The lack of clarity prompts Edward Vacek to observe that "most philosophical and

16. Sigmund Freud, *Civilization and Its Discontents*, trans. James Strachey (New York: W. W. Norton, 1961), 55.

17. Mildred Bangs Wynkoop, *A Theology of Love: The Dynamic of Wesleyanism* (Kansas City, MO: Beacon Hill Press, 1972), 9.

18. For an analytic approach to love, see Robert Brown, *Analyzing Love* (Cambridge: Cambridge University Press, 1987).

19. Jules Toner, *The Experience of Love* (Washington, DC: Corpus Books, 1968), 8.

theological writing, when it speaks of 'love,' does not analyze what love is, but rather assumes it has an evident meaning."[20] Irving Singer argues that "the analysis of love has been neglected more than almost any other subject in philosophy."[21] A dearth of definitions remains.

Some philosophers abandon any attempt to provide love a normative definition.[22] They rest content in simply trying to figure out what love means given the context or language game in which it is used. This practice is important because love has so many meanings and context largely determines these precise meanings. But refusing to identify a general definition leaves central assumptions about the nature of love unacknowledged. This in turn leads to incoherence and further ambiguity. In the extreme, love might be indistinguishable from hate if a normative definition is not offered.

One need not think that love has an absolute, for-all-time meaning. But some definitions of love are superior. A good general definition could become the conceptual mooring to which researchers might tie other, more-specific types of love. Researchers need a good general definition to avoid unnecessary misunderstanding and incoherence. Otherwise, confusion reigns.

It would be foolish, of course, to think that even the best definition of love can capture fully love's richness. We should be skeptical of any claim that language corresponds perfectly to diverse experiences. Language is at least one step removed. Postmodernisms of virtually every type have shown that words themselves, even when not narrowly associated with experience, have multiple meanings. Words are inherently ambiguous.[23]

But the inherent limitations of language do not negate the central importance of offering and defending a definition of love. We should not expect any definition to be perfect in all ways and for all

20. Edward Collins Vacek, *Love, Human and Divine: The Heart of Christian Ethics* (Washington, DC: Georgetown University Press, 1994), 34.

21. Irving Singer, *The Nature of Love*, vol. 1, *Plato to Luther*, 2nd ed. (Chicago: University of Chicago Press, 1987), xi.

22. See, for example, John Armstrong, *Conditions of Love: The Philosophy of Intimacy* (New York: W. W. Norton, 2002), 12.

23. Many postmodern philosophers and theologians express this concern with the ambiguity of language. Jacques Derrida perhaps expresses it best in his work. See, for instance, the critical reader of his work, *Derrida: A Critical Reader*, ed. David Wood (Oxford: Blackwell, 1992), and Derrida's other writings.

times, but some definitions are better than others. And progress in understanding and promoting love can be made if we gain clarity about love's nature. We need an adequate definition of love now more than ever.

A growing number of scholars offer hypotheses pertaining to love as it relates to particular fields of inquiry. For instance, psychologists and sociologists consider what kind of person is capable of love and what social conditions are conducive to love. They explore the fundamental drives and relationships characteristic of altruistic, prosocial, and loving behavior. Biologists explore the social interaction of species and suggest hypotheses about the altruism driving such interaction. They offer theories to account for altruism, such as kin-selection theory, reciprocal-altruism theory, group-selection theory, and game theory. Cosmologists speculate about the kind of universe required for free and loving creatures to emerge. Religious scholars in the theistic traditions suggest hypotheses and creeds about divine action and human responses as these pertain to love. And a few philosophers classify various types of love according to their motivations and/or objects.

If researchers fail to affirm a clear definition of love, the present surge in love studies will not produce the positive results that it otherwise might. When we are not relatively lucid about love, it becomes difficult to judge the value or contribution of any particular love investigation. It becomes difficult to compare the theories and research of one discipline with another when researchers employ widely divergent definitions. And the absence of a clear definition of love can undermine the work of those who call us all to express and promote love.

In light of the need for a definition of love, the major concern of the remainder of this chapter is to provide and defend a definition of love adequate for those doing research in the love, science, and theology symbiosis. This definition is meant to be adequate for a wide swath of academic disciplines, including the natural sciences, social sciences, and theological sciences. It has already proven beneficial for both those inside and outside the research academy. The proffered love definition might be regarded as preferable to the relatively few other definitions offered and preferable to no definition at all.

My own definition of love, and the one I will employ in various ways throughout the book, is this:

> To love is to act intentionally, in sympathetic response to others (including God), to promote overall well-being.

To say this differently: loving actions are influenced by the previous actions of others, oneself, and God, and these actions are purposefully executed in the hope of encouraging flourishing.

To explain better what this simple definition entails, I explore its three main phrases. This definition will arise from time to time in later chapters on research in natural and social sciences. It will play a role in the final chapter, which offers a theology of love consonant with research on love in the natural and social sciences. The first phrase in the love definition is . . .

To Act Intentionally

Intention is a multifaceted and multivalent word. I use the word *intentionally* to refer to three facets of love: deliberateness, motive, and self-determination. The three facets overlap, but each one offers something distinctive to a robust notion of intentionality.

With regard to deliberateness, I mean that love involves a decisional aspect.[24] This decisional aspect need not entail long, drawn-out contemplation. We often express love in split-second decisions. Philosopher Robert Kane notes that deliberateness is present in an instant when he says that we should accept "the possibility of impulsive, spur-of-the-moment, or snap decisions, which also settle conditions of indecision."[25] The decisionality of deliberating suggests that a degree of mentality accompanies action that we should regard as loving, but this mentality need not be complex or deep.

The decisional aspect does not mean that those who love repeatedly step back to survey thoroughly the wide range of pos-

---

24. I use the word *deliberateness* rather than *deliberation* because the latter carries connotations of a long, drawn-out process of reflection. Although love sometimes may involve such deliberation, more often love emerges from fleeting decisions.

25. Robert Kane, *The Significance of Free Will* (New York: Oxford University Press, 1998), 23. For a helpful collection of philosophical essays on the issues of freedom, agency, and responsibility, see Laura Waddell Ekstrom, ed., *Agency and Responsibility: Essays on the Metaphysics of Freedom* (Boulder, CO: Westview Press, 2001); Kevin Timpe, *Free Will: Sourcehood and Its Alternatives* (London: Continuum, 2008).

sible alternatives before deciding what action to take. Although those who love reflect occasionally on a wide array of options, most often they decide between only a few options of which they are aware. One or more of those options may seem more compelling than others. Creatures need not be omniscient to express love.

The decisional aspect in my definition of love opposes the idea that a person loves when, by coincidence, a positive outcome results from that person's actions. Action without any judgment whatsoever, even when that action results in good, should not be regarded as loving. Love is not accidental. Of course, the good that results from accidental or inadvertent activity is still valuable, and unintentional good can be appreciated. I reserve the label "loving action," however, for deeds purposefully done to promote well-being. Like John B. Cobb Jr., I affirm that love requires "conscious psychic activity."[26] Love is intentional.

With regard to the motive aspect of intentional action, love requires a noble purpose to do good. We should not say that a person has acted lovingly when a positive outcome results from actions that the person meant for harm.[27] Motives matter, even though actions done with good motives sometimes can produce ill-being, and actions done with evil motives can inadvertently produce well-being. Ill will is incompatible with actions that we should deem loving.

By emphasizing the importance of motives, I reject ethical theories that judge actions as good or evil solely by their consequences. Consequences matter and may or may not be indicators of love, but lovers cannot entirely control the consequences of their actions. The aspirations of those who love are fundamental, and lovers have some end or purpose in mind. Love assesses prospectively what actions promise to do rather than retrospectively whether actions have actually yielded the greatest good.[28]

26. John B. Cobb Jr., *The Structure of Christian Existence* (Philadelphia: Westminster, 1967), 127.

27. It also makes little sense to say that someone loves whose motives are neutral.

28. In this sense, my theory of love is similar to the ethical theory of proportionalism that Garth Hallett champions in his book *Greater Good: The Case for Proportionalism* (Washington, DC: Georgetown University Press, 1995).

Admittedly, we cannot be absolutely certain of someone else's motives. In fact, discerning our own true motives can be tricky. Harry Frankfurt, for instance, has suggested that we can have multiple levels of motivations, with one or some dominant.[29] The weight of scientific research on love, however, does not depend on discerning motives flawlessly. The claim that love requires good motives simply reminds us of what seems obvious: actions done with negative motives should not be considered acts of love.

I use the phrase "to act intentionally," third, to account for the self-determination, or freedom, inherent in love. To say it another way: love is meaningless if individuals are not free to choose one action rather than others. In philosophical circles, this understanding of self-determination fits best in the libertarian or incompatiblist traditions.[30] To be free is to make choices that are not entirely dependent on external conditions that make it the case that one cannot do otherwise. Free choices entail that choosers are in some sense genuinely responsible for their actions. Coercion, in the sense of the unilateral determination of the chooser, is antithetical to love.

Freedom does not, however, involve total spontaneity and completely random choice. Concrete circumstances limit what is genuinely possible as options for action.[31] Libertarian freedom should not be equated with unconstrained freedom. Unfortunately, the freewill tradition sometimes has been thought to require unfettered personal autonomy. Theologian Daniel Day Williams helps when he says that "freedom is never absent from love, [but] neither is it ever unconditional freedom."[32] Freedom to love includes being

29. Harry Frankfurt, *The Importance of What We Care About: Philosophical Essays* (Cambridge: Cambridge University Press, 1988).

30. A number of philosophers defend the importance and cogency of self-determination in terms of libertarian freedom. See especially William Hasker, *God, Time, and Knowledge* (Ithaca, NY: Cornell University Press, 1989); Peter Van Inwagen, *An Essay on Free Will* (Oxford: Clarendon Press, 1983); Kane, *Significance of Free Will*.

31. This claim is developed in terms of neurology in Nancey C. Murphy and Warren S. Brown, *Did My Neurons Make Me Do It? Philosophical and Neurobiological Perspectives on Moral Responsibility and Free Will* (Oxford: Oxford University Press, 2007).

32. Daniel Day Williams, *The Spirit and the Forms of Love* (New York: Harper & Row, 1968), 116. Williams was influenced by Alfred North Whitehead, who argued that "there is no such fact as absolute freedom; every actual entity

17

impelled to choose between a limited number of possibilities that pertain to the chooser's immediate context. We might best call this "limited freedom."

To call love an action is not to claim that love always entails an imposition, interference, or intervention into the affairs of others. Sometimes love entails acting in ways that do not directly impact others. Nor does calling love an action mean that love always entails deeds perceptible to our five senses. Thinking and praying, for instance, can be acts of love. Deciding to remain calm is an action; listening is acting.[33] I use the word *act* to cover a broad range of activities, both seen and unseen, both proactive and restrained.

Earlier in our brief exploration of science, we noted that many factors influence our perception of and reflection on the world. These factors influence but do not entirely determine intentional actions. For instance, one's bodily characteristics, emotions, neural substrates, hormonal constitution, dispositions, genetic framework, and other factors influence greatly but, I argue, do not entirely control one's intentional actions. Environmental dynamics beyond the lover's own body, such as political, communal, and ecological relationships, also greatly shape intentional activity. The claim that agents feel a variety of influences and yet remain genuinely free suggests that intentional action occurs in a context and with constraints.

In the chapters that follow, we examine scientific research that strengthens the claim that the expressions of love possible for any particular individual are partly dependent on physical and emotional factors both within and beyond a lover's body. This idea is presented concisely in the second phrase of the definition of love I offer, however, and an introduction to it is now required. The second phrase in my definition of love is . . .

---

possesses only such freedom as is inherent in the primary phase 'given' by its standpoint of relativity to its actual universe. Freedom, givenness, potentiality, are notions which presuppose each other and limit each other" (*Process and Reality: An Essay in Cosmology*, ed. David Ray Griffin and Donald W. Sherburne, corrected ed. [1929; repr., New York: Free Press, 1978], 133).

33. Jay McDaniel develops the importance of listening for love in his book *Gandhi's Hope: Learning from Other Religions as a Path to Peace* (Maryknoll, NY: Orbis Books, 2005).

In Sympathetic Response to Others (Including God)

Love requires actual relations with others. Entirely isolated individuals, if such existed, could not love. To say that love involves sympathetic response is to presuppose that individuals are mutually influencing. It is to assume that others—people, nonhumans, one's own past actions, entities in the environment, or God—influence the one who loves. No one expresses love in a vacuum. The relations of love are more than merely logical. They are causal in that they involve genuine sway or effect of one agent on another. Real, not just relative, influence occurs.

I use the word *sympathy* in my definition as a technical word to refer to the internal, constituting influence of one or more objects or individuals on the loving actor. Many twentieth-century American and British philosophers use the word in this way. It derives from the Greek word *sympatheō* (*syn*, "with" or "together"; *patheō*, "feel" or "suffer").

The process philosophical tradition has been especially powerful in describing the philosophical and theological dimensions of real relatedness in sympathy. Philosopher Charles Hartshorne, for instance, explains what sympathy entails by saying that "the doctrine of sympathy . . . is that all feeling feels other feeling, all reaction has an object which itself is reactive, [and] that we have objects at all is due entirely to the . . . immanent sociality of experience."[34] Alfred North Whitehead refers to sympathy as "prehension," and other philosophers, such as George Herbert Mead and Herbert Spencer, call it "fellow feeling." Because of this sympathy, or what Hartshorne also calls "the social nature of reality," the very being of each lover is partly decided by others.[35]

What I have described as sympathy—"feeling with"—is in some scientific disciplines called "empathy." Especially in the disciplines of psychology and sociology, sympathy carries overtones of pity and condescension rather than the philosophical idea of feeling the feelings of others. Sociologists Pearl and Samuel Oliner, for

34. Charles Hartshorne, *Beyond Humanism: Essays in the New Philosophy of Nature* (1937; repr., Gloucester, MA: Peter Smith, 1975), 185.
35. Charles Hartshorne, "Whitehead's Idea of God," in *The Philosophy of Alfred North Whitehead*, ed. Paul Arthur Schilpp, 2nd ed. (New York: Tudor, 1951), 527.

instance, suggest that sympathy "means pity or commiseration *for* another's condition." Sympathy implies looking at another person "at a distance." By contrast, say the Oliners, "empathy means feeling *with* the other person."[36]

Some social psychologists, such as L. G. Wispe, dissect the two words even further. Wispe suggests that "sympathy refers to the heightened awareness of the suffering of another person," while "empathy, on the other hand, refers to the attempt by one self-aware self to comprehend unjudgmentally the positive and negative experiences of another self." Wispe concludes that in empathy we substitute ourselves for others, but in sympathy we substitute others for ourselves.[37]

My use of "sympathy" is not meant to be equated with looking at others from afar, as if detached. Nor do I mean for sympathy to connote an absolute substitution of oneself for another (if this were even possible). Rather, to sympathize is to be internally influenced by the other such that one's own experience is partially constituted by the one or ones perceived. A creature's sympathetic response to others entails reaction to what has occurred in both the immediate and distant past.[38] The one who loves is internally related to what has happened in the past, as past actions influence

36. Pearl M. Oliner and Samuel P. Oliner, *Toward a Caring Society: Ideas in Action* (Westport, CT: Praeger, 1995), 32.

37. L. G. Wispe, "The Distinction between Sympathy and Empathy," *Journal of Personality and Social Psychology* 50 (1986): 318.

38. I find Whitehead's thought on internal and external relations most helpful when proposing a theory of relatedness. "Every actual entity is what it is and is with its definite status in the universe," says Whitehead, because "its internal relations to other actual entities" shape it (*Process and Reality*, 59). Each experiential organism begins with an openness to the past, and this open window makes possible the organism's internal relations. Once the influence from the past has entered in, the window closes. Whitehead likes to explain external relations as an organism's influence on future others by saying that "it belongs to the nature of a 'being' that it is a potential for every 'becoming'" (ibid., 22). Just as each organism, through its internal relations, drew on its relations with others as it came into existence, each organism subsequently becomes datum for future organisms as they come into being. See also my own work on the importance of internal and external relations (Thomas Jay Oord, "Morals, Love, and Relations in Evolutionary Theory," in *Evolution and Ethics: Human Morality in Biological and Religious Perspective*, ed. Philip Clayton and Jeffrey Schloss [Grand Rapids: Eerdmans, 2004], 287–301).

that individual's moment-by-moment identity. The interdependence of sympathy—or empathy, if you prefer—is essential to what it means to love.

Just as many factors influence one's intentional actions, many factors also influence the nature of one's sympathetic response. Our responses to our environment are partly dependent on the makeup of our brains, our bodies, and causes beyond ourselves. Just as bodily and environmental factors greatly shape our intentions, these same factors also greatly shape our sympathetic responses. This shaping is addressed frequently in contemporary discussions of emotions, biological constraints, and affect. This shaping will also be discussed in later chapters.

An important feature of the phrase "in sympathetic response to others (including God)" is the parenthetical acknowledgment of divine influence. The final chapter offers a proposal for how best to conceive of the causal role that God plays in love. I simply note here that I consider God an actual, causal agent to whose inspiration, or "call," creatures respond appropriately when expressing love. I will claim that this causal influence does not violate the dominant methods of science, which rely primarily on observation through sense perception.[39] Rightly understood, science and theology can be complementary.

The phrases of my love definition explored thus far—"to act intentionally" and "in sympathetic response"—reflect two dominant ways that philosophers, theologians, scientists, and even poets have thought about the nature of love. Philosopher Robert Hazo, in his classic study *The Idea of Love*, refers to these two ways as "tendency" and "judgment."

Those who understand love primarily or exclusively as tendency identify love with feeling or emotion. They use words such as *instinct* and *impulse*. Lovers might say that they "fell in love," that they feel as though they have been "overwhelmed by love," or that some object or person is "just *so* lovable."[40] Neurologist Antonio Damasio argues for this understanding of love, and he endorses

---

39. Thomas Jay Oord, "Love as a Methodological and Metaphysical Source for Science and Theology," *Wesleyan Theological Journal* 45, no. 1 (Spring 2010).

40. For an analytic look at love as an emotion, see Robert C. Roberts, *Emotions: An Essay in Aid of Moral Psychology* (Cambridge: Cambridge University Press, 2003).

proposals that philosopher Baruch Spinoza offered centuries ago.[41] I account for this and what Hazo calls the "tendency" aspect of love in my phrase "sympathetic response."

Those who understand love primarily or exclusively as judgment typically use the words *will, choice,* or *cognition* when talking about love. Love is a decision, they say. We must choose to love no matter what emotions we feel. This claim typically gains traction when coupled with the claim that one should love despite experiencing negative feelings or emotions. Reflecting the idea that love is a matter of the will, psychologists Robert Hemfelt, Frank Minirth, and Paul Meier give their best-selling book the title *Love Is a Choice.* They argue that one must choose to break free from addictive or unhealthy codependent relationships if they are to love.[42] I account for this choice, or what Hazo calls the "judgment" aspect of love, in my phrase "act intentionally."

I argue that love necessarily involves both spheres: tendential and judgmental. Or, as I prefer, love involves both sympathetic and intentional aspects. Martha Nussbaum gets at this when she argues that emotions are essential elements of human intelligence and choice when humans love.[43] Theologians John B. Cobb Jr. and David Ray Griffin use the label "creative-responsive love" to account for both of these necessary dimensions.[44] I join these scholars by claiming that love has both passive and active elements. Both sympathy and intentionality are necessarily present in an act of love.

As I see it, sympathetic feeling logically but not temporally precedes decisional intentionality. An act of love logically begins with an individual's feeling of or being influenced by past others and the relevant possibilities arising from that past. The love act is consummated, however, by the lover's decision about how that past will be appropriated in light of an expected contribution to the future. The initial feeling requires subsequent decision.

41. Antonio Damasio, *Looking for Spinoza: Joy, Sorrow, and the Feeling Brain* (Orlando, FL: Harcourt, 2003).

42. Robert Hemfelt, Frank Minirth, and Paul Meier, *Love Is a Choice: Breaking the Cycle of Addictive Relationships* (Nashville: Thomas Nelson, 1992).

43. Martha C. Nussbaum, *Upheavals of Thought: The Intelligence of Emotions* (Cambridge: Cambridge University Press, 2001).

44. John B. Cobb Jr. and David Ray Griffin, *Process Theology: An Introductory Exposition* (Philadelphia: Westminster, 1976), chap. 3.

This progression is only logical, however, not temporal. Lovers do not simply feel in one moment and then simply choose in the next. Both aspects are present in each moment, although one may dominate. This way of understanding the relation between feeling and decision is consonant with Stephen Post's proposal that "an even balance or co-primacy between emotion and reason is the fitting alternative to those who would diminish the importance of either capacity."[45] But I afford feeling—the sympathetic response to factors and agents in one's environment—a logical priority.

This discussion of intentionality and sympathy is primarily an analysis of the necessary conditions for the possibility for deeming any particular activity an expression of love. But these conditions themselves are not love. In fact, I would argue that intentionality and sympathy are also necessary conditions for hate and indifference. The final phrase in my definition of love points to the element required for deeming some intentional responses as loving and others as not. The final phrase of my love definition is . . .

To Promote Overall Well-Being

The first thing to notice in my definition's last phrase is the positive character of love's aim. This positive character is captured in the label "well-being."[46] To say that love promotes well-being requires an explanation of what well-being entails. Moral philosopher James Griffin defines well-being minimally as "the level to which basic needs are met."[47] Philosopher Partha Dasgupta, however, says that what we regard as well-being exceeds the bare minimum of meeting basic needs. Well-being pertains to a quality of life.[48] In other contexts, well-being denotes health, happiness, wholeness, and flourishing. Aristotle called it *eudaimonia*. Theistic traditions have sometimes spoken of it as "blessedness" or "shalom." Jesus called it "abundant life."

45. Post, *Unlimited Love*, 67.

46. Others also define love so as to make this orientation toward well-being love's central aspect. For instance, Gary Chartier defines love as "a positive orientation on the other" (*The Analogy of Love: Divine and Human Love at the Center of Christian Theology* [Charlottesville, VA: Imprint Academic, 2007], 1).

47. James Griffin, *Well-Being: Its Meaning, Measurement, and Moral Importance* (Oxford: Oxford University Press, 1986), 42.

48. Partha Dasgupta, *Human Well-Being and the Natural Environment* (Oxford: Oxford University Press, 2001), 13.

Promoting well-being involves enhancing the mental and physical aspects of reality. It may involve acting to attain sufficient food, clean air and water, adequate clothing and living conditions, personal security, and the opportunity for intellectual development. It may involve attaining the satisfaction of being cared for and the sense of belonging, diversity of life forms and cultural expressions, an appropriate level of leisure and entertainment, and economic stability. Promoting well-being may involve acting responsively to secure a feeling of worth, medical soundness and physical fitness, deep personal relationships, social and political harmony, and the opportunity to develop spiritual/religious sensibilities and practices. Acting responsively to increase well-being may involve acting in ways that develop a person's virtuous dispositions, habits, and character. To promote well-being is to act to increase flourishing in at least one but often many of these dimensions of existence.[49]

Love takes into account, to varying degrees, the life of the individual, local community, and global community. As far as they apply, acting to promote overall well-being includes considering the flourishing of nonhuman organisms and ecological systems. It even includes intensifying God's own happiness. Acting to promote overall well-being can pertain to any dimension of life. I affirm what Dasgupta calls a "pluralist outlook," insofar as I acknowledge that love can pertain to the multifarious dimensions of a life well lived.[50] An act of love establishes or increases well-being.

Promoting overall well-being is roughly the same as promoting the common good. Of course, determining how to calculate what the common good requires and the various dimensions that compose it is exceedingly difficult, if not impossible. A recent Princeton University think tank consisting of scholars from various academic disciplines discovered that a comprehensive definition, let alone calculation, was beyond their grasp.[51] Nevertheless, a deep com-

---

49. For strategies and research in promoting well-being in humans, see Margaret Schneider Jamner and Daniel Stokols, eds., *Promoting Human Wellness: New Frontiers for Research, Practice, and Policy* (Berkeley: University of California Press, 2000).

50. Dasgupta, *Human Well-Being*, 14.

51. See the product of the Princeton three-year discussion, Patrick D. Miller and Dennis P. McCann, eds., *In Search of the Common Good* (New York: T&T Clark, 2005).

mitment to promoting the common good or overall well-being in the various dimensions of life and for the good of the whole persists among scholars and religious leaders today. A recent papal encyclical underscores the Christian commitment to promoting the common good.[52] Love demands that we pay attention to concerns beyond those near and relatively few. Love's vision is deep and wide.

One factor that makes defining love so difficult is that at least three divergent linguistic traditions influence our love vocabulary. The reference to "well-being" requires that we address the love vocabulary of these traditions. By "love vocabulary" I mean the actual way people use the word *love* in their communication. I identify these three linguistic traditions as (1) the proper/improper tradition, (2) the mutuality tradition, and (3) the *ḥesed* tradition. Coming to terms with the love vocabulary of these three will help us analyze the ways we use the word *love*.

The proper/improper love tradition, identified initially with the ancient Greeks, has primarily affected the way some Westerners use the word *love*. We see its influence in the earliest Greek philosophers, a little bit in the Christian New Testament, in the Qur'an, and sometimes in common language of the West. What is distinctive about the proper/improper linguistic tradition is that the word *love* can describe any purposive action whatsoever. To love is to act purposively or to desire.

Thomas Aquinas, who was greatly influenced by Aristotle's language on this issue, expresses well the purposive action aspect of the proper/improper tradition's understanding of love. He argues that "every agent, whatever it be, does every action from love of some kind."[53] We see the proper/improper linguistic tradition at play in Augustine's famous directive "Love, but see to it what

52. Pope Benedict XVI, *God Is Love* (*Deus Caritas Est*) (Washington, DC: USCCB, 2006).

53. Thomas Aquinas, *Summa Theologica* (Westminster, MD: Christian Classics, 1981), parts I–II, q. 28, a. 6. My use of this quotation from Aquinas (and the next from Augustine) are not meant to claim that Aquinas or Augustine thought of love only as proper/improper or as will. We find the other linguistic traditions employed in their thought as well, which means that they contribute to linguistic confusion surrounding the use of the word *love*.

you love."[54] According to the proper/improper linguistic tradition, merely to act intentionally is to love.

Søren Kierkegaard sometimes uses the word *love* to express a second way some in the proper/improper tradition understand love. Instead of emphasizing love as purposive action, Kierkegaard thinks of love as first and foremost a desire or passion. He puts it succinctly when he says that "love is a passion of the emotions."[55] To desire an object or individual is to love that object or individual. Desire is love.

When someone from the proper/improper tradition uses the word *love*, a qualifier of some sort is or should be employed. An adjective such as "proper" and "improper," "perfect" and "imperfect," "appropriate" and "inappropriate," or "fitting" and "unfitting" precedes the word *love*.[56] Saints love properly; sinners love improperly. Wise people love objects appropriately; fools love objects inappropriately. The word *love* requires a qualifier if laden with moral or value connotations, because love in this linguistic tradition can refer to actions and desires that are good or evil.

One of the most common problems arising in the proper/improper tradition of love language is the tendency for those in the tradition not to use a qualifier consistently. Sometimes they mean for love to have a positive sense, but they forget to include the qualifier with the word *love*. Readers and listeners are unsure then how "love" is being used. They wonder if "love" is value-positive, value-negative, or value-neutral. When those in this tradition use "love" to refer to that which is value-negative, readers are confused. Bewilderment ensues.

Although the proper/improper tradition rightly emphasizes the idea that love is an action or passion, the qualifiers prior to the word

54. Augustine, *Commentaries on the Psalms* 90.31.5. The following sentence reads, "*Caritas* says: love of God and love of neighbor; *cupiditas* says: love of the world and love of this age."

55. Søren Kierkegaard, *Works of Love: Some Christian Reflections in the Form of Discourses*, trans. Howard and Edna Hong (New York: Harper & Row, 1962), 117.

56. A long and noble tradition exists within Christian theology that uses the phrase "perfect love" and "holy love." Two books that operate from that tradition are William G. Greathouse, *Love Made Perfect: Foundations for the Holy Life* (Kansas City, MO: Beacon Hill Press, 1997); and Kenneth J. Collins, *The Theology of John Wesley: Holy Love and the Shape of Grace* (Nashville: Abingdon, 2007).

love also make it rhetorically problematic. It strikes most people, including me, as odd to talk of "improper love," "inappropriate love," "inauthentic love," or even "evil love."[57] Although we can make some sense out of what a speaker means when using "love" in these ways, these uses more often confuse. Telling our spouses, children, or even God that we love them properly seems an odd practice. A consistent and rhetorically sensible use of "love" seems important for making progress in the study and promotion of love.

We often find the second linguistic tradition—mutuality—in the philosophies of the East. It is also evident in the West's amorous literature. According to the mutuality tradition, to love is to engage in personal interaction or relationship. Love *is* relation.

The mutuality linguistic tradition says that the reciprocity inherent in any relationship is, itself, love. For instance, contemporary theologian Vincent Brümmer calls love "a reciprocal relation," and he claims that love "must by its very nature be a relationship of free mutual give and take."[58] Philosopher Charles Hartshorne offers a similar understanding of love as mutuality when he says that "love means realization in oneself of the desires and experiences of others, so that one who loves can in so far inflict suffering only by undergoing this suffering himself."[59] Hartshorne also uses the phrase "life sharing" to define love as mutuality.[60] Wherever we see reciprocal relationships, says the mutuality tradition, love is present. To be mutually related is to love.

Although the mutuality tradition rightly emphasizes the importance of relationships, few of us, including me, would describe

57. One could also use the word *love* to speak of proper and improper relations. In this way of speaking, proper relations is correct moral response, while improper relations are morally incorrect. My objection to this relational use of "love" is the same as my objection to the proper/improper linguist tradition.

58. Vincent Brümmer, *The Model of Love: A Study in Philosophical Theology* (Cambridge: Cambridge University Press, 1993), 162, 161.

59. Charles Hartshorne, *Man's Vision of God, and the Logic of Theism* (Chicago: Willett, Clark, 1941), 31. Hartshorne, like most in the mutuality (and proper/improper) tradition, is inconsistent in his use of the word *love*. Sometimes he uses the word to speak of simple mutuality; other times he uses the word to speak of acting for the good. And he does not believe that mutuality always promotes the good.

60. Charles Hartshorne, *Wisdom as Moderation: A Philosophy of the Middle Way* (Albany: State University of New York Press, 1987), 119.

all relationships as loving. Some relationships generate evil. Some relationships are not healthy, and at least temporarily severing such unhealthy relationships may be the loving path one should take. Taken to its rhetorical extreme, the mutuality tradition would identify a relationship promoting evil as a relationship of love. By contrast, I suggest that we should not equate love with mutuality, despite the necessary role that mutuality plays in love. Robust research requires rhetorical consistency.

In my definition of love, the phrase "to promote overall well-being" places my understanding of love in the third linguistic tradition, *ḥesed*. Love is doing good. In this linguistic tradition, "love" is reserved for descriptions of ideal ethical actions or what the Hebrew authors called "righteousness." Such loving actions promote well-being. When I use the word *love*, therefore, I follow the practice of the love-as-doing-good tradition and therefore refer to action that engenders well-being. This use corresponds with a widespread tendency to understand love as doing good or acting in beneficial ways.

A key word in the last phrase of my love definition is "overall." The next chapter addresses the importance of this word in greater detail. Here I will simply say that the reference to overall well-being is meant to indicate that actions intended to benefit the self or the few at the obvious expense of the many should not be considered acts of love. In chapter 2 we will explore this notion as it pertains to loving oneself.

It will be obvious to many that my reference to well-being implicates most if not all versions of metaethics and moral theories. As is appropriate, ethicists, theologians, and moral philosophers debate the value of ethical theories when deciding how to best understand morality and the pursuit of the good life. And as is typical, a variety of approaches exist among scholars.

I mean for my definition of love to fit comfortably within most if not all the dominant metaethical frameworks and moral theories. Advocates of differing approaches should find my definition helpful, even as they employ it in differing ways. For instance, advocates of feminist ethics will appreciate the central role of sympathy/empathy in my definition of love. Advocates of divine command ethics should find my reference to divine action helpful as they consider love as the appropriate response to God's will. Those who propose various ethics of care should find helpful my emphasis on relationality and response. Advocates of metatheories such as natural law ethics, virtue ethics, and Kantianism should also find my definition of love helpful in various ways for their own deliberations.[61]

To be adequate to a wide range of concrete activities that should rightly be regarded as loving while also being fruitful for a wide variety of metaethical theories, an acceptable definition of love must be sufficiently abstract. To say it another way: a definition that seeks to be relevant to a comprehensive set of actions and theories requires generalization. A helpful abstraction should not be so general, however, that it allows for any action or theory whatsoever. It must be able to account for those actions that, after careful reflection, we justifiably deem loving. And yet it must exclude those actions that we justifiably deem unloving. A good definition should be both broadly inclusive and appropriately exclusive.

Conclusion

I suggest that my definition of love—to love is to act intentionally, in sympathetic response to others (including God), to promote overall well-being—can provide the practical benefit and intellectual satisfaction needed of a definition helpful for the love, science, and theology symbiosis. Scientific and theological research on love requires more than this, but an adequate definition can be fruitful for research in many ways. Although we can express love without having a well-conceived definition, my hope is that this definition

61. For particularly good sources for these various metaethical theories, see, for instance, Craig Boyd, *A Shared Morality: A Narrative Defense of Natural Law Ethics* (Grand Rapids: Brazos Press, 2007); Paul M. Cooey, Sharon A. Farmer, and Mary Ellen Ross, eds., *Embodied Love: Sensuality and Relationship as Feminist Values* (San Francisco: Harper & Row, 1987); Andrew Michael Flescher, *Heroes, Saints, and Ordinary Morality* (Washington, DC: Georgetown University Press, 2003); Robin Gill, ed., *The Cambridge Companion to Christian Ethics* (Cambridge: Cambridge University Press, 2001); Ruth Groenhout, *Connected Lives: Human Nature and an Ethics of Care* (Lanham, MD: Rowman & Littlefield, 2004); Timothy Jackson, *The Priority of Love: Christian Charity and Social Justice* (Princeton, NJ: Princeton University Press, 2003); Alasdair MacIntyre, *After Virtue: A Study in Moral Theory*, 2nd ed. (Notre Dame, IN: University of Notre Dame Press, 1984); Robert C. Solomon and Kathleen M. Higgins, eds., *The Philosophy of (Erotic) Love* (Lawrence: University Press of Kansas, 1991).

itself can be an act that promotes well-being. My hope is that it can help those who wish to promote well-being.

Other pressing issues must still be addressed. In the next chapter we look at the forms of love and acting for one's own good in relation to others. These issues must be carefully sorted if the love, science, and theology symbiosis is to gain necessary traction. This chapter, however, provides an important piece of the process—a definition of love—for the depth and breadth of research possible for the love, science, and theology symbiosis.

2

Love's Diverse Forms and Multiple Recipients

Providing a definition of love for the love, science, and theology symbiosis is crucial. I have done this in the previous chapter. But a good definition does not go far enough to clarify issues of love and answer key questions posed previously. In particular, we want to know what general kinds of actions promote well-being. We want to know whose well-being we should consider when deciding how to respond intentionally. This chapter addresses these issues by looking at the general forms of love and those individuals and entities whom we should consider when deciding what love requires.

Diverse Forms of Love

The seventeenth-century French philosopher François de La Rochefoucauld wisely said, "There is only one kind of love, but there are a thousand different versions."[1] Today we might say that love

1. François de La Rochefoucauld, *Reflections; Or, Sentences and Moral Maxims*, trans. J. W. Willis Bund and J. Hain Friswell (New York: Scribner, Welford, 1871), 11.

has millions, billions, or even trillions of versions. Love is pluralistic in the sense that many actions, depending on their motives and circumstances, can be acts of love. Love is multiform and multiexpressive.

It has become increasingly common, however, to place the multifarious versions of love under three general forms: *agape, eros,* and *philia.*[2] These Greek-derived words prevail in theological and philosophical research on love but arise only occasionally in the natural and social sciences. However, many of the sciences either presuppose the meanings of these general love forms or provide important research pertaining to these meanings. An examination of these words reveals that the theological and philosophical sciences are more closely related to the natural and social sciences than many may have thought. We will explore these three forms of love in the first half of this chapter.

Agape

Agape is by far the form of love to which the love, science, and theology symbiosis literature, at least literature influenced by Christianity, most refers. Philip Hefner, for instance, identifies *agape* and altruism and argues that "the most pressing question that arises in conversation with the sciences is . . . Can we entertain the hypothesis that altruistic love is rooted in the fundamental nature of reality, including the reality we call nature?"[3] Stephen Post uses the word *agape* for his work as he oversees various scientific and religious investigations.

2. There are other words in the Greek language sometimes translated "love." However, like most scholars, I do not consider these others to have archetypal status. Instead, they are subforms or expressions of one or more of the three archetypes that I list. Other Greek words sometimes translated "love" include *storge* and *epithymia. Storge* is not used in Christian Scripture except in the negative *astorgos* (Rom. 1:31; 2 Tim. 3:3) and the *phil*-prefixed *philostorgos* (Rom. 12:10). My definition of *philia* is intended to incorporate subtle differences that *storge* might denote. I subsume *epithymia* under *eros,* or what Paul Tillich calls "the normal drive towards vital self-fulfillment" (*Love, Power, and Justice: Ontological Analyses and Ethical Applications* [New York: Oxford University Press, 1963], 25; see also 91–114).

3. Philip Hefner, *The Human Factor: Evolution, Culture, and Religion* (Minneapolis: Fortress, 1993), 208–9.

Theologians, philosophers, and scientists who speak of *agape* typically believe it means something beyond or distinct from the simple word *love*. Many adopt *agape* to distinguish their notion of love from romantic or popular understandings. Some adopt *agape* because for them it entails special reference to divine action. Others identify it with altruism. Still others, including me, use *agape* to distinguish some actions from others that might also promote well-being.

Widespread contemporary use of *agape* should be credited to the influential writing of theologian Anders Nygren, although the word dates to antiquity. Nygren's mid-twentieth-century book *Agape and Eros* set off wide-ranging debates. These debates placed the word at the center of scholarly attention in an unprecedented way. Nygren "so effectively posed issues about love," Gene Outka claimed in the 1970s, "that they have had a prominence in theology and ethics they never had before. . . . Thus, whatever the reader may think of [Nygren's book], one may justifiably regard his work as the beginning of the modern treatment of the subject."[4] In the 1990s Edward Collins Vacek acknowledged that Nygren's "insights are splendid, his mistakes are instructive, and his views are still very much alive."[5] Colin Grant, an advocate of Nygren's general *agape* scheme, calls Nygren's emphasis on *agape* "indispensable," saying that he "deserves to be heard clearly in his insistence on the distinctively theological significance of *agape*."[6]

Two main features of Nygren's understanding of *agape* influence both scholarly and popular understandings. The first feature is his complex theological and philosophical hypotheses pertaining to *agape*. According to him, *agape* is rightly understood as

- unconditioned, spontaneous, groundless, or unmotivated
- indifferent to, but creative of, value
- directed toward sinners

4. Gene Outka, *Agape: An Ethical Analysis* (New Haven: Yale University Press, 1972), 1.

5. Edward Collins Vacek, *Love, Human and Divine: The Heart of Christian Ethics* (Washington, DC: Georgetown University Press, 1994), 159.

6. Colin Grant, "For the Love of God: Agape," *Journal of Religious Ethics* 24, no. 1 (1996): 21.

- the sole initiator of creaturely fellowship with God
- in opposition to all that can be called self-love
- sacrificial giving to others
- and expressed only by God.[7]

Scholars routinely criticize each of these *agape* hypotheses.[8] Some reject the argument that *agape* opposes all that can be called self-love. Others reject Nygren's claim that *agape* is the only love that should be called "Christian." The emphasis on *agape* as the only appropriate Christian love, say critics, neglects legitimate *philia* and *eros*. Others reject the notion that *agape* requires sacrificial giving, arguing that love can also involve receiving from others. Some note that Nygren's argument that *agape* is exclusively divine love implies a form of divine determinism or predestination. I join these critics and argue that love extends beyond *agape*, and the hypotheses Nygren offers do not describe *agape* well.

Those familiar with *agape* debates typically are aware of these and other criticisms. Consequently, few biblical and theological scholars today fully endorse Nygren's *agape* hypotheses or his

7. Anders Nygren, *Agape and Eros*, trans. Philip S. Watson (1930; repr., New York: Harper & Row, 1957), 27–240.

8. Among the many scholars who disagree with aspects of Nygren's thesis are Paul Avis, *Eros and the Sacred* (Harrisburg, PA: Morehouse, 1990), chap. 15; John Burnaby, *Amor Dei: A Study in the Religion of St. Augustine* (London: Hodder & Stoughton, 1938), 18; idem, *"Amor* in St. Augustine," in *The Philosophy and Theology of Anders Nygren*, ed. Charles W. Kegley (Carbondale: Southern Illinois University Press, 1970), 174–86; Martin C. D'Arcy, *The Mind and Heart of Love: Lion and Unicorn; A Study in Eros and Agape* (London: Faber & Faber, 1945); Carter Heyward, "Lamenting the Loss of Love: A Response to Colin Grant," *Journal of Religious Ethics* 24, no. 1 (1996): 23–28; Douglas N. Morgan, *Love: Plato, the Bible, and Freud* (Englewood Cliffs, NJ: Prentice-Hall, 1964), chap. 2; Stephen G. Post, *A Theory of Agape: On the Meaning of Christian Love* (Lewisburg, PA: Bucknell University Press, 1990), chap. 3; John M. Rist, "Some Interpretations of *Agape* and *Eros*," in Kegley, *Philosophy and Theology of Anders Nygren*, 156–73; George F. Thomas, *Christian Ethics and Moral Philosophy* (New York: Scribner, 1955), 54; Tillich, *Love, Power, and Justice*, chap. 2; Edward Collins Vacek, "Love, Christian and Diverse," *Journal of Religious Ethics* 24, no. 1 (1996): 29–34; idem, *Love, Human and Divine*, chap. 5; Victor Warnach, "*Agape* in the New Testament," in Kegley, *Philosophy and Theology of Anders Nygren*, 143–55; Daniel Day Williams, *The Spirit and the Forms of Love* (New York: Harper & Row, 1968), chap. 4.

theological and philosophical views.[9] However, Nygren's general understanding of *agape* and the word itself retain significant cachet in the broader science and theology dialogue as well as in popular theological discussions.

Scholars and laity typically are less familiar with criticisms of the second feature of Nygren's concept of *agape*. That feature is his claim that *agape* represents the distinctively Christian understanding of love. Following Nygren, philosophers David L. Norton and Mary F. Kille state that "from a strict Christian standpoint" we find that "*agape* is God's love"; and the fact that "*agape* is God's nature, wholly independent of man, is a principle which aligns perfectly with the Christian doctrine of grace."[10] Theologian Emil Brunner observes that "the statement that God is *agape* is found only in the New Testament," and God loves with *agape* and not with *eros*.[11] Brunner also draws from Nygren and his belief that the Bible proposes a relatively unique and uniform understanding of *agape*.

An examination of Christian Scripture, however, reveals that Nygren's exegesis is faulty.[12] Biblical authors actually use *agape* to convey a wide variety and sometimes contradictory set of meanings. For instance, biblical writers sometimes use *agape* to refer to ideal ethical action and other times to sinful action.[13] To express *agape* is not always a good thing, according to biblical authors.

9. For an in-depth analysis of *agape* as used in the New Testament, see Ceslas Spicq, *Agape in the New Testament*, trans. Maria Aquinas McNamara and Mary Honoria Richter, 3 vols. (New York: Herder, 1963–1966).

10. David L. Norton and Mary F. Kille, *Philosophies of Love* (Totowa, NJ: Rowman & Allanheld, 1983), 157, 154.

11. Emil Brunner, *Faith, Hope, and Love* (Philadelphia: Westminster, 1956), 64–67.

12. See my chapter on Nygren's work in Thomas Jay Oord, *Essential Kenosis: An Open and Relational Theology of Love* (St. Louis: Chalice Press, forthcoming).

13. Although Nygren claims that Paul "knows nothing of any distinction between true and false *agape*" (*Agape and Eros*, 156), Paul does speak of false *agape* when he speaks of being deserted by Demas, who "loved [*agapaō*] this present world" (2 Tim. 4:10). Paul implies that false *agape* is possible when he twice urges his readers to have sincere *agape* (Rom. 12:9; 2 Cor. 8:8) and also urges them to express genuine *agape* (2 Cor. 6:6). Writings attributed to other authors and biblical figures also refer to inappropriate *agape*. Examples include love of darkness (John 3:19), prestige (Luke 11:43; John 12:43), wages of unrighteousness (2 Pet. 2:15), and the world (2 Tim. 4:10; 1 John 2:15).

In addition, sometimes biblical authors use *agape* to talk about unconditional love and other times about conditioned, response-dependent love.[14] *Agape* is not necessarily disinterested, according to Scripture. Some biblical authors use *agape* to talk about self-sacrifice; others use *agape* to talk about activity that is not self-sacrificial. *Agape*, as biblical writers understand it, is not necessarily altruistic. The apostle Paul, whom Nygren believes most supports his theory that *agape* is opposed to all self-love, sometimes uses the word *agape* to talk about appropriate self-love.[15] The biblical witness does not uniformly or even predominantly support Nygren's claims.

To complicate things even more, biblical scholars translate the Greek word *agape* in ways that we typically think *eros* or *philia* would be translated. *Agape* is translated as "to long for," "to prefer," "to desire," "to prize," "to value," and "to be fond of."[16] Each of these translations fits more easily in *eros*-oriented forms of love. Sometimes *agape* is used to convey meanings traditionally assigned *philia*, and in many contexts the two words are interchangeable.[17] Biblical authors are inconsistent in their use of *agape* and *philia*. These authors can have the meaning of *philia* and *eros* in mind when they employ the word *agape*.

Neither the narrow claim that *agape* possesses a single meaning in the Bible nor the broader claim that one meaning of *agape* predominates in Christian Scripture finds textual support. The

14. Nygren suggests that at least Paul reserves use of *agape* to talk about unconditional love when he says that "no words are too strong for [Paul] to use in order to press home [*agape*'s] spontaneous and unmotivated character" (*Agape and Eros*, 155). However, Paul's admonition to give cheerfully grows out of his reasoning that God *agape* loves those who do so (2 Cor. 9:7). In other words, Paul claims that God's love is motivated by the activity of humans, and this is not unconditional love.

15. Nygren says that a feature "especially characteristic of the Pauline idea of *agape*" is its "opposition to all that can be called 'self-love'" (*Agape and Eros*, 130). He then quotes Paul's words: "Love seeketh not its own" (1 Cor. 13:5). Paul, however, is not opposed to a healthy self-love, and he even speaks of it in terms of *agape*. He commands, for instance, that husbands "love" (*agapaō*) their wives in the same way they love their own bodies (Eph. 5:28).

16. See the use of the verb *agapaō* in Luke 7:5; John 3:19; 12:43; 2 Tim. 4:8, 10; Heb. 1:9; Rev. 12:11.

17. On this, see James Moffatt, *Love in the New Testament* (London: Hodder & Stoughton, 1929), 51–56.

meanings of *philia* and *eros* often are present when we encounter the word *agape*. To be true to Christian Scripture, we should not talk about *the* biblical understanding of *agape* or think that *agape* is a definitively Christian form of love.

Despite the objections of Nygren's critics and the diverse meanings of *agape* found in Christian Scripture, many contemporary researchers, although rarely biblical scholars, consider *agape* to have privileged status or unique meaning. Those aligned with the Christian tradition are especially prone to afford *agape* such high honor.[18] As a love word, *agape* continues to exert influence.

The meanings that scholars assign *agape* vary greatly. This fact is well illustrated in the various ways scholars have defined *agape*. Consider these sixteen examples drawn from these contemporary writers: *Agape* is . . .

"the simple yet profound recognition of the worthiness of and goodness in persons."[19]—Bernard Brady

"ordinary human affection and compassion."[20]—Don Cupitt

"self-giving" or "a person's spending himself freely and carelessly for the other person."[21]—Paul Fiddes

"the principle of beneficence, that is, of doing good."[22]—William Frankena

"unconditional willing of the good."[23]—Timothy Jackson

a representation of "the divine extravagance of giving that does not take the self into account."[24]—Colin Grant

18. For a fine exploration of the relationship between divine and human love under the notion of *agape*, see Craig A. Boyd, ed., *Visions of Agapé: Problems and Possibilities in Human and Divine Love* (Burlington, VT: Ashgate, 2008).

19. Bernard V. Brady, *Christian Love: How Christians through the Ages Have Understood Love* (Washington, DC: Georgetown University Press, 2003), 268.

20. Don Cupitt, *The New Christian Ethics* (London: SCM Press, 1988), 57.

21. Paul Fiddes, *The Creative Suffering of God* (Oxford: Clarendon Press, 1988), 170.

22. William K. Frankena, *Ethics*, 2nd ed. (Englewood Cliffs, NJ: Prentice-Hall, 1973), 44.

23. Timothy Jackson, *Love Disconsoled: Meditations on Christian Charity* (Cambridge: Cambridge University Press, 1999), 15.

24. Colin Grant, *Altruism and Christian Ethics* (Cambridge: Cambridge University Press, 2001), 188.

"understanding, redeeming good will for all men."[25]—Martin Luther King Jr.

"letting-be."[26]—John Macquarrie

"selfless altruism."[27]—Mike Martin

"self-sacrifice."[28]—Reinhold Niebuhr

"equal regard"[29] or "the attribution to everyone alike of an irreducible worth and dignity."[30]—Gene Outka

"the overriding, unconditional claim of God's utterly gracious yet utterly demanding rule of righteous love."[31]—John A. T. Robinson

"God giving himself" or "divine bestowal."[32]—Irving Singer

"x loves y independently of y's merit, and any merit of y's that plays a role in x's love is value that x attributes to or creates in y as a result of x's love."[33]—Alan Soble

to act "for the sake of the beloved."[34]—Edward Collins Vacek

"identification with the neighbor and meeting his needs."[35] —Daniel Day Williams

The foregoing list illustrates well Gene Outka's observation that "the meaning ascribed in the literature to love, in general, and to

25. Martin Luther King Jr., *A Testament of Hope: The Essential Writings of Martin Luther King, Jr.*, ed. James Melvin Washington (San Francisco: Harper & Row, 1986), 19.

26. John Macquarrie, *Principles of Christian Theology*, 2nd ed. (New York: Scribner, 1977), 349.

27. Mike W. Martin, *Love's Virtues* (Lawrence: University Press of Kansas, 1996), 14.

28. Reinhold Niebuhr, *The Nature and Destiny of Man: A Christian Interpretation*, 2 vols. (New York: Scribner, 1964), 2:82.

29. Outka, *Agape*, 9–12.

30. Ibid., 260.

31. John A. T. Robinson, *Christian Morals Today* (London: SCM Press, 1964), 12.

32. Irving Singer, *The Nature of Love*, vol. 1, *Plato to Luther*, 2nd ed. (Chicago: University of Chicago Press, 1987), 269.

33. Alan Soble, *Agape, Eros, and Philia: Readings in the Philosophy of Love* (New York: Paragon House, 1989), xxiv.

34. Vacek, *Love, Human and Divine*, 157. Vacek also writes, "Agape is directed to the beloved's full value for the beloved's own sake" (ibid., 179).

35. Williams, *Spirit and the Forms of Love*, 262.

agape, in particular, is often characterized by both variance and ambiguity."[36] Robert Adams notes the diverse understandings of *agape* that scholars offer, and he concludes that "*agape* is a blank canvas on which one can paint whatever ideal of Christian love one favors."[37] I suggest that this variance arises from the theological, ethical, anthropological, scientific, and metaphysical commitments of those who use *agape* to identify something distinctive when compared with other forms of love. These diverse understandings suggest that we should not think that *agape* has a uniform or obvious meaning.

With all this diversity, one might wonder whether the word *agape* is redeemable. Should we toss it in the garbage pile of overused, worn-out, and ambiguous words? Does it make sense to use the word *agape* anymore to talk about a particular form of love?

Given that the Bible and Greek tradition offers no uniform meaning for *agape* and that scholars of love offer divergent definitions, one might be tempted to pass over *agape* altogether to overcome the variance and discord. This is the same temptation, however, to which many have succumbed when passing over the even-more general word *love*. Yet *love* remains a uniquely powerful word, a rallying word for people of many religious and ethical persuasions. Despite the divergent meanings of *agape*, it too carries significant rhetorical weight in many communities. It seems unwise to squander the value that this word has accumulated. *Agape*'s day is not done.

Those who employ the word *agape*—and I count myself among them—seem obligated to be careful about using the word. They should

1. define clearly what they mean by *agape* and then employ that meaning consistently;
2. show how this meaning differs from the other love forms (especially *philia* and *eros*);
3. show how their definition of *agape* fits with and does not contradict their definition of love in general.

36. Outka, *Agape*, 257–58.
37. Robert Merrihew Adams, *Finite and Infinite Goods: A Framework for Ethics* (New York: Oxford University Press, 1999), 136.

Only by meeting these three criteria can *agape* retain well its usefulness as one form of love in relation to other forms and its proper relation to love itself.

I find some merit in all definitions of *agape* listed above. But for one reason or another, few are adequate. Most of the definitions add to the confusion by failing to meet the three obligations I have just suggested. A quick look at how these three obligations function relative to *agape* definitions seems helpful.

Some of the sixteen definitions of *agape* are flawed, because they make it difficult to see how these definitions allow for other love forms to really be loves. For instance, some equate *agape* with doing what is good or promoting the good. William Frankena defines *agape* as "the principle of benevolence, that is, of doing good."[38] I too believe that *agape* should be understood as a love that promotes good, but this definition is not specific enough. After all, when *agape* is equated with or claimed to be identical with doing good, this implies that the other forms of love (*philia*, *eros*) are not actions that promote good. Either these other forms are not forms of love at all or Frankena's definition of *agape* provides no clear way to distinguish *agape* from the other forms.[39]

Some definitions of *agape* are less adequate because they equate it with self-sacrifice or selfless altruism. In fact, this is the most common use of *agape* in love, theology, and science research. The equation of *agape* and self-sacrifice is also found in some philosophical and theological traditions. On the list of sixteen definitions, for instance, Reinhold Niebuhr identifies *agape* with self-sacrifice and Mike Martin equates it with selfless altruism.

38. Frankena, *Ethics*, 44.
39. Of course, one might respond to my criticism and say that love is best defined simply as acting (proper/improper tradition) or being in relation (relational tradition). What makes *agape* unique, one might contend, is that *agape* promotes what is good. But as I argued in the previous chapter, this use of "love" is counterintuitive and contributes to the general confusion pertaining to the meaning of love. When we say that Mother Teresa expressed love, we do not typically mean that she simply acted or was related to someone else. We do not usually say that she loved properly. When we say that Mother Teresa was loving, we mean that what she did was good. Her actions promoted well-being. And to say that only *agape* promotes good is to disparage other forms of action, such as friendship (*philia*), that also promote good.

There are a host of problems with equating *agape* with self-sacrifice and selfless altruism. First, self-sacrifice is untenable in ongoing love relationships. If two persons tried always to act self-sacrificially toward one another, neither could act self-sacrificially. "In a completely self-sacrificing community," argues Vacek, "we would want to give to and not receive from persons who would want to give to and not receive from us."[40] Neil Cooper illustrates the problem of understanding constant self-sacrifice as love by imagining two relentless altruists who find a cup of water in the desert. The two pass the cup back and forth, each insisting that the other drink first. The water eventually evaporates in this relentless display of altruism. Both die of thirst.[41]

Love sometimes shuns altruism. In the same way that we want others to satisfy themselves by receiving our gifts, so we ought to receive gifts given us. If the satisfaction that comes from such give-and-take relations is thwarted because all parties insist on acting altruistically, Dietrich Bonhoeffer's retort seems appropriate: "Too much altruism is a bore."[42] And boredom may be the least of our worries. Failing to receive good gifts can be rude, arrogant, and mean.

Second, equating *agape* with self-sacrifice or altruism denies what seems obvious: sometimes we must *not* sacrifice ourselves so that in the long run we can provide more benefits to others. Love sometimes requires self-realization, which is a form of self-affirmation. Feminists in many disciplines seem especially aware of the fact that love sometimes demands that the individual eschew self-sacrifice and act instead in self-authenticating ways for the good of the individual and the whole.[43] Choosing to act as a doormat on whom others stomp can be a negative enabling act that fails to promote overall well-being.

Third, the idea that a loving person always engages in self-sacrifice may actually keep those at the margins of society from

40. Vacek, *Love, Human and Divine*, 184.

41. Neil Cooper, *The Diversity of Moral Thinking* (Oxford: Clarendon Press, 1981), 274.

42. Dietrich Bonhoeffer, *Letters and Papers from Prison* (London: Collins, 1953), 96.

43. One of the first to make this claim was Valerie Saiving, "The Human Situation: A Feminine View," *Journal of Religion* 40, no. 2 (1960): 100–112.

experiencing justice. If the poor and oppressed always act self-sacrificially, they would remain in their impoverished and unjust existence. To think that all people, even the poorest of the poor, ought always to act self-sacrificially is to fall victim to what Arthur McGill calls "the illusion of perpetual affluence."[44] The demand that love in general or *agape* in particular requires unceasing self-sacrifice can become the means for keeping the oppressed from contributing to their own liberation.

If *agape* is a form of love, it must be an action that promotes rather than prevents the attainment of overall well-being. While self-sacrificial, self-subordinating, or altruistic action can be an expression of love, these actions can also generate overall ill-being. *Agape*, if it is to be understood as a form of love, does not generate overall ill-being. A more precise and yet robust definition of *agape* is required.

Still others place a great deal of emphasis on *agape* as having unique identification with God. Nygren's influence is evident in this emphasis. Some argue that only God expresses *agape*. Others contend that *agape* is the recognition that God gives love to the world. The first argument places in jeopardy the Christian claim that God wants humans to love God, others, and themselves. How can humans love with *agape* if only God can express this type of love?

The argument that *agape* should be defined as God's bestowal of love on creatures, present in Irving Singer's quote on the list of sixteen, suggests that God does not give or express other forms of love (*philia, eros*). According to the Christian Scriptures, however, God both inspires creatures to love with *philia* and *eros* and expresses these forms of love for creation. Provided that *philia* and *eros* are defined adequately, one should regard God as expressing these forms of love if God is also concerned with promoting overall well-being. I will expand later on the claim that God expresses multiple forms of love, or what I call "full-orbed love."

Whereas many if not all the *agape* definitions fail to meet the three obligations necessary for an adequate definition of *agape*, I intend for my definition to meet these demands. Before looking at

44. Arthur C. McGill, Charles A. Wilson, and Per M. Anderson, *Death and Life: An American Theology* (Philadelphia: Fortress, 1987), 89.

it, however, I should note that I do not claim that my definition is the only one that could be adequate. Although my definition fits well with some ways biblical authors employ *agape*, and my definition reflects important themes in ethics in general and Christian ethics in particular, I do not claim it is the only biblical, Christian, or generally adequate definition of *agape*.

Having made these qualifications, I define *agape* as acting intentionally, in sympathetic response to others (including God), to promote overall well-being when responding to acts, persons, or structures of existence that promote ill-being. To put it more concisely:

> *agape* is intentional sympathetic response to promote overall well-being when confronted by that which generates ill-being.

As I define it, *agape* repays evil with good, to use a phrase attributed to Jesus. When we love our enemies and pray for those who persecute us, we express *agape*. In an effort to promote overall well-being, *agape* turns the other cheek. *Agape* acts to promote well-being despite the ill-being or evil—whether directed toward the lover, the lover's community, or society at large—that it encounters.

Acts that rightly bear the label *agape* range from those we deem exceptional to those we consider mundane. Many who risked their lives to save Jews during the Nazi Holocaust, for instance, expressed *agape*. They responded intentionally to promote overall well-being when confronted with the ill-being generated by Nazi ideals, structures, and activity. A father who puts a bandage on his child's cut finger also responds intentionally to promote overall well-being when confronted by unnecessary pain. A teacher who refuses to retaliate when a student lodges false accusations against her is also likely expressing *agape*. In a world full of activity that generates ill-being, numerous opportunities to express *agape* arise.

As soon as we offer concrete examples, of course, we wonder about the intentions of the ones doing the loving. These questions are legitimate, because as I pointed out when explaining what I mean by love, motives matter. Acts done with evil intentions are not loving. We could imagine, for instance, that instead of responding intentionally to promote overall well-being, perhaps the rescuers of Jews were motivated primarily by the desire to gain a burnished reputation or the wish to avoid divine wrath. Or we could imagine a case in which the father responding with a bandage wants his child healthy primarily so that his genetic lineage will continue at the expense of the whole. Or perhaps the teacher refuses to retaliate against the accusing student because she relishes being abused.

All these are possible motives, but they may not be plausible. We typically judge on a case-by-case basis, given the information we have, what a person's primary motives might be. And the person typically knows best what his or her primary motives might be. Unless we are prepared to accept the claim that no one ever acts to promote well-being when confronted by ill-being, it seems plausible that most rescuers, fathers, and teachers in the situations noted above express *agape*. Those acting in these ways often have a good idea what their motives are, and onlookers can come to plausible judgments given a reasonable amount of observation. When these actors respond to that which is negative by seeking to promote what is positive, they express *agape*.

My definition of *agape*—intentional sympathetic response to promote overall well-being when confronted by that which generates ill-being—fulfills the three obligations necessary for an adequate notion of *agape*. First, I offer what I hope is a reasonably clear definition. Surely there are additional questions to resolve (e.g., What motivates one to express *agape*? What role, if any, does God play in expressing or inspiring *agape*? What kind of person expresses *agape*?). But the fact that *agape* promotes overall well-being in response to that which generates ill-being should be a reasonably clear description of *agape*.

Second, I hope to have indicated, albeit briefly, that what makes *agape* a unique form or version of love in contrast to other forms is its response to ill-being. *Agape* repays evil with good. Other forms of love are not responses to ill-being; they are intentional responses to something else. This will become clearer as I examine and define *philia* and *eros*.

I meet the third obligation by defining *agape* as one form of love rather than love itself. *Agape* is just one way love can be expressed. *Agape* is one way that we might respond intentionally to others (including God) to promote overall well-being. The other forms

44

represent other ways to love, and none should be regarded as the only or correct love form.

Eros

While *agape* garners significant attention from love, science, and theology researchers, *eros* receives little attention. That is, it receives little attention unless one regards *eros* as equivalent with sexual activity, reproduction, or selfishness. Like most scholars, however, I do not equate *eros* with such behavior and motivation, although such behavior and motivation may be important for love in its *eros* form. Here I need to discuss *eros* briefly before suggesting how this form of love might best be defined.

Plato is either directly or indirectly the source of most scholarly understandings of *eros*, although his use of the word involves differing meanings. Sometimes Plato uses *eros* to denote the general desire to possess beauty. Other times *eros* pertains to one's desire for a specific object of value.[45] In both the general and the specific cases, the desire inherent in *eros* implies some need on the part of the lover. Desire and need do not necessarily indicate that the lover is selfish, however. At least the lover is not selfish in the narrow sense of wanting something to the detriment of others. One can desire that others become more beautiful or desire that others enjoy value and beauty for themselves. For instance, a mother might desire something good for her son for his own sake.[46] Or an artist might desire to paint a beautiful picture for others to enjoy. In these cases, *eros* has in mind promoting values in others, although a sense of need in the one expressing love is implied.

As classically understood, the affirmation of value is the core of *eros*. Jules Toner captures this when he defines *eros* as "affective affirmation of its object."[47] *Eros* is directed toward affirming what one regards as valuable and good; it desires worth. Martha Nussbaum says that *eros* "involves an opening of the self toward

45. See Plato's discussion of *eros* in his *Symposium*. For a detailed analysis, see A. W. Price, *Love and Friendship in Plato and Aristotle* (Oxford: Clarendon Press, 1989). See also Catherine Osborne, *Eros Unveiled: Plato and the God of Love* (Oxford: Clarendon Press, 1994).

46. In addition to Plato's *Symposium*, see his *Phaedrus*.

47. Jules Toner, *The Experience of Love* (Washington, DC: Corpus Books, 1968), 177.

an object, a conception of the self that pictures the self as incomplete and reaching out for something valued."[48] When *eros* is expressed, the responsive, affective, or emotional element in love often exerts considerable influence, but intentionality is never completely absent.

Due in part to Plato, many throughout history have regarded *eros* as equivalent with desire. But this equivalence is problematic *if* we consider *eros* a form of love. Love as I define it and as often understood promotes overall well-being. Desire, as such, does not always promote well-being. We can desire the humiliation of others, the destruction of beautiful creatures, or even our own annihilation. To speak consistently of *eros* as a form of love, we must not equate or entirely identify *eros* with desire.

Others equate *eros* with acquisitiveness. Anders Nygren, for instance, claims that *eros* is the action we take to accumulate for ourselves what we find valuable.[49] But accumulating objects for ourselves does not always promote well-being, especially overall well-being. Hoarding is rarely good. Those who accumulate wealth at the expense of the impoverished, for example, are not expressing the love form *eros*. Therefore, regarding *eros* as equivalent with acquisitiveness is not helpful, if *eros* is truly a form of love.

The popular use of *eros*, of course, has to do with romance and sexual activity. If something or someone is erotic, it displays or excites sexual images and urges. Few, upon careful consideration, would finally equate *eros* with sex and romance, but it is easy to see why we frequently identify *eros* in this way. We often (but not always) regard sexual activity and romance as including the desire for something valuable, whether those values be union with another, sexual gratification, or something else. Of course, not everyone who engages in sex and romance seeks to promote well-being, let alone well-being in others. This is one reason *eros* as a form of love should not be equated or identified solely with sex and romance. Even more importantly, however, we should not regard *eros* as equivalent with sex and romance because *eros* as affirmation of what is valuable often has nothing to do with

48. Martha C. Nussbaum, *Upheavals of Thought: The Intelligence of Emotions* (Cambridge: Cambridge University Press, 2001), 460.
49. Nygren, *Agape and Eros*, 210. For an argument for divine *eros*, see Paul Avis, *Eros and the Sacred* (Harrisburg, PA: Morehouse, 1989).

46

romance and sexuality. Romance and sex may or may not be expressions of *eros*.

Sometimes *eros* is defined as an inclination toward the lover's own wishes or orientation. In this use, *eros* often is called "self-love." Edward Vacek identifies *eros* in this way when he speaks of *eros* as loving the beloved "for our own sake."[50] This is an unfortunate use of *eros*, however, because it ignores the truth that we can desire that value be increased in others for their sakes. While it surely is true that *eros* includes the self's appraisal of values either already or possibly evident, the intentional response that promotes well-being resulting from such appraisal need not be primarily for one's own sake. One may well recognize the value in another and act in ways to increase that value despite sacrifice to oneself. *Eros* can be self-sacrificial.

Each of these understandings of *eros* expresses partial truth, but each also misses something important. To account faithfully for the core notion of *eros* as affirmation of value while also conceiving it as a form of love, I define *eros* as acting intentionally, in sympathetic response to others (including God), to promote overall well-being when affirming what is valuable, beautiful, or excellent. To put it more concisely:

> *eros* is intentional sympathetic response to promote overall well-being when affirming what is valuable.

Not just any affirmation of value is an act of love. One can affirm that sexual activity is valuable yet also recognize that such activity, when expressed by particular individuals in particular situations (e.g., adultery), does not promote overall well-being. Sometimes sexual activity is an expression of *eros* love; sometimes it is an expression of lust. The murderer who arranges his victims in an aesthetically interesting way has affirmed some forms of value, but murder probably is never *eros*. The murderer is likely not promoting overall well-being. To express *eros*, one must affirm what is valuable as part of the aim to promote overall well-being. Whatever values are present in adultery or murder do not exceed the greater loss of well-being that such actions cause.

50. Vacek, *Love, Human and Divine*, 157–58.

The words *covetousness* and *lust* capture the promoting of ill-being when one affirms what is valuable. To covet is to desire or value an object or person at the expense of overall well-being. To lust is to do the same, although typically we associate lust with sexual activity. If *eros* is truly an expression of love, it is something different from covetousness and lust. And it must be more than desire, acquisitiveness, attraction, sex, or self-love. *Eros* involves the intentional response that promotes overall well-being when affirming what we deem valuable or worthwhile.

An adequate definition of *eros* fulfills the obligations noted in the previous discussion of *agape*. To avoid confusion, I define *eros* as intentional sympathetic response to promote overall well-being when affirming what is valuable. Given its relations to other definitions of *eros*, it should be noted that *eros* is not equivalent with desire, self-love, or acquisitiveness. And like all forms of love, *eros* promotes overall well-being. *Eros* differs from *agape* and *philia* because it sees value—whether in the self, others, the enemy, nature, or God—and seeks to promote overall well-being in response. Whereas *agape* repays evil with good, *eros* affirms the good perceived and promotes it. And *eros* as I understand it is not equated with love itself. *Eros* is just one form of love among others.

Philia

Although classic understandings of *eros* emerge from Plato, credit should be given Aristotle for shaping how we view *philia*. The word *philia* rarely appears in the love, science, and theology literature, however.[51] Yet its connotation, especially with regard to the interrelatedness of the created order, is often present. We turn to a brief explanation and definition of *philia*.

Throughout history, the *philia* love form typically has been identified with friendship. Friendship "is very necessary for living," says Aristotle, and "no one would choose to live without friends."[52] Ar-

51. An exception to this is my discussion of *philia* in chapter 5 of my book *Science of Love: The Wisdom of Well-Being* (Radnor, PA: Templeton Foundation Press, 2004).

52. Aristotle, *Nichomachean Ethics* 1155a, in *Aristotle: Nichomachean Ethics*, ed. and trans. Sarah Broadie and Christopher Rowe (Oxford: Oxford University Press, 2002).

istotle follows this statement with relatively complex explanations of how friendship emerges, how friendship is sustained, and with whom one can be a friend. Aristotle even suggests that nonhuman animals express *philia*.[53]

Philosophers and theologians after Aristotle often speak of "special" relationships as a way of accounting for *philia*.[54] These special relationships are ones in which those involved are attached in some unique way and cooperate. By speaking of special relationships, scholars analyze a wide array of personal bonds between those different in age, gender, intellect, socioeconomic status, and even species.

One of the most important contemporary scholars of *philia*, Edward Vacek, argues that *philia* is the foundation and goal of the good life.[55] "In *philia*," says Vacek, "persons give themselves over to the relationship . . . and thereby create a good that they could not separately achieve."[56] He notes that while some scholars say that covenant and community are central, they describe love primarily in terms of selflessness, engaging enemies and strangers, or acting for the good of universal humanity. In this, the love expressed in communal life is neglected.[57] *Philia*, says Vacek, has often been "rejected or displaced in favor of an individualistic, nonmutual, and task-oriented love."[58]

The special relationships of *philia* are well identified with the categories of mutuality, reciprocity, and cooperation. *Philia* understood in this broader sense—beyond simple friendship—is evident in varying levels or degrees. Those who cooperate for long periods to promote well-being express rich forms of *philia*. Understanding *philia* as having primarily to do with mutuality, reciprocity, or cooperation also proves beneficial for understanding this form of love as important for love, theology, and science research. Both humans

53. See ibid.
54. For powerful arguments for the role of *philia* in Christianity, see Liz Carmichael, *Friendship: Interpreting Christian Love* (London: T&T Clark, 2004); Thomas A. F. Kelly and Philipp W. Rosemann, eds., *Amor amicitiae: On the Love That Is Friendship* (Leuven: Peeters, 2004); Gilbert Meilaender, *Friendship: A Study in Theological Ethics* (Notre Dame, IN: University of Notre Dame Press, 1981).
55. Vacek, *Love, Human and Divine*, 280.
56. Ibid., 288.
57. Ibid., 280.
58. Ibid., 284.

and nonhumans often rely on others to secure well-being. In fact, we will see in later chapters that some scientists regard creaturely cooperation as more fundamental than competition.

Mutuality, reciprocity, and cooperation are not always entered into with the purpose of promoting overall well-being, however. We can cooperate with or befriend others while intending to wreak havoc and cause evil. Thieves, thugs, and killers can join together to do dastardly deeds. Gang rape requires a degree of cooperation. Coalition and solidarity are not good in themselves. If *philia* is truly a form of love, it must be expressed with the purpose of promoting overall well-being.

With this brief introduction, I define *philia* as acting intentionally, in sympathetic response to others (including God), to promote overall well-being when working to establish deeper levels of mutuality, reciprocity, or cooperation. To put it more concisely:

> *philia* is intentional sympathetic response to promote overall well-being by cooperating with others.

In the community of *philia*, says Linell E. Cady, persons "share a commitment to the continued well-being of the relational life uniting them."[59] *Philia* expressions secure a level of well-being that individuals cannot secure acting alone. The nature of one's relations with others, especially within specific communities, greatly influences what kind of persons love and what specific acts of love are required. In fact, ongoing expressions of *philia* profoundly shape the character and habits of individuals, both human and nonhuman. Community matters.

The emotional or affective tone of *philia* expressions vary. *Philia* can involve warm and tender feelings for the one or ones with whom we cooperate. But *philia* does not require warmth and tenderness. Sometimes a deep sense of collegiality emerges among those who express *philia* when working cooperatively. But *philia* does not require great depth of feeling. While greater warmth, tenderness, and depth may be important goals in a long-lasting relationship of

59. Linell E. Cady, "Relational Love," in *Embodied Love: Sensuality and Relationship as Feminist Values*, ed. Paul Cooey, Sharon A. Farmer, and Mary Ellen Ross (San Francisco: Harper & Row, 1987), 141.

cooperation, *philia* can be expressed when accompanied by much milder feelings. *Philia* can involve multiple kinds and degrees of emotion.

I aim for my definition of *philia* to meet the obligations of an adequate definition I identified in my explanations of *agape* and *eros*. What makes *philia* an act of love is its intentional response to promote overall well-being. What distinguishes it from the other forms of love is its cooperative aspect. While *agape* and *eros* may benefit from cooperation from others, these forms of love do not require cooperation. *Philia* is a form of love—rather than love itself—that expresses one's intentional response by cooperating with others to promote what is good.

Mixed Love

The tendency when discussing each of the three main forms of love is to think of a single act as expressing only a single form. We can assume either that we are single minded in our intentional responses or that only one form of love promotes well-being in a given situation. These assumptions often are mistaken.

Our tendency to think of promoting well-being with a single love form is unfortunate because our motives are often mixed and the relations we have with others are complex. An *agape* response, for instance, often also entails cooperating with others (*philia*) to promote overall well-being in response to the evil encountered. People might work cooperatively to combat prostitution and the forces that support it, for instance, and thereby express both *agape* and *philia*. One can appreciate something of value in the other when seeking to promote well-being (*eros*) while simultaneously opposing the ill-being that the other has generated (*agape*). Parents often express multiple forms of love when loving rebellious and unappreciative children. They affirm the value of their children and simultaneously oppose the ill-being that the children may cause. In working cooperatively with others to promote overall well-being, we can affirm the value of our co-workers and the value of the recipients of our work. When we do so, we express both *philia* and *eros*. In the interrelated universe in which we live, the forms of love often mix in our intentional responses to promote overall well-being.

Admitting that many forms of love might be present in an act does not preclude the possibility that one form predominates. It may be that the overwhelming sense of solidarity to cooperate to make the world better (*philia*) may predominate over the *agape* and *eros* love forms also present. Or one's primary motivation to promote well-being in the face of tragedy, pain, or evil may be *agape*, although the other forms of love also emerge. For example, a mother may be primarily compelled to express *agape* in response to her drunken teenager, but the presence of *eros* that affirms the child's value is also likely present as a secondary motivation. Working with other family members to help the errant teenager likely will entail *philia*. Although many forms may be present in the lover's intentional response to promote overall well-being, one form may and often does predominate.

It is difficult to imagine an enduring and flourishing human being (perhaps even a nonhuman mammalian) who did not include all three forms of love: *agape*, *eros*, and *philia*. The three are likely expressed every day by every able-minded human on the planet. In addition, we often consider some people especially good at expressing one love form, realizing that such people also likely express the other forms. These forms seem present in the activity of many nonhumans. Vacek puts it this way: "Life typically includes all three loves in rhythmically occurring ways."[60]

Instead of considering one love form superior to the others or advocating the exclusive expression of one form, a typical individual can promote overall well-being by expressing each love often in life. Those who consistently promote overall well-being might best be said to express full-orbed love. Full-orbed love is a way to talk about the importance of each love form, the appropriate expression of which depends on the context. But all three—*agape*, *eros*, *philia*—typically are necessary for a lifetime devoted to enhancing the common good. The good life, whether creaturely or divine, is characterized by full-orbed love.

Acknowledging that more than one love form can be present in the promotion of well-being allows one to overcome some paradoxes that arise in discussions of egoism and altruism. Affirming the value of oneself or one's own feeling of satisfaction when doing

60. Vacek, *Love, Human and Divine*, 310.

good can accompany one's primary intention to promote well-being in others at some cost to oneself. The paradox of psychological hedonism with regard to altruism is overcome when we see that the forms of love often are mixed in any particular action. Altruism and egoism need not and often cannot be neatly distinguished in any act of love. But one form may predominate.

Love's Multiple Recipients

It seems helpful to identify love with intentional responses that promote overall well-being and to show that love takes a variety of forms. I have explored three main forms and suggested that overall well-being often means expressing full-orbed love. But an important question remains unanswered: Whose well-being does love promote?

Our first response to this question might be "Love promotes the well-being of others." If only an adequate answer were so simple! This answer does not resolve the question, "Which others ought to be loved when competing interests arise?" Should we love family and friends first? What about love of enemies? Can we promote the well-being of every human on planet Earth? What about all creatures great and small? The entire universe? God? Whose well-being does love promote?

One way to begin addressing this set of questions is to consider a vexing question: What is the proper way to act for one's own good in relation to promoting the good of others? Is there such a thing as self-love? If so, what does it mean?[61]

Some argue that acting to benefit oneself—self-love—is antithetical to love. We earlier noted Anders Nygren's understanding of *agape* as the only legitimate form of love. Nygren says that legitimate love opposes all that can be called self-love. In his view, "If there were not a desire on other grounds to include self-love among the ethical demands of Christianity, no one would be able to find in the commandment of love any reason for doing so. Self-love is . . . the reason for the perversity of [human] will."[62] Søren

61. For insightful prose on this subject, see Darlene Fozard Weaver, *Self Love and Christian Ethics* (Cambridge: Cambridge University Press, 2002).
62. Nygren, *Agape and Eros*, 100–101.

Kierkegaard argues similarly (although he is inconsistent on this point in his writing) that "wherever Christianity is, there is self-renunciation, which is Christianity's essential form."[63] According to Nygren and Kierkegaard, love excludes promoting one's own well-being. They say love denies well-being to oneself.

Others affirm a role for self-love, but only as a secondary and unintended good. On this view, we devote ourselves wholly to promoting the well-being of others. Our sole motive is the good of the other. This view admits that other-devotion often inadvertently enhances our own well-being. But benefiting oneself is unintentional. Stephen Post expresses this idea when he says that "in the genuine giving of self lies the unsought discovery of a higher self."[64] This approach views love as self-forgetfulness, but it acknowledges that despite self-forgetting, one's own well-being often is unintentionally promoted. Its main point, however, is that love aims for the good of others, not the good of oneself.

Others who consider self-love reverse the order of primacy. They say that in acting for one's own well-being first, the good of others will subsequently be enhanced. "The first function of the moral good will be to direct the individual toward his real happiness," argues Jean Rohmer.[65] Love's first inclination is self-preference, say proponents of this view, and the effects derived from promoting one's own well-being spill over to enhance the well-being of others. In an interrelated universe, self-love has positive consequences for others.

Theologian John Macmurray offers yet another view of self-love. Macmurray acknowledges a place for promoting one's own well-being, but he believes that one should love oneself only to promote the well-being of others. The lover "has no value for himself, but only for the other," argues Macmurray; "consequently he cares for

63. Søren Kierkegaard, *Works of Love: Some Christian Reflections in the Form of Discourses*, trans. Howard and Edna Hong (New York: Harper & Row, 1962), 68. Stephen Evans argues that Kierkegaard's overall view has a place for proper self-love (*Kierkegaard's Ethic of Love: Divine Commands and Moral Obligations* [Oxford: Oxford University Press, 2004]).

64. Stephen G. Post, *Unlimited Love: Altruism, Compassion, and Service* (Philadelphia: Templeton Foundation Press, 2003), 60.

65. Cited in Gérard Gilleman, *The Primacy of Charity in Moral Theology*, trans. William F. Ryan and André Vachon (Westminster, MD: Newman Press, 1959), 104.

himself only for the sake of the other."[66] Philosopher Garth Hallett argues for a view of proper self-love similar to Macmurray's. Hallett believes that self-subordination best describes what love demands, because the lover puts the well-being of others before his or her own well-being. Others come first, says Hallett, and the lover gets any leftovers. In this way of thinking, one can intentionally promote one's own well-being. But promoting one's own well-being cannot be considered love if such promoting is an end in itself. Self-love is only a means to enhance the well-being of others.

I find none of these views of self-love fully adequate. I draw on Vacek's work to help explain the inadequacies of each. First, says Vacek, theists who typically are the only ones who denounce self-love entirely need to consider some theological anomalies that follow from this denunciation. These anomalies can be posed in the form of questions: Do they really think that God does not have self-love? And if Jesus and his Father can love themselves and accept being loved, the question arises "Why can't believers do the same?"[67] Vacek believes that creatures should follow God's example of self-love by loving themselves. Self-love has a strong theological basis.

A similar argument can be made from a nontheological perspective. We might ask if we really hoped that others deny themselves any expression of love. After all, looking after one's own basic needs is a benefit both to the individual and to society. And if we think that some measure of self-love is appropriate for others, it makes little sense to make an exception of ourselves. Self-love, in some form, seems required.

In response to those who regard love as self-forgetfulness, Vacek argues from a Christian perspective that "a strict policy of self-forgetfulness is neither possible nor desirable. The Gospel, which so often offers us the prospect of a more abundant life, is not very supportive of such a policy."[68] From a theological perspective, self-forgetfulness amounts to not valuing what God values and what others should rightfully value. "Not to love ourselves," adds Vacek,

66. John Macmurray, *Persons in Relation* (Atlantic Highlands, NJ: Humanities Press International, 1983), 158.
67. Vacek, *Love, Human and Divine*, 201.
68. Ibid., 204.

"is *prima facie* not to cooperate with the love that God has for us. It is sinful."[69] What God affirms we ought also affirm.

In response to those who start with love of self and hope that self-love overflows to others, Vacek argues that love sometimes requires self-sacrifice. The context sometimes demands altruism. Although acting for one's own well-being is sometimes required, acting for the good of others, even to the point of choosing death, may also be necessary if one's goal is the promotion of overall well-being. Considering self-love as the exclusive channel by which love for others can overflow will not suffice; others sometimes come first.

We should also reject the view that self-love is a necessary evil. "Some allow self-love," argues Vacek, "but only as a way of keeping the beast alive so it can love others for yet another day." But this "is a denigration or neglect of one's own God-given value," Vacek says. "A lack of self-love is ultimately un-Christian. It is a refusal to cooperate with God's love for us."[70] In nontheological terms, this view of self-love treats oneself only as a means to some other end. But sometimes the self should be the primary end.

To Hallett and those who say that self-subordination is the proper way to understand love of self in relation to others, Vacek responds that such a view is finally indefensible. "A strict criterion of self-subordination holds that only when others' needs are met may we fulfill our own needs," says Vacek. "But it is almost always the case that there is someone who is in need, indeed, in much greater need than we are."[71] In a world of immense need, continual self-subordination deprives oneself of basic needs. Suicide is justified if self-subordination is one's sole ethical concern.

Upon examining a wide range of positions related to self-love, everything from self-denial to self-preference, Vacek concludes that "there are roughly equivalent dangers of excessive self-assertion and self-giving. The danger of self-love is selfishness. The danger of other-love is that we treat ourselves merely as a *means* for the fulfillment of others."[72] We need a view of self-love that allows for multiple responses depending on the contexts.

69. Ibid., 261.
70. Ibid., 60.
71. Ibid., 271.
72. Ibid.

How does love for oneself figure into love's intentional response to promote well-being? My own position begins by acknowledging that it is difficult, if not impossible, to separate love for others and love for oneself entirely. It is difficult both psychologically and ontologically.

With regard to the psychological aspect, we sometimes feel deeply satisfied, and thus enjoy a measure of well-being, when we benefit others. We gain this satisfaction even though we may choose significant physical, monetary, or social loss. Deep down, we often feel good about ourselves when we help. If we expect to feel good when doing good for others, we should not say that we are acting *entirely* for the good of others. We should acknowledge that we may benefit as well.

We also have difficulty separating ourselves completely from others in the ontological sense. Who we are is largely shaped by the relations we have with those around us. It is as true to say that we are ontologically shaped by our environments as it is to say that we are ontologically shaped by what we eat. As interrelated beings, we are partly constituted by our relations with others.

There remains a difference, of course, between us and those with whom we relate. But to say that we are essentially related to others entails that we are not isolated atoms, disconnected from and uninfluenced by others. If what we do partly determines who others become, and others partly determine what we become, our attempts to promote well-being in others often will increase our own well-being. In short, the well-being of the lover is tied up in large part with the well-being of the ones loved.

Because the lover's own well-being is part of the whole, loving action done to promote overall well-being often results in the lover enjoying benefits secured for others. Jesus expressed this concept when he urged his listeners, "Give, and it will be given to you. A good measure, pressed down, shaken together, running over will be put into your lap; for the measure you give will be the measure you get back" (Luke 6:38).

There are two basic ways in which we act for our own good. When we respond intentionally to promote our own well-being, we might promote our bodily and mental well-being. For example, we might brush our teeth, enhance our cardiovascular capacities through exercise, eat some vegetables, or clip our toenails. In one sense, our teeth, lungs, stomach, or toenails are us. In another sense, however, our bodily members are not simply identical to us. When we have clipped a toenail, for instance, we do not think that we have decreased in some way. When we diet successfully, we might say, "I have lost weight," but we also might say, "My hips are smaller" or "My belly is shrinking." In the first sense, the self seems identical to the body; in the second sense, we distinguish ourselves from our bodily parts. In either sense, however, we love ourselves when we act in ways that promote our own bodily well-being.

Acting to promote our own well-being frequently entails, second, promoting our future well-being—the selves (whether bodily or subjective experiences) we will be. In this episodic sense, we are a self related to past selves and anticipating future selves. When we put aside money for retirement, for instance, we are considering the well-being of the person we will (hopefully) someday become. When we get an education, we are likely securing this learning so that we can benefit in the future. In these ways, we act for the good of another, even though that other will be directly related to the person we currently are.

Thinking of ourselves as being composed of episodes or as a connected series of event-experiences is important for understanding central religious claims about love. For instance, Christians are commanded to love others as they love themselves. If love for oneself is understood in terms of one's future selves, this commandment becomes understandable. Our future selves are, in one sense, others or neighbors whom we should consider as future recipients of our loving actions in the present. Charles Hartshorne puts it this way: "We can love the other *as ourselves* because even the self as future is also another."[73]

Thinking of ourselves in terms of our relations with our bodily members also helps to understand what it means to love our neighbors as ourselves. If we consider our bodily members—teeth, lungs, stomach, toenails, and so on—as others and not simply identical to ourselves, we might realize that we should love other persons in the way we love our bodily members. If I care for my own physical

73. Charles Hartshorne, *Creative Synthesis and Philosophic Method* (LaSalle, IL: Open Court, 1970), 198.

well-being, I should also care for the physical well-being of my neighbor.

All of these positive instances of self-love express interrelatedness. In loving our bodies, relations exist between our subjective self and our own bodily members. Our minds and bodies interrelate. In loving our future selves, we assume that a future self (whether bodily self or subjective self or both) will someday exist and be affected by our present self. All of these actions to promote one's own well-being involve relations with our own moments of existence and the existence of others.

Sometimes, however, the call to promote overall well-being involves acting in ways that do not promote our own present or future well-being. We typically label such self-sacrificial action as altruistic, although definitions of altruism vary. Jesus says in one of his more memorable lines, "There is no greater love than this: to lay down one's life for one's friends" (John 15:13). Philosopher Kenneth Cauthen puts it this way: "It is not always true that the highest good of the self is coincident with service of others. . . . The soldier who dies for his country in a just war cannot live to become the poet his soul longs to be." Cauthen concludes that "sacrifice of self is not always the road to self-realization in every sense of the word."[74]

Sometimes the good of the whole requires that the lover be self-sacrificial and act in ways that promote the well-being of others at significant cost to the lover's own well-being. Finite creatures in an interrelated universe do not always receive just deserts. Self-sacrifice may be what the common good requires. Self-sacrifice may be what God desires, for we cannot conclude, as Vacek puts it, "that what God is doing in the world will always be entirely for our [personal] good. Some loss to our own well-being will be necessary."[75] Self-sacrifice may be in order if we seek to promote the good of the whole.

The foregoing provides the rationale for the position on self-love versus other-love that I advocate. This position is pluralistic.[76] Love sometimes requires that we be self-sacrificial, in the sense of

74. Kenneth Cauthen, *Process Ethics: A Constructive System* (New York: Mellen, 1984), 167–68.

75. Vacek, *Love, Human and Divine*, 188.

76. This emphasis on multiplicity is similar to the argument that Kristen Renwick Monroe makes about the multiple motivations and expressions of altru-

denying something good for ourselves so that the well-being of others is enhanced. Sometimes love requires that we act in relatively neutral ways. In these cases, we act to promote the well-being of others with no measurable gain or loss to our personal well-being. Sometimes love requires that we act to promote well-being equally for others and for ourselves. Sometimes love requires that we be self-enhancing, in the sense that acting for our own good promotes the common good. In fact, acting for our own good may mean that some with whom we relate will not directly benefit from our intentional response to promote overall well-being.

To say that love promotes overall well-being acknowledges that perpetually boosting one's own flourishing at the overall expense of others is unjustified. When we perceive that acting for one's own good is clearly at odds with what the common good requires, we should not regard this acting as an act of love.

A common way to speak of the concern to promote overall well-being, not just the well-being of one or a few, is to speak of love as including justice. To act unjustly is to grant excessive goods to the self or the few at the expense of the many. The justice aspect of love can entail giving to the few the rights and privileges rightly afforded the many. In both cases, it is overall well-being that justice seeks and love requires.[77] Justice is not antithetical to love. Justice is the fairness involved in promoting overall well-being.

My emphasis on love as promoting overall well-being does not mean that only those who are thinking about the entire universe or considering all dimensions of well-being can express love. Only an all-encompassing Mind could do this. But responding intentionally for the good of the one, the few, or the in-group to the obvious detriment of the whole should not be considered an act of love. When global concerns clearly outweigh local ones, love requires acting for the common good.

I use the phrase "overall well-being" to argue that the multidimensional flourishing of the whole trumps the flourishing of the individual. And the good of all others is often more important than

---

ism (*The Heart of Altruism: Perceptions of a Common Humanity* [Princeton, NJ: Princeton University Press, 1996]).

77. An important book exploring the connection between justice and love is Timothy P. Jackson, *The Priority of Love: Christian Charity and Social Justice* (Princeton, NJ: Princeton University Press, 2003).

the good of the self, with the exceptions noted above. Philosopher Drew Christiansen explains the function of my phrase "overall well-being" in his reference to its synonym, the common good:

> The common good functions above all as a coordinating principle, and the weight of relevant norms will alter depending on the circumstances. The goal of the coordination, however, remains clear: *Everyone in society ought to be able to share in an advancing quality of life.* . . . The principle of solidarity charges privileged individuals, groups, and nations with making sacrifices, even from their substance, to close the gap between themselves and the poor.[78]

Since the nineteenth century, talk of promoting "overall well-being" or "the common good" has, unfortunately, sometimes been identified solely with utilitarian ethics. This is understandable in part, since utilitarian ethics is concerned with the greatest good for the greatest number. However, this equation is not entirely accurate. Strict utilitarianism is not possible for finite creatures. If the world is characterized by interrelatedness, precise calculation by localized individuals of the greatest good for the greatest number is inherently impossible. Despite the impossibility of precise calculations, however, we use measurements, both intuitive and scientific, to gauge the relative enhancement or undermining of overall well-being.[79]

We ought to act for the common good, and this implies that we must make rough assessments of how our actions might affect the whole. The justice element of love calls us to such rough assessments. If it is clear that our actions toward the one or the few will be detrimental to the whole, we should not regard such intentional responses as loving.

Of course, we frequently love with one or a few others specifically in mind. We love spouses, children, family, friends, associates, victims, enemies, pets, and so on. As we become aware of the experiences of family, friends, and close associates, we see the

---

78. Drew Christiansen, "The Common Good and the Politics of Self-Interest," in *Beyond Individualism: Toward a Retrieval of Moral Discourse in America*, ed. Donald L. Gelpi (Notre Dame, IN: University of Notre Dame Press, 1989), 81; emphasis original.

79. See Partha Dasgupta, *Human Well-Being and the Natural Environment* (Oxford: Oxford University Press, 2001).

need to act for their good. Sometimes this loving action involves personal expense, sometimes not. When a distressed friend calls seeking comfort, for instance, love often requires that we sacrifice some personal pleasure to come to our friend's aide. When a sibling needs money to pay unexpected bills, love often requires that we provide resources to meet that need, even when the provision of such resources entails cost to ourselves.

As we will see in my later discussion of sociobiology, the tendency to promote the well-being of those near and dear appears to be a natural part of our evolutionary development. Parents often sacrifice some measure of their own well-being, occasionally even choosing death, for the good of their children. Relatives come to the aid of kin in crisis. Acting intentionally, in response to others (including God), to promote overall well-being seems to occur often in the relations among family and friends.

Love sometimes requires that we seek the well-being of enemies and strangers. Their well-being cannot be ignored. We cannot be concerned solely with our own well-being or with that of our family, friends, and group members. In fact, sometimes love demands that we refrain from enhancing the well-being of friends so that we can enhance the well-being of foes. The well-being of many others, including the developmentally disadvantaged or socially impaired, strangers, nonhuman creatures great and small, and even God, needs to be considered if love requires that we act in ways that promote overall well-being.

Considering what acting for overall well-being might entail can be difficult. How do we know what love requires when we feel obligated to promote the well-being of so many? About whose well-being should we localized beings with limited resources be most concerned? Conflicting responsibilities and legitimate needs from many quarters call for loving responses. In my later discussion of a doctrine of God, we will look at what love might require in the face of competing needs.

Conclusion

Love, as we have observed in this chapter, has many forms. Sometimes, when confronted with evil, we must respond intentionally to promote well-being (*agape*). Other times, love affirms what is valuable and promotes well-being in response (*eros*). And promoting well-being sometimes means cooperating with others (*philia*). Often these forms of love are mixed, although one form may predominate in our effort to promote overall well-being. Flourishing lives express full-orbed love.

Acting to promote one's own well-being is sometimes appropriate, but sometimes we must be self-sacrificial. Promoting the good of friends and family is sometimes appropriate, but sometimes acting for the good of strangers or enemies takes priority. A pluralist approach to love suggests that the context determines whose well-being must primarily be promoted. In all, love responds intentionally to promote overall well-being. Actions that clearly undermine the common good should not be considered loving.

3

Love and the Social Sciences

The natural place to begin exploring recent research on love is that collection of sciences examining what we seem to know best: our own human experiences. Psychology and sociology are two scientific domains that take human experience, especially behavior and mental processes, as their primary interest. Because of this, the experiments, data, and hypotheses in these domains deserve careful attention.

Beginning an examination of scientific love research with psychology and sociology also seems appropriate, because in many ways these disciplines are the children of ethics. Over time, however, most social scientists distanced themselves from questions of virtue in their endeavor to place their disciplines on what they believed were respectable scientific foundations. Yet ethical dimensions remain. And an increasing number of psychologists and sociologists embrace these ethical concerns.[1] Given these factors, we begin our exploration of recent scientific literature about love by investigating representative quantitative and qualitative love research in the social sciences.[2]

1. For an argument on the close relationship between psychology and ethics, see Alan C. Tjeltveit, "Christian Ethics and Psychological Research," in *Science and the Soul: Christian Perspectives on Psychological Science*, ed. Scott W. VanderStoep (Lanham, MD: University Press of America, 2003), 73–92.

2. For excellent essays on love and altruism from the perspective of mental and physical health, see Stephen G. Post, ed., *Altruism and Health: Perspectives from Empirical Research* (Oxford: Oxford University Press, 2007).

Psychology of Love

A representative sampling of how psychologists view love is *The Psychology of Love*, a collection of essays edited by Robert J. Sternberg and Michael L. Barnes. The book offers diverse materials, but the final essay provides a critical overview of the field's recent love research. Its author, Ellen Berscheid, is a pioneer in love studies.

Berscheid says that providing her overview of psychological love research is difficult, because "love is not a single distinct behavioral phenomenon with clearly recognizable outlines and boundaries." Instead, "love is a huge and motley collection of many different behavior events whose only commonalities are that they take place in a relationship with another person . . . and that they have some sort of positive quality to them."[3]

Most psychologists take one of two approaches when studying love, says Berscheid. The first approach begins by asking a sample of people to describe their thoughts, feelings, and actions toward those they love. These diverse descriptions are subsequently analyzed to identify common properties. This analysis results in a statistical summary of the properties found in love as described by those in the sample. For instance, a high percentage of people report that caring is a foundational quality of love.[4] I call this approach the "Common Denominator" method for studying love.

The significance of the Common Denominator approach is that it begins with the actual self-reports of lovers. Self-reports have the advantage of offering an insider's view of human experience—in this case, the experience of loving others. The data do not come from external observers speculating about the lover's intentions, motivations, and deliberate responses. Self-reports give firsthand information about intentional acts or feelings of love.

Love research based on self-reports also has its downsides, of course. The primary problem of the Common Denominator approach is the limitation in the investigator's own preconceptions of love. Berscheid explains the problem: "What appears in the sample is, naturally, heavily determined by the investigator's [prior] notion of

---

3. Ellen Berscheid, "Some Comments on Love's Anatomy: Or, Whatever Happened to Old-Fashioned Lust?" in *The Psychology of Love*, ed. Robert J. Sternberg and Michael L. Barnes (New Haven: Yale University Press, 1988), 362.

4. Ibid., 363.

what love is. . . . If 'caring' is part of that conception," she observes, "one can be certain that respondents will be asked to tell whether they exhibit caring behaviors toward the loved ones."[5] In other words, the investigator's questions arise from his or her assumptions about what love is, and these assumptions significantly influence the results.

The second general approach to studying love is more common among psychologists. In this approach, says Berscheid, "the love theorist mulls over his or her own life experiences and personal observations of the experiences of others . . . , attends to their similarities and differences, and comes up with some sort of classification scheme that purports to distinguish among the varieties of love."[6] I call this the "Classification" approach to studying love.

Examples of the Classification approach abound. For instance, psychologist Abraham Maslow distinguished between "B-love" and "D-love." B-love is love for the being of the other, and D-love is love driven by one's own deficiencies.[7] Psychologist John Alan Lee distinguishes between the loves *eros*, *ludus*, and *storge* and suggests a typology with eight different "love-styles."[8] In his own chapter and in other work, *Psychology of Love* coeditor Sternberg suggests a triangular theory of love. The components of the triangle are intimacy, passion, and decision/commitment. These components may be combined in various ways, resulting in seven love-type combinations.[9] All are examples of the Classification approach to love studies.

The Classification approach to love research is a theoretical guide. Psychologists must do additional work to determine if a particular classification actually describes the phenomena. The Classification approach becomes particularly complicated when the scientist assigns actual expressions of love to particular classes. To classify an act of love correctly, one must determine its causes. If the lover's intention, which the outside observer cannot know well, is

5. Ibid.

6. Ibid., 364.

7. Abraham H. Maslow, *The Farther Reaches of Human Nature* (Harmondsworth: Penguin, 1973).

8. John Alan Lee, "Love-Styles," in Sternberg and Barnes, *Psychology of Love*, 38–67.

9. Robert J. Sternberg, "Triangulating Love," in Sternberg and Barnes, *Psychology of Love*, 119–38. See also Sternberg, *Cupid's Arrow: The Course of Love through Time* (Cambridge: Cambridge University Press, 1998); idem, *Love Is a Story: A New Theory of Relationships* (Oxford: Oxford University Press, 1998).

a necessary cause in any genuine act of love, the work of assigning love expressions to particular classes is by nature subjective.

Psychologists Susan S. Hendrick and Clyde Hendrick combined the self-report method of the Common Denominator approach with the Classification approach's love-type scheme to explore the relation of love to religious belief. They asked over five hundred participants in two separate studies to complete a self-rating of religiousness alongside a forty-two-item love-styles scale. The scale addressed six types of love defined in particular ways: *eros* (romantic), *ludus* (game-playing), *storge* (compassionate), *mania* (possessive), *pragma* (practical), and *agape* (selfless/religious).

The Hendricks found that participants who rated themselves as very religious also rated themselves as expressing more *storge*, *pragma*, and *agape* love-styles than did nonreligious participants. Very religious participants self-rated as having much less *ludus* than nonreligious participants. The psychologists concluded from these studies that "subjects who were more religious endorsed the more 'dependable' love-styles of storge (compassionate), pragma (practical), and agape (selfless), while they relatively rejected ludus (game-playing)."[10] These studies do not demonstrate, however, whether those individuals who naturally tend toward *storge*, *pragma*, and *agape* also tend to be religious or if religious traditions and teachings influence individuals to express or favor these love-types.

The Common Denominator and Classification approaches have their advantages and disadvantages. Both typically consider the promotion of well-being in some form, a central aspect of how love should be understood. And both consider love a relational phenomenon.

Both are less clear, however, about the proper role of motives and intentions. The Common Denominator approach relies on self-reports and believes that clearer insight into love will emerge when collecting a respectable sample from those who report having loved. But self-reports are not always reliable, and an investigator's own assumptions about love can skew the study. By contrast, the Classification approach assigns expressions of love to particular classes based on the classifier's own experiences. But it does not provide an adequate gauge to assess the motives of those whose

10. Susan S. Hendrick and Clyde Hendrick, "Love and Sex Attitudes and Religious Beliefs," *Journal of Social and Clinical Psychology* 5, no. 3 (1987): 391–98.

love is observed. Without some indication of an actor's intent, it becomes difficult to know if an action should really be regarded as loving and, therefore, difficult to classify various loves accurately.

Positive Psychology and Attachment Theory

At the turn of the twenty-first century, a new focus to psychological research appeared. This focus—positive psychology—sees itself returning to the field's early research agenda. Positive psychologists argue that researchers after World War II concentrated on studying and treating pathology and mental illness. Earlier psychologists regarded their clients as passive victims, with conflicts in childhood or later life largely controlling their victims.[11]

By contrast, positive psychology intends to study and promote positive subjective experiences. "The aim of positive psychology," says its chief proponent, Martin E. P. Seligman, "is to catalyze a change in psychology from a preoccupation only with repairing the worst things in life to also building the best qualities in life."[12] Treating clients is not only about fixing what is wrong but also about building what is right. "In the quest for what is best," says Seligman, "positive psychology does not rely on wishful thinking, self-deception, or hand waving; instead, it tries to adapt what is best in the scientific method to the unique problems that human behavior presents in all of its complexity."[13]

Positive psychologists investigate a wide variety of positive human traits. "We have discovered," says Seligman, "that there are human strengths that act as buffers against mental illness: courage, future-mindedness, optimism, interpersonal skill, faith, work ethic, hope, honesty, perseverance, the capacity for flow and insight, to name several."[14]

The work of Patricia L. Bruininks serves as an example of one positive psychology research agenda. Many humans have remarkable capacities to represent future events flexibly, imagine diverse

11. Martin E. P. Seligman, "Positive Psychology, Positive Prevention, and Positive Therapy," in *Handbook of Positive Psychology*, ed. C. R. Snyder and Shane J. Lopez (Oxford: Oxford University Press, 2002), 4.

12. Ibid., 3.

13. Ibid., 4.

14. Ibid.

possible outcomes, and act in light of those representations. These positive appraisals of the future typically are identified by the categories of optimism and hope. Bruininks thinks that these two categories are distinguishable, and her research demonstrates this.

In a series of studies Bruininks asked participants to describe hope, optimism, and similar anticipatory states, such as wanting, desiring, and wishing. The studies reveal that participants typically identified optimism with general outcomes (e.g., the expectation of a good day) and hope with specific outcomes (e.g., the expectation of receiving a paycheck). In addition, participants understood optimism to involve circumstances in which the odds were good that something positive would result. But participants identified hope with outcomes whose likelihood of occurrence may be great or slim. Bruininks's work on hope makes it possible to study hope's antecedents and consequences more precisely.[15] Such study may be useful for encouraging hope in those who feel hopeless.

In addition to work on hope,[16] the most compelling research in positive psychology relates to traits or actions such as forgiveness,[17] positive emotions,[18] gratitude,[19] and optimism.[20] Unfortunately,

15. Patricia L. Bruininks, "Distinguishing Hope from Optimism and Related Affective States," *Motivation and Emotion* 29, no. 4 (2005): 327–55.

16. See Shane J. Lopez, ed., *The Encyclopedia of Positive Psychology* (Malden, MA: Wiley-Blackwell, 2009); Diane McDermott and C. R. Snyder, *Making Hope Happen: A Workbook for Turning Possibilities into Reality* (Oakland, CA: New Harbinger Publications, 1999); C. R. Snyder, *The Psychology of Hope: You Can Get There from Here* (New York: Free Press, 1994).

17. See Robert D. Enright, *Forgiveness*, DVD, American Psychological Association, 2004; Michael E. McCullough, *Beyond Revenge: The Evolution of the Forgiveness Instinct* (San Francisco: Jossey-Bass, 2008); Michael E. McCullough, Steven J. Sandage, and Everett L. Worthington, *To Forgive Is Human: How to Put Your Past in the Past* (Downers Grove, IL: InterVarsity Press, 1997); Everett J. Worthington, *Dimensions of Forgiveness: Psychological Research and Theological Perspectives* (Philadelphia: Templeton Foundation Press, 1998).

18. See Barbara Fredrickson, *Positivity: Groundbreaking Research Reveals How to Embrace the Hidden Strength of Positive Emotions, Overcome Negativity, and Thrive* (New York: Crown, 2009).

19. See Robert A. Emmons, *Thanks! How the New Science of Gratitude Can Make You Happier* (Boston: Houghton Mifflin, 2007); Robert A. Emmons and Michael E. McCullough, *The Psychology of Gratitude* (New York: Oxford University Press, 2004).

20. See Charles S. Carver and Michael F. Scheier, *Perspectives on Personality*, 6th ed. (Boston: Allyn & Bacon, 2007); Christopher Peterson, *A Primer in Positive*

however, positive psychologists typically do not regard love as the overarching category to describe a wide variety of acts that promote well-being. They generally use the word *love* to describe particular romantic or sexual feelings and expressions.[21] Because romance and sex do not always promote overall well-being, this way of describing love is not particularly helpful.

Some positive psychology research draws on or assumes the value of another branch of psychology influencing contemporary love research: attachment theory. Social scientists often regard attachment theory as a theoretical explanation for why some individuals are capable of establishing positive relationships that promote well-being. Given that love involves relationships (as Berscheid points out and as I asserted in earlier chapters), investigating attachments between individuals is a natural agenda for social scientists.

John Bowlby is widely regarded as the originator of attachment theory. His work and the work of Mary Ainsworth provided empirical data that refined the theory's basic concepts.[22] In the mid-twentieth century, Bowlby came to believe that the relationship an infant enjoys with its mother (or significant caregiver) greatly influenced the infant's development throughout life. Evolution has endowed infants with particular learning and loving abilities that seek expression in the relationship between infant and caregiver. The nature of this relationship establishes a prototype that shapes later relationships.[23] Today, developmental psychologists employ Bowlby's basic theory in their research on relationships at all stages of life.

Bowlby suggested that humans have evolved an attachment behavior system as part of the human biological substrate. This

Psychology (New York: Oxford University Press, 2006); Christopher Peterson and Martin Seligman, *Character Strengths and Virtues: A Handbook and Classification* (New York: Oxford University Press, 2004); P. Alex Linley and Stephen Joseph, eds., *Positive Psychology in Practice* (Hoboken, NJ: Wiley, 2004).

21. See the essay on love by Susan Hendrick and Clyde Hendrick in Snyder and Lopez, *Handbook of Positive Psychology*. See also Arthur Aron and Elaine N. Aron, *Statistics for the Behavioral and Social Sciences: A Brief Course*, 2nd ed. (Upper Saddle River, NJ: Prentice Hall, 2002).

22. Along with their books, see their classic essay, Mary Ainsworth and John Bowlby Jr., "An Ethological Approach to Child Development," *American Psychologist* 46 (1991): 333–41.

23. See John Bowlby, *Attachment and Loss*, vol. 1, *Attachment* (New York: Basic Books, 1969).

system activates when humans (especially infants) perceive a threat. In response to this evolved system, humans seek close proximity and protection in their efforts to find relief and a sense of safety. The attachment system naturally elicits in humans a positive mental representation of those who protect them. When the system functions well, individuals feel relaxed and confident and are more likely to care for self and others.

Testing the appropriateness of an individual's attachment security is done in various ways. A common way is the self-report system, by which test participants complete a questionnaire designed to gauge their sense of attachment security. The self-report approach has advantages, but it is difficult to link directly a participant's reaction to particular laboratory scenarios with the participant's sense of attachment. Many nonattachment factors may motivate participants to respond to the stimuli.[24]

Recent research in attachment theory has turned to a technique called "priming." Psychologists Mario Mikulincer and Phillip R. Shaver, for instance, use priming techniques. Such techniques expose experiment participants to the names of supportive others, conveying proximity or intimacy words and bringing memories of attachment security to the participant's mind. After researchers prime the participants with attachment-inducing techniques, they subject participants to a variety of act-based or self-report tests.[25]

In one study, Mikulincer and Shaver exposed a group of participants for twenty milliseconds to names of people whom the participants had previously nominated as security-enhancing attachment figures. The scientists compared this group to another group of people subliminally primed with names of close partners who were not security-enhancing. The researchers also compared these two groups to a third group of people subliminally primed with names of mere acquaintances who did not serve as security-enhancement attachment

24. Bowlby and Ainsworth's ideas found confirmation in the work of primatologist Harry Harlow. For an account of Harlow's work, life, and contribution to attachment theory research, see Deborah Blum, *Love at Goon Park: Harry Harlow and the Science of Affection* (Cambridge, MA: Perseus, 2002).

25. Mario Mikulincer and Phillip R. Shaver, "Attachment Theory and Intergroup Bias: Evidence That Priming the Secure Base Schema Attenuates Negative Reactions to Out-Groups," *Journal of Personality and Social Psychology* 81, no. 1 (2001): 97–115.

figures. After all three groups were primed, researchers exposed all participants to a videotape showing a woman in great need.[26]

Mikulincer and Shaver found in this study, and others, that those who feel a proper sense of attachment are more likely to act compassionately than the less-secure participants. "Our findings indicate," say Mikulincer and Shaver, "that the attachment behavior system affects the caregiving system, making it likely that heightening security will yield benefits in the realm of compassionate altruistic behavior."[27] The temporary activation of the sense of attachment security through priming "allows even chronically insecure people to react to others' needs in ways similar to those of people with a more secure attachment style."[28] The activation of a particular mental representation of attachment security may spread throughout a person's memory network, say Mikulincer and Shaver, causing the person temporarily to become more compassionate or helpful.[29]

By contrast, anxious people are prone to wallow in personal distress in response to a needy person's plight. Anxiety typically does not lead to helping behavior. A lack of attachment or attachment avoidance, report Mikulincer and Shaver, "was consistently associated with less compassion and less willingness to help a suffering woman."[30]

The two psychologists summarize their research by saying that "attachment security, whether dispositionally present or contextually enhanced, fosters compassion and altruism."[31] And "what begins as a caring tendency toward specific figures (especially offspring) can become transformed and generalized into a prosocial disposition or trait that is applied very broadly."[32] Attachments at least sometimes play a role in love and altruism.

Research in positive psychology and attachment theory illustrates well the basic structures of love. Positive psychology emphasizes the

26. Ibid.
27. Mario Mikulincer, Phillip R. Shaver, Omri Gillath, and Rachel A. Nitzberg, "Attachment, Caregiving, and Altruism: Boosting Attachment Security Increases Compassion and Helping," *Journal of Personality and Social Psychology* 89, no. 5 (2005): 833.
28. Ibid., 834.
29. Ibid.
30. Ibid., 832.
31. Ibid., 834.
32. Ibid.

point that promoting well-being should be a major goal in psychological research. Various expressions of positive and prosocial behavior suggest that individuals and groups have some degree of power to pursue such loving activity.[33] Positive psychology research can be used to promote wider and more-complex expressions of love.

Attachment theory emphasizes the relationality of love. It studies the types and qualities of relationships between individuals, noting in particular when secure attachments heighten the proclivity to express love. Attachment theory suggests that damaged or disconnected relationships constrain our capacities to love. Research in attachment theory can become the means for developing structures and techniques that promote love.

In short, positive psychology and attachment theory support well an understanding of love as intentional response that promotes overall well-being. These research approaches, along with the Common Denominator and Classification approaches, are methods by which psychologists have, as Berscheid puts it, understood love as requiring "a relationship" that has "some sort of positive quality."[34]

Emergency Intervention

Researchers on love, helping, and prosocial behavior often cite a tragic murder in Queens, New York, as important for a particular type of sociopsychological research. On March 13, 1964, Catherine "Kitty" Genovese was stabbed, raped, and robbed as she arrived home from work just after three o'clock in the morning. Although at least thirty-eight people saw or heard the attack, no one came to Kitty's assistance. An anonymous caller reported the incident a half hour later. Before help could arrive, Kitty bled to death.

33. Research psychologists and sociologists call much of what falls under the category of love "prosocial behavior." J. A. Piliavin, J. F. Dovidio, S. L. Gaertner, and R. D. Clark III define prosocial actions as "generally beneficial to other people and to the ongoing political system" (Jane Allyn Piliavin et al., *Emergency Intervention* [New York: Academic Press, 1981], 4). The similarities between prosocial behavior and love defined as acting intentionally in sympathetic response to others (including God) to promote overall well-being, are fairly obvious. We should regard most behavior labeled prosocial as loving, mainly because of its relationship to love's goal to promote overall well-being.

34. Berscheid, "Some Comments on Love's Anatomy," 362.

When the public heard that thirty-eight witnesses did not intervene to help, a flurry of questions emerged. People wondered if this unresponsiveness indicted New Yorkers and was indicative of urban culture generally. They wondered if the tragic event reveals a profound lack of compassion fundamental to human nature. Judging by the public outrage, most people assumed the incident to confirm their view that humans are basically apathetic, callous, and indifferent.

Social psychologists Bibb Latané and John Darley, along with other researchers, sought experimental answers to why onlookers and witnesses failed to respond to the attack on Kitty Genovese. Their research takes the name "emergency intervention." Latané and Darley conducted research on the decision-making processes humans typically use when deciding whether to help during situation-specific tragedies. The research explores what the social sciences might tell us about interpersonal and collective factors that may or may not influence people to act lovingly in response to emergencies.

Although the media and the public at large portrayed the thirty-eight witnesses who did not help as uncaring, indifferent, and cold, researchers found a much more complex set of factors at play. As a result of interviews and research projects, Latané and Darley developed a five-step model for how bystanders decide whether to help in an emergency.[35]

The first step in the decision model for bystander intervention is simply noticing the emergency event. Various factors influence a bystander's ability to notice. For instance, bystanders experiencing bad moods are less likely to be sensitive to their surroundings than bystanders in a good mood.[36] Bystanders are also more likely to notice events that are sensually stimulating or vivid.[37] Thus the chance increases that a bystander will intervene in an emergency if

35. Bibb Latané and John Darley, *The Unresponsive Bystander: Why Doesn't He Help?* (New York: Appleton-Century Crofts, 1970).

36. P. Salovey, J. D. Mayer, and D. L. Rosenhan, "Mood and Helping: Mood as a Motivator of Helping and Helping as a Regulator of Mood," in *Review of Personality and Social Psychology*, vol. 12, *Prosocial Behavior*, ed. Margaret Sydnor Clark (Newbury Park, CA: Sage, 1991), 215–37.

37. J. A. Piliavin, I. M. Piliavin, and L. Broll, "Time of Arrival at an Emergency and the Likelihood of Helping," *Personality and Social Psychology Bulletin* 2, no. 3 (1976): 273–76.

moodiness does not hamper the bystander and if the event grabs the bystander's attention.

The second step in the model is interpretation. A bystander must not only notice a tragic incident but also interpret it as requiring assistance. Researchers document that bystanders are more likely to intervene when victims express strong distress cues. Screaming is a strong distress cue. Those who observe an event and are confused by the victim's silent or passive actions wonder if they should intervene. The confused bystander is less likely to help.[38]

The behavior of fellow witnesses also influences bystanders who perceive signs of distress. In ambiguous situations, bystanders seek social information to interpret better the event taking place. A number of experiments have shown that a bystander will not intervene if those in the same environment appear indifferent to or unconcerned about the situation. If fellow bystanders act alarmed in response to distress signals, however, the bystander in question will likely intervene to provide assistance. Bystanders who interpret themselves as the sole witness to a tragic event are much more likely to intervene to provide help.[39]

Sometimes environmental factors confuse or distract emergency witnesses. In one study, a person wearing a cast dropped books on the sidewalk directly in front of oncoming strangers. In some instances, these books were dropped as a power lawn mower roared nearby. In other instances, books were dropped when the mower was not running. When the power lawn mower was silent, bystanders helped the injured book dropper 80 percent of the time. When the power mower was running loudly, however, bystanders helped only 15 percent of the time.[40] This study suggests that excessive stimulation hampers a person's ability to interpret what to do in an emergency.

38. R. L. Shotland and T. L. Huston, "Emergencies: What Are They and How Do They Influence Bystanders to Intervene?" *Journal of Personality and Social Psychology* 37, no. 10 (1979): 1822–34.

39. B. Latané, S. A. Nida, and D. W. Wilson, "The Effects of Group Size on Helping Behavior," in *Altruism and Helping Behavior: Social, Personality, and Developmental Perspectives*, ed. J. P. Rushton and R. M. Sorrentino (Hillsdale, NJ: Lawrence Erlbaum, 1981), 287–313.

40. K. E. Mathews and L. K. Canon, "Environmental Noise Level as a Determinant of Helping Behavior," *Journal of Personality and Social Psychology* 32, no. 4 (1975): 571–77.

The third step in Latané and Darley's model for emergency intervention decision-making is the taking of responsibility. Experiments show that bystanders who believe themselves to be the only witness to an emergency are more likely to help than bystanders who believe themselves to be one of many witnesses. Bystanders may shirk responsibility, because they assume others are better equipped or have more knowledge for helping victims. This phenomenon, labeled "diffusion of responsibility," may account largely for why no one helped Kitty Genovese.

Psychologist Leonard Bickman's research confirms that witnesses are less likely to intervene if they believe that others also have witnessed the emergency. In one of Bickman's studies, college students heard over an intercom system about an emergency nearby. Students who believed themselves to be the only one hearing the emergency were more likely to take responsibility to help than students who believed that others also heard the message. Students who believed that people in nearby buildings had heard the intercom message but that these people were unable to intervene were as likely to help as students who heard the intercom message and believed themselves to be the only one hearing it.[41]

Step four in the decision-making process for intervention involves deciding what kind of help to give. Here the issue is not so much willingness to help; instead, the issue is ascertaining the best way bystanders might aid in an emergency.

Little research has been done on the process that bystanders use to decide what kind of help to give. One study, however, tested the effectiveness of those with first-aid training compared to those without this training when encountering an emergency. The study showed that both those with training and those without it were equally as likely to respond to help a bleeding person. Not surprisingly, the medical assistance of those with first-aid training was most effective in the emergency situation. Those without such training often made the emergency worse.[42] It could be, therefore, that those who believe that they lack the expertise to help effectively

41. Leonard Bickman, "The Effect of Another Bystander's Ability to Help on Bystander Intervention in an Emergency," *Journal of Experimental Social Psychology* 7 (1971): 367–79.

42. R. L. Shotland and W. D. Heinold, "Bystander Response to Arterial Bleeding: Helping Skills, the Decision-Making Process, and Differentiating the Help-

fail to intervene in emergency situations like the one involving Kitty Genovese. Bystanders may worry that intervening will cause more harm than good.

The fifth and final step in the process of emergency intervention is the actual implementation of the decision to help. Of course, the actualization of this step is also at stake in the previous steps. But implementing one's decision to help as noted in this fifth step brings to the fore the question of costs and rewards for a potential helper's decision.

A number of experiments have been done under the general rubric of assessing costs and rewards to those who help the needy. Many experiments are based on the notion that people generally want to maximize rewards and minimize costs in life. The cost-reward approach is associated with an economic view of social interaction, and one of its strengths is its capacity for measurement.

When implementing the decision to help a suffering victim, bystanders may consider costs and benefits related to the time and effort that giving aid will require. Some may decide that the risk for personal harm is too great. Others may intervene to avoid negative emotional consequences (e.g., guilt) that they may face should they choose not to help. Other bystanders may help because they know that helping will likely put them in a good mood. Some may help in emergency situations because they find the victim in some way attractive, similar to themselves, friendly, or a fellow member of a group. Generally speaking, as costs increase, the likelihood that a bystander will help a victim decreases. As rewards increase, so does the likelihood that a bystander will help.[43]

The cost-benefit aspect of decision-making has its limits, of course. For instance, the scheme seems not to account well for the actions of bystanders who help despite the costs seeming to outweigh the benefits. These limits and others will become more evident in our examination of other psychological and sociological

ing Response," *Journal of Personality and Social Psychology* 49, no. 2 (1985): 347–56.

43. For a summary of the issues and recent research related to costs and rewards of helping behavior, see John F. Dovidio, Jane Allyn Piliavin, David A. Schroeder, and Louis A. Penner, *The Social Psychology of Prosocial Behavior* (Mahwah, NJ: Lawrence Erlbaum, 2006), 85–103.

research. The point here, however, is that some may not intervene in an emergency, because they perceive the cost of helping too high given the possible reward.

In their book, *The Social Psychology of Prosocial Behavior*, authors John F. Dovidio, Jane Allyn Piliavin, David A. Schroeder, and Louis A. Penner summarize the key role that Latané and Darley's work has played in emergency intervention research. "Overall, the Latané and Darley decision model of intervention provides a valuable framework for understanding when bystanders will or will not help others in need."[44] Through analysis and research, say these authors, emergency intervention researchers show "how behaviors that might appear abnormal can be understood using principles of normal behavior." The problem often is that emergency situations are "complex and confusing, and bystanders must make a series of decisions, make them quickly, and make them in a very specific way before they will intervene."[45] This research suggests that those who do not intervene in emergency situations, including the witnesses to the attack on Kitty Genovese, may not be apathetic, callous, or indifferent after all. The conditions that frame one's decision to love in emergency situations are complex.

A Social-Psychological Answer to Altruistic Love

The foregoing research does not always address well a form of love that some regard as quintessential to understanding love in general: altruism. If strict quantitative measures could show that some people intentionally act altruistically, the study of love would likely become more widely regarded as a significant scientific research program.

One problem scholars face when investigating altruism is that the word *altruism*, like the word *love*, has been defined variously. The word *altruism* (*altruisme* in French) was coined by social scientist and philosopher Auguste Comte in the nineteenth century. Its barest meaning is its reference to "the other" or what sometimes is labeled "other-regard."

44. Ibid., 81. The model has also been applied to research on other situations of social interaction.
45. Ibid.

79

One problem in research on altruism is the definition that some scholars give to it. Some define altruism in a way that makes acting altruistically a virtual impossibility. Altruism so defined entails acting to benefit another person with no benefit whatsoever to the actor. I call this "absolute altruism." Such a definition eliminates as altruistic any action that provides a sense of self-motivation, self-satisfaction, self-gain, or any reward in the afterlife. Absolute altruism presupposes that existence is composed of isolated selves. In my view, this way of defining altruism is untenable. Others agree.[46]

Social scientist C. Daniel Batson addresses the issue of altruism squarely in his sociopsychological research. Batson recognizes that altruism in late twentieth-century psychology is such that the territory "allotted to altruism [since 1970] is no more than a quaint province in an egoistic empire." Batson believes, however, that this is changing. "A small group of contemporary psychologists," he reports, "has begun once again to take seriously the possibility that altruism may be part of human nature."[47]

Batson's landmark book, *The Altruism Question: Toward a Social-Psychological Answer*, brings together a number of strict quantitative studies on altruism, including his own research. Batson seeks to answer this question: Could it be that we are capable of having another person's welfare as a primary goal and that not all of our efforts are directed toward looking out for ourselves?[48]

Batson defines altruism as "a motivational state with the ultimate goal of increasing another's welfare."[49] This definition makes altruism's measuring stick the actor's primary motives to increase the welfare of another. If the actor's primary goal is to increase another's welfare, the actor is altruistic, even if the actor also benefits in some way. Altruism so understood is not absolute altruism, since it does not require, but may include, total self-sacrifice. Moving

46. See Jacob Neusner and Bruce Chilton, eds., *Altruism in World Religions* (Washington, DC: Georgetown University Press, 2005). This collection of essays of religion on altruism demonstrates the problems that arise in defining altruism in an absolute sense. The collection provides essays from a variety of religious perspectives, but the introduction and the epilogue by William Scott Green spell out the problems with absolute altruism most succinctly.

47. C. Daniel Batson, *The Altruism Question: Toward a Social-Psychological Answer* (Hillsdale, NJ: Lawrence Erlbaum, 1991), 62.

48. Ibid., vii.

49. Ibid., 6.

the discussion from measuring consequences to assessing primary motives allows Batson to engage critics who argue that humans always act with self-interest as their primary goal.[50]

Batson says that three principles should guide researchers as they seek to identify primary goals of altruism. First, researchers infer a person's motives from the person's behavior. Researchers use inference because they cannot observe the motives of others directly. Second, if a person's behavior is directed toward several possible goals (e.g., self-benefit and other-benefit), researchers will not discern well which goal is actually primary. But, third, if researchers witness a person's behavior in two or more different situations, they can draw reasonable inferences about the person's primary goal. Such inferences can be drawn if these situations provide differing relationships with the primary goals apparently at play.[51] Batson explains this crucial third principle in this way:

> We must vary the helping situation in a way that disentangles the confounding of the benefit to other[s] and the benefit to self. We might do this by, for example, providing a behavior means of obtaining the self-benefit that does not involve helping [others] and, moreover, is less costly than helping. If we do this and the individual no longer helps [others], then we have reason to believe that his or her ultimate goal was self-benefit. . . . If the individual still helps [others], then we have reason to believe that this self-benefit was not an ultimate goal.[52]

If benefiting others is a person's primary goal, we have good grounds to claim that the helping person's motive, in the situation observed, is altruistic.

Batson brings a specific theory to his experiments on altruism. He calls it the "empathy-altruism hypothesis." At its root, the hypothesis states that altruistic motives are evoked by an emotional reaction of empathy, sympathy, or tenderness toward the person in

---

50. An excellent source for exploring the various ways altruism is understood is Andrew Michael Flescher and Daniel Worthen, *The Altruistic Species: Scientific, Philosophical, and Religious Perspectives on Human Benevolence* (Philadelphia: Templeton Foundation Press, 2007).

51. Batson, *Altruism Question*, 65.

52. Ibid., 66.

need.[53] A person's unique emotional response to perceived distress results from adopting the needy person's perspective. As empathetic feeling for a person in need increases, says Batson, one's altruistic motivation increases to have that need relieved.[54]

Experience tells us that not every person who seeks to relieve another person's need is acting with primary motives that are altruistic. It could be, for instance, that the helper's primary motive is social and/or personal rewards. After all, helpers are often praised by others or engage in self-congratulatory behavior when aiding the needy. A helper's primary motive may also be avoiding punishments of various kinds, whether externally or internally inflicted. Or a helper's primary motive may be to reduce his or her own feelings of personal distress. If reducing personal stress is one's primary motive, an egoistic rather than an altruistic desire largely motivates giving aid to others. The refined version of Batson's empathy-altruism hypothesis, therefore, claims "that feeling empathy for the person in need evokes motivation to help in which these benefits to self are not the ultimate goal of helping."[55]

To test his hypothesis, Batson creates various situations in which he can manipulate the factors that will indicate whether one's primary motives are egoistic or altruistic. These indicators become the basis for his quantitative research.

In one experiment, undergraduates were told that they would help test resiliency to stress. Before the experiment, participants were told that Batson and colleagues would study performance under stressful conditions. The research project required teams of two participants, and these participants would draw lots to determine roles. One participant would perform a task consisting of up to, but not more than, ten trials under averse conditions. These conditions were created by electric shocks at random intervals. The second participant was to observe the first participant being subjected to these shocks.[56] All participants were told that they could withdraw from the experiment at any time.

Unbeknownst to the participants, the drawing was rigged. All participants drew the observer role; none were subjected to shocks.

53. Ibid., 14.
54. Ibid., 72.
55. Ibid., 87.
56. Ibid., 113.

As participants were escorted to an observation room, they learned that they would be watching on closed-circuit television a young woman, Elaine, receive the series of ten moderately uncomfortable electric shocks. Some participants were told that they would only need to observe Elaine receiving two of the ten shocks. Others were told that they would observe Elaine receiving all ten shocks.

Participants were also given access to Elaine's fourteen-item personal values and interests questionnaire. This questionnaire was identical to the questionnaire that each participant had completed weeks earlier. However, Batson actually had prepared a variety of questionnaires himself. He told participants that the questionnaire he placed in front of them was Elaine's. The rigged results of the questionnaires reflected values and interests either very similar or very dissimilar to each participant's own values and interests. Batson speculated that those who saw themselves similar to Elaine would feel a high degree of empathy, and those who saw themselves dissimilar would feel a low degree of empathy.

Participants watched Elaine undergo what they thought were real-time shock treatments, but in fact what they watched had been prerecorded. By the end of the second treatment, Elaine's reactions to the shocks were so strong that the assistant administering the treatment "interrupted" to ask Elaine if she was feeling okay. A (prerecorded) conversation ensued in which Elaine confessed that as a child she had been thrown from a horse onto an electric fence. After the (fictitious) fence incident, a doctor said that in the future she might react strongly to even mild shocks. Hearing this, the assistant wondered aloud to Elaine if the participant watching the shocks might take her place. With a mixture of reluctance and relief, Elaine consented to having the assistant check on this possibility.

After a brief moment, the assistant entered the room in which the participant was watching the shock treatments on closed-circuit television. The assistant asked the participant if he or she would be willing to take Elaine's place. The option to remain an observer was also given.[57] The assistant concluded by saying, "If you decide to help Elaine by taking her place, what will happen is that she'll come in here and observe you. You will go in and perform the recall

57. Ibid., 115.

trials while receiving the shocks. Once you have completed the trials, you'll be free to go. What would you like to do?"

Batson found that most observers who judged themselves very dissimilar to Elaine (based on questionnaires) opted out of taking her shocks. These participants escaped the situation presumably because they felt little empathy for Elaine, and because the least costly way to reduce their personal distress was simply to answer the final questions and leave.

More significantly, however, Batson found that observers who were highly empathetic toward Elaine—an empathy apparently based on similarities evident in the questionnaires—were very likely to help even when they could easily escape the situation. Whereas only 18 percent of low-empathy observers helped Elaine when given an easy escape, 91 percent of high-empathy observers helped Elaine when given an easy escape.[58] These results give reason to believe that the primary motive of some people in some situations is genuinely altruistic.

Batson cites the results of five other experiments designed to test if people sometimes act altruistically or always act egoistically to reduce personal distress. In five of the six studies, the results were remarkably consistent: the majority of highly empathetic participants were willing to help at some cost to themselves. In the only study whose results were not consistent with the others, the cost of helping was apparently too high. The abnormal study suggests that there are limits, due to excessive costs, to what people will do to help others.[59]

We noted earlier that a helper's primary motive may be egoistic even when acting for the benefit of another. In addition to acting to reduce one's own anxiety or stress, the helper may have as primary motive the gain of social and/or personal rewards. Or a helper's primary motive may be to avoid penalties and punishments of various kinds.

Batson cites experiments designed to measure if altruism can be sufficiently explained away as behavior whose primary goal is to avoid punishment or seek reward. He cites seven studies showing that at least some of the time those who empathize with the needy

58. Ibid., 116.
59. Ibid., 126–27.

are not primarily motivated to avoid punishment. The claim that the altruist's motivation was "directed toward the egoistic goal of avoiding empathy-specific punishments," says Batson, "must, it seems, be rejected."[60]

Studies done to discover if altruists are always primarily motivated to gain rewards reveal that sometimes altruists act for the good of others despite gaining no obvious reward. Batson concludes that in the approximately twenty-five empirical studies examined "we find no clear support for any of the three egoistic alternatives to the empathy-altruism hypothesis."[61] Instead, the studies support the hypothesis that those who strongly empathize with a needy other will sometimes act with the well-being of that other as their primary motive.

Batson's strict quantitative methods provide valuable data to social scientific love research. He is quick to say, however, that the studies on altruism do not prove irrefutably that humans express altruistic love. After all, experiments that test human motivations are highly unlikely to prove irrefutably any general claim about human nature. Nevertheless, these studies provide strong support for the claim that some humans sometimes express altruistic love. If humans are actually capable of altruism, argues Batson, "possibilities arise for the development of more caring individuals, and a more compassionate, humane society."[62]

Loving Personality

Batson's scientific approach sets up experiments wherein the motives of participants are inferred by examining actions. But others suggest that research on love should focus on the kind of person who loves, not simply on actions analyzed in controlled experiments. In particular, social scientists do well to study those whose behavior emerges from a loving personality or character. Loving persons are the most fitting examples for scientific research, say some. Research on what makes a loving person is best done by examining expressions of love in the real world, not by constructing contrived circumstances.

60. Ibid., 149.
61. Ibid., 174.
62. Ibid., 4.

Sociologist Samuel Oliner and his wife, Pearl, have collected real-world data and proposed hypotheses related to what they call "the altruistic personality." The Oliners and their assistants interviewed almost seven hundred persons who lived in Nazi-occupied Europe. Most interviewees were from Poland, Germany, France, and Holland. Those interviewed included 406 individuals who had rescued Jews, 126 individuals who had chosen not to rescue Jews, and 150 Jewish survivors. Most who rescued Jews during the Nazi regime did so for more than two years, and most helped individuals of a different culture, ethnicity, and religious persuasion. Nonrescuers were included in the study to address how rescuers and nonrescuers differ.[63] The research done by the Oliners is highly suggestive of what kind of person acts lovingly and what influences humans to become loving people.

The Oliners questioned rescuers who had voluntarily risked their lives in some way, seeking no material gain. Implicit in the questions was whether those who rescued Jews possessed, as the Oliners put it, "a relatively enduring disposition to act selflessly on behalf of others."[64] The Oliners believe this selfless behavior is altruistic. They define altruism as (1) directed toward helping another, (2) involving a high risk or sacrifice to the actor, (3) accompanied by no external reward, and (4) voluntary.[65] "We view an altruistic behavior," explain the Oliners, "as the outcome of a decision-making process in which the internal characteristics of actors as well as the external environments in which they find themselves influence each other."[66]

In their book *The Altruistic Personality: Rescuers of Jews in Nazi Europe*, the Oliners provide firsthand accounts of those who risked their lives rescuing Jews. The following account given by a Dutch rescuer serves as an example of these testimonials:

> The Germans came and took a look at our house. They told us we had to take in a German couple who were living on the coast. We were worried because they would find out we were keeping Jewish

63. Samuel P. Oliner and Pearl M. Oliner, *The Altruistic Personality: Rescuers of Jews in Nazi Europe* (New York: Free Press, 1988), 2.
64. Ibid., 3.
65. Ibid., 6.
66. Ibid., 10.

people. They took the living room, bedroom, bathroom, and kitchen upstairs. Slowly they found out the truth.

One day we had soup on the kitchen stove. The German woman came downstairs and lifted the lid to see what was in the pot. Willy—the Jewish guy—saw that. He said, "It's not ladylike to lift the lid from the pot." I told him, "Be careful what you say; don't make trouble!"

I had the feeling something would happen. I told my husband, "Let's go away, let's find a place," but he said, "You're crazy!" But I had a feeling. My husband should have listened to me.

This woman, the German lady, went to the police. She told them we had a Jew in hiding. She said, "I would like to have the Jew taken away from there, but don't do anything to the people." She was referring to us. She thought the police were safe. But the guy she spoke to worked for the NSB, the Nazis. She didn't know that.

It was four o'clock on a clear Sunday afternoon. My husband had just come home from taking our little girl on a sled ride. He was home just ten minutes when the Gestapo came—with a dog. The dog ran upstairs, and there was shooting. My little girl was crying because her Daddy was screaming. I took my little girl and ran out the door. The dog smelled out the hiding place. My husband wouldn't say anything, so they set the dog on him. It bit off his hand. They shot my husband and one of the Jews.[67]

This Dutch rescuer and her husband knew the great risk associated with helping Jews. Yet they chose to take this risk at their own peril.

One altruistic Polish woman took on a Jewish infant at the request of its mother. She tells of her experience protecting the young child:

One time I was arrested on the train. The policeman took my baby and went to examine it. He discovered it was circumcised and said to me, "You are a Jew."

I said, "No, I am not a Jew, but this is my baby." They took us to jail. I was able to run away when the policeman was distracted by ten pounds of butter.

I had to move many times. The baby was so emaciated and sickly. He did not have a good diet. When the war ended, I contacted the Red Cross and found out that the mother was alive and lived in

67. Ibid., 74–75.

Borislaw. In 1945, the mother came. We made contact. We met. I gave her back the child. It is very difficult for me to tell you how I felt then.[68]

A French rescuer recounts the initial events that prompted him to pursue the risky rescue of Jews:

> I had a deep friendship with a classmate, a Jewish girl, who was very exceptional. During my visit to Frankfurt in Germany, I stayed with a Jewish family. I saw some horrible things. I saw some people coming back from the camps. I was at the train station in Frankfurt when these people were coming back. Some had very marked and bruised faces, swollen legs—hardly a human face anymore. I was very shocked by this. So when the war started, I looked for a way to help.[69]

The Oliners present hundreds of stories of altruistic rescuers. The risks that these people took to secure well-being for others often were astounding. These accounts lead naturally to this question: Why did some people in Nazi Europe choose to risk their lives to help Jews? Or to put the question more generally: Why do some people sometimes act altruistically and other people do not?

According to the Oliners, those who consistently act altruistically have an altruistic personality. When the Oliners say that people have altruistic personalities, however, they do not mean that these people invariably act altruistically. Rather, they mean that some people are more likely than others to make altruistic decisions.[70] Those who act altruistically more often have an altruistic personality.

People who see themselves as closely related to others are more likely to act for the good of others at some cost to themselves. "What distinguished rescuers was not their lack of concern with self, external approval, or achievement," say the Oliners, "but rather their capacity for extensive relationships—their stronger sense of attachment to others and their feeling of responsibility for the welfare of others, including those outside their immediate familial or

68. Ibid., 92.
69. Ibid., 134.
70. Ibid., 12.

communal circles."[71] Rescuers were not constantly self-sacrificial, but they felt a stronger general sense of attachment to others.

Altruistic rescuers developed this sense of deep relatedness to others during childhood. "An examination of the early family lives and personality characteristics of both rescuers and nonrescuers suggests that their respective wartime behavior grew out of their general patterns of relating to others," say the Oliners. Rescuers developed what the Oliners call greater "extensivity," while non-rescuers constricted their relations to a small group or themselves. The result is that "those who were inclined toward extensive attachments—feeling committed to and responsible for diverse groups of people—were predisposed to accept feelings of responsibility to Jews, whatever danger to themselves." Conversely, "those who were inclined toward constrictedness—detachment and exclusiveness—were particularly unlikely to reject this behavior when doing so might have exposed them to personal threat."[72]

Those with an altruistic personality are typically both inclusive of and attached to others. The Oliners speak of two strands: "inclusiveness—a predisposition to regard all people as equals and to apply similar standards of right and wrong to them without regard to social status or ethnicity—and attachment—a belief in the value of personal relationships and caring for the needy."[73] For most rescuers, helping Jews was an expression of ethical principles that extended to all humanity.

A person's identification with religion was not strongly related to whether the person chose to rescue Jews. However, the way in which the person interpreted his or her religious teaching and commitment did influence his or her proclivity to help. Those who believed that religion instructed them to care for all humans were more likely to rescue Jewish victims. "For the overwhelming majority (87 percent) of rescuers," observe the Oliners, "helping Jews was motivated by concerns of *equity* and *care*."[74] The Oliners characterize equity as directed toward the welfare of society as a whole and care as concerned with the welfare of people without regard for repayment.

71. Ibid., 249.
72. Ibid., 186.
73. Ibid., 144.
74. Ibid., 163.

Parental guidance served as a major factor in the development of people with altruistic personalities. Rescuers report that their childhood relationships were characterized by strong and cohesive family bonds. Many rescuers developed close contact with Jews. Rescuers "lived among [Jews], worked with them, and had close Jewish friends while growing up and in their adult years," the Oliners report.[75] Some rescuers were taught early that they were connected to society as a whole and that they were similar to Jews. Nonrescuers more often reported poor family relationships, a feeling that Jews were distant objects, less inclination to identify with the larger society, and a feeling that Jews were outsiders.[76]

The Oliners conclude that those who rescued Jews were fairly ordinary people. "What distinguished them [from nonrescuers and bystanders] were their connections with others in relationships of commitment and care. It is out of such relationships that they became aware of what was occurring around them and mustered their human and material resources to relieve the pain." Those who rescued Jews "remind us that courage . . . is available to all through the virtues of connectedness, commitment, and the quality of relationships developed in ordinary human interactions."[77]

Love, Virtues, and Character Formation

The idea that some people exhibit personalities characterized by love has been a subject of interest in moral philosophy for centuries. In contemporary philosophy, the study of why some people characteristically love and others do not has been an ongoing question in virtue ethics. Psychologists sometimes refer to this as "character formation."[78] Philosophers often talk about developing virtues or living a virtuous life.

75. Ibid., 184.
76. Ibid., 186.
77. Ibid., 260.
78. See, for instance, Anne Colby, Jacquelyn James, and Daniel Hart, eds., *Competence and Character through Life* (Chicago: University of Chicago Press, 1998); Nicholas Emler, "Moral Character," in *Personality: Contemporary Theory and Research*, ed. V. J. Derlega, B. A. Winstead, and W. H. Jones, 2nd ed. (Chicago: Nelson-Hall, 1999), 376–404.

Psychologists Blaine J. Fowers and Alan C. Tjeltveit identify virtues as "the particular character strengths that make it possible for individuals to flourish as human beings and to pursue uniquely human aims and goods."[79] The study of virtue ethics explores what it means to become "the kind of person who wants to act virtuously because it is clear that doing so will help us and those around us flourish as human beings."[80] After all, individual good is inextricably tied to the common good. Fowers and Tjeltveit lament, however, that social scientists typically present the virtues as an "idiosyncratically chosen assortment of traits that have some beneficial outcome but seldom have a systematic coherence or unity."[81]

Nancy Eisenberg is one social scientist doing research on virtues and character formation. Eisenberg has spent a career studying character formation and prosocial behavior in children.[82] Her work addresses issues of benevolence, altruism, and empathy in infants, toddlers, young schoolchildren, and adolescents. In addition to her own research, Eisenberg acts as a spokesperson for those doing research in the study of prosocial behavior among children.[83]

Eisenberg notes the importance of empathy in the prosocial behavior of children, and she cites evidence that empathy is present in the very young. One study of six-month-olds revealed that about half of those examined responded to distressed peers with actions indicating empathy. Researchers wonder whether this empathy-based action is intentional, however, and they question whether infants can clearly differentiate between themselves and others.

79. Blaine J. Fowers and Alan C. Tjeltveit, "Virtue Obscured and Retrieved," *American Behavior Scientist* 47, no. 4 (2003): 2. See also Blaine J. Fowers, *Virtue and Psychology: Pursuing Excellence in Ordinary Practices* (Washington, DC: American Psychological Association, 2005); Alan C. Tjeltveit, *Ethics and Values in Psychotherapy* (London: Routledge, 1999).

80. Fowers and Tjeltveit, "Virtue Obscured and Retrieved," 4.

81. Ibid., 2.

82. For a summary of recent research in prosocial behavior, see Nancy Eisenberg, Sandra Losoya, and Tracy Spinrad, "Affect and Prosocial Responding," in *The Altruism Reader: Selections from Writings on Love, Religion, and Science*, ed. Thomas Jay Oord (West Conshohocken, PA: Templeton Foundation Press, 2008), 285–312.

83. See especially Nancy Eisenberg, *Altruistic Emotion, Cognition, and Behavior* (Hillsdale, NJ: Lawrence Erlbaum, 1986); idem, *The Caring Child* (Cambridge, MA: Harvard University Press, 1992); idem, ed., *The Development of Pro-Social Behavior* (New York: Academic Press, 1982).

But the evidence suggests that even at an early age humans are hardwired to respond to those in their environment.

The apparently involuntary response of children to another's distress decreases through childhood.[84] In a study of children aged sixteen to thirty-three months, for instance, toddlers responded to the distress of others during playtime only about 25 percent of the time. Most of the time, toddlers ignored distressed peers. Children of this age group were, however, three times as likely to help friends as to help nonfriends.[85]

The voluntary empathetic responses of children increase as they grow older. "Because preschool children are better able than younger children to take the perspective of others," says Eisenberg, "they are more motivated and better able to pinpoint the source of another's distress and to help in ways that are appropriate to the other's need."[86] As children move through their school years, their ability also to help others in a more-sophisticated manner increases. Older children are more likely than younger children to take the perspective of the distressed people whom they encounter. This increase in helping behavior with the increase in age also applies to helping in an emergency situation involving an injury or someone else falling.[87] Preadolescents and adolescents are more likely to sympathize with and comfort a wider range of people than younger people. "It appears that the *quality* of children's motives for their pro-social behaviors changes considerably with age," says Eisenberg.[88]

To say that some empathetic response is voluntary leads one to wonder what motives children may have for their actions. Eisenberg finds that generally speaking, the moral reasoning of children seems to go through changes from preschool years into adolescence. Older children seem more capable than younger of understanding another person's perspective. Older children seem to grasp abstract

84. C. Zahn Waxler and M. Radke Yarrow, "Development of Altruism: Alternative Research Strategies," in Eisenberg, *Development of Pro-Social Behavior*, 109–38.

85. C. Howes and J. Farver, "Toddlers' Responses to the Distress of Their Peers," *Journal of Applied Developmental Psychology* 8 (1987): 441–52.

86. Eisenberg, *Caring Child*, 13.

87. Ibid., 17.

88. Ibid., 18.

values related to helping others and altruism. And older children understand better how their own behaviors may be viewed by the wider public. All of these factors contribute to the motives that children express indicating why they help others.[89]

Like the Oliners, Eisenberg wonders what kind of character and characteristics are common among prosocial or altruistic children. She notes that any given child may share and act to help others in one situation and not in another. But research indicates that some children are consistent in their prosocial responding.

Eisenberg cites studies showing other interesting prosocial responding research. Boys are as likely to be consistently prosocial as girls.[90] It does not appear that social class plays a role in consistent prosocial behavior among children. And the common view that children in larger families are more helpful has also not been supported by research.[91]

Eisenberg does find that those children with certain personalities appear to be more social than others. Generally speaking, "gregarious children engage in more pro-social behavior than do shyer children," says Eisenberg, "especially in behavior outside the home, and especially in behavior that is offered spontaneously."[92] Eisenberg speculates that introverted children may not help as often because they want to avoid social interaction and attention. She cites studies about preschoolers who are assertive and notes that this assertiveness seems to be associated with relatively high levels of prosocial behavior.[93]

Prosocial children also tend to fit a particular cognitive profile. Research suggests, for instance, that smarter children are more likely to help, comfort, and share.[94] This may be because smarter children are more able to take the perspective of a larger number of others or may be more adept at the moral reasoning skills required in complex situations.

89. Ibid., chap. 3.
90. Ibid., 39.
91. Ibid., 40.
92. Ibid., 41.
93. Lois B. Murphy, *Social Behavior and Child Personality: An Exploratory Study of Some Roots of Sympathy* (New York: Columbia University Press, 1937); M. R. Yarrow and C. Z. Waxler, "Dimensions and Correlates of Prosocial Behavior in Children," *Child Development* 47 (1976): 118–25.
94. Eisenberg, *Caring Child*, 55.

Eisenberg stresses the role that adults have in developing proso-cial children. Research shows, for instance, that children tend to copy the moral or immoral behavior of parents and other adults. "It is clear that parental modeling of altruism can have a powerful effect on the altruistic tendencies of children," says Eisenberg. "Children exposed to altruistic care-givers apparently learn pro-social behavior and frequently seem to adopt the caring orientation of their parents."[95] Parents who are supportive, use indicative dis-ciplines (e.g., purposive formation exercises), provide opportuni-ties for prosocial activities, encourage other-oriented behavior, have high standards, and encourage sympathy are most likely to rear prosocial children.[96]

Research on the role of parents in raising moral children suggests that there are three foundations for moral development in children. First, children must internalize the parental standards of right and wrong; second, they must develop empathetic reactions; third, they must acquire personal standards.[97] "Caregivers can promote posi-tive behaviors and values in their children not only through their own interactions with the children," adds Eisenberg, "but also by influencing school curricula, monitoring children's use of media, and taking steps to influence public policy related to schools and television."[98]

The work of developmental psychologists Anne Colby and William Damon in their book *Some Do Care: Contemporary Lives of Moral Commitment* offers a look at twenty-three people whose lives serve as moral examples of love. Colby and Damon not only report on the activities and testimonies of these exem-plars but also draw some conclusions from their investigations. Exemplars demonstrated "unremitting faith and positivity in the face of the most dismal circumstances," the two report. They

95. Ibid., 91.

96. Nancy Eisenberg, "Empathy-Related Emotional Responses, Altruism, and Their Socialization," in *Visions of Compassion: Western Scientists and Tibetan Buddhists Examine Human Nature*, ed. Richard J. Davidson and Anne Harrington (Oxford: Oxford University Press, 2002), 155.

97. Michael Schulman and Eva Meckler, *Bringing Up a Moral Child: A New Approach for Teaching Your Child to Be Kind, Just, and Responsible* (Reading, MA: Addison-Wesley, 1985), 76.

98. Eisenberg, *Caring Child*, 131.

were motivated by their unswerving commitment to principles, and this motivation led them to take great risks to help those in need.[99]

Colby and Damon argue that the exemplars they studied were different from the typical person, but this difference was not one of kind. "The unusual feature of our exemplars' personal development is the strength of this integration and the extensivity of the moral engagements," Colby and Damon observe. "This is unusual and admirable, but it still does not set moral exemplars wholly apart from other people."[100]

What makes moral exemplars different from those who act in usual moral ways is that "over the course of their lives," say Colby and Damon, "there is a progressive uniting of self and morality. Exemplars come to see morality and self as inextricably intertwined, so that concerns of the self become defined by their moral sensibilities." Exemplars begin to see themselves as so intertwined with their moral obligation that self-identity and moral identity are nearly fused.[101]

Colby and Damon note that moral exemplars also have "a common sense of faith in the human potential to realize its ideals." The exemplars believed in something above and beyond the self. This faith "provides the glue joining all the self's systems of action and reflection." Faith in the human potential to attain something better is "what made the center hold throughout all the decades of the exemplars' uniquely consequential lives."[102]

Research on the virtues and character formation depends heavily on narrative. As such, this research lacks some of the precision of other research methods. The methods for studying specific loving actions, for instance, are available and possess a higher degree of exactness. Methods with precise measurements for studying character formation—the question of what kind of person loves—are not readily available. Yet the issues

99. Anne Colby and William Damon, *Some Do Care: Contemporary Lives of Moral Commitment* (New York: Free Press, 1992), 293ff.

100. Ibid., 301.

101. Ibid., 304. For a philosophical perspective on the differences between exemplars and others, see Andrew Michael Flescher, *Heroes, Saints, and Ordinary Morality* (Washington, DC: Georgetown University Press, 2003).

102. Colby and Damon, *Some Do Care*, 311.

of character formation are central to a robust understanding of love. Research in how persons develop virtuous lives is of great interest to the human enterprise and often is inspiring to those who engage in it. For this reason, new methodologies in the social sciences seem now required for the holistic study of persons and communities.[103]

Conclusion

The research on love reviewed in this chapter prompts an increasing number of social scientists to be skeptical of the claim that humans are inevitably and invariably egoistic. In their literature survey titled "Altruism: A Review of Recent Theory and Research," J. A. Piliavin and H.-W. Charng conclude that they "are now seeing a 'paradigm shift' away from the assumption that humans are inherently self-interested."[104] Although love is not equivalent with other-interest, the shift in psychological and sociological research is significant for what it means for exploring the promotion of well-being for the self, the near and dear, and the world.

An increasing number of social scientists consider research on love worthwhile and productive. Social scientists are ideally suited to identify values and virtues present in individuals and communities. This work is crucial for identifying what it means to promote overall well-being. Promoting overall well-being, I have been suggesting, is an essential aspect of what it means to love. Social science research tells us something important about what it means to be human and how we might generate a better today and tomorrow.

103. A classic text that moved the conversation forward in this regard is Don S. Browning, *Religious Thought and the Modern Psychologies: A Critical Conversation in the Theology of Culture* (Philadelphia: Fortress, 1987).
104. J. A. Piliavin and H.-W. Charng, "Altruism: A Review of Recent Theory and Research," *Annual Review of Sociology* 16, no. 1 (1990): 28.

4

Love and the Biological Sciences

In recent decades, biology has moved to the fore of love research. The role of evolution, the function of genes, selection pressures, and group interaction play a prominent role in contemporary biological discussions of the possibility and nature of love. In this chapter we explore a sampling of biological research as it pertains to love.

Contemporary biologists typically use the language of altruism when formulating theories and hypotheses related to love. In most cases, this preference of language is understandable. The language of love carries connotations that most biologists want to avoid. For instance, love typically connotes intent and motive. Most biologists do not consider an organism's intent or motive a factor for which they should or even could account in their research. The disregard for intent is especially evident, at least in theory, in scientific research on genetics. Some researchers distinguish biological altruism from psychological altruism by assuming that the latter involves motives and intention while the former does not.[1]

---

1. See, for example, the work of Elliott Sober, available in many formats. For a brief explanation of the difference between psychological and biological

Much of this chapter is spent exploring Charles Darwin's thoughts on the theory of evolution as it relates to love and altruism. Evolution suggests that continuities exist between humans and their nonhuman predecessors, and the data and theories of biology and related disciplines must be considered for a satisfactory account of love. I intersperse in the discussion, amid my descriptions of Darwin's theories, recent biological research related to Darwinian themes.[2]

Contemporary discussions of altruism in biology often center on the role of genes. The second part of this chapter explores genetic aspects of biological research on love and altruism. The emphasis on genes affects various biological accounts of agency and creaturely freedom. Throughout the chapter, I note how biological research and the theories of biology either inform, affirm, or oppose theories of love.

Love and the Origin of Species

The dominant theories of contemporary biology have their beginning in Charles Darwin. He firmly established evolution as biology's theoretical superstructure. At its bare bones, evolutionary theory says that all species descended from common ancestors, and this evolution occurred over a very long time. Contemporary scientists and philosophers of science debate how best to account for common descent. They suggest various "mechanisms" as the components or engines of evolution, and these mechanisms typically include natural selection, genetic mutation, and self-organization. Darwin, however, characteristically described evolution simply as "descent with modification"[3]

---

altruism, see Sober's "The ABCs of Altruism," in *Altruism and Altruistic Love: Science, Philosophy, and Religion in Dialogue*, ed. Stephen G. Post et al. (Oxford: Oxford University Press, 2002), 17–28.

2. Some of the better introductions to how evolutionary theory and altruism relate include John Cartwright, *Evolution and Human Behavior: Darwinian Perspective on Human Nature* (Cambridge, MA: MIT Press, 2000), and other books cited later in this chapter. One of the best explorations of the compatibility of evolution and altruism is Stephen J. Pope, *The Evolution of Altruism and the Ordering of Love* (Washington, DC: Georgetown University Press, 1994).

3. Charles Darwin, *On the Origin of Species by Means of Natural Selection, or the Preservation of Favoured Races in the Struggle for Life* (1859), reprinted

or "slow and gradual modification, through descent and natural selection."[4]

Darwin begins his most famous work, *On the Origin of Species*,[5] by arguing that his theory of evolution derives from observation. His work as a naturalist provided the raw material for his theory, and five years aboard HMS *Beagle* allowed him to encounter empirical data unknown in European scientific circles. Darwin's insights into the emergence of and changes in species so powerfully affect contemporary biology that scholars today approvingly cite Theodosius Dobzhansky's comment that "nothing in biology makes sense except in the light of evolution."[6]

In the book's introduction, Darwin offers a summary of natural selection's role in evolution. "As many more individuals of each species are born than can possibly survive," he writes, "and as, consequently, there is a frequently recurring struggle for existence, it follows that any being, if it vary however slightly in any manner profitable to itself, under the complex and sometimes varying conditions of life, will have a better chance of surviving, and thus be *naturally selected*." Darwin adds that "from the strong principle of inheritance, any selected variety will tend to propagate its new and modified form."[7]

A key to Darwin's evolutionary theory is the emergence of variations within species. He is forthright about his ignorance of how such variations occur.[8] He speculates that they derived from repro-

---

in *From So Simple a Beginning: The Four Great Books of Charles Darwin*, ed. Edward O. Wilson (New York: W. W. Norton, 2006), 660.

4. Ibid., 648.

5. The full name of the manuscript is *On the Origin of Species by Means of Natural Selection, or the Preservation of Favoured Races in the Struggle for Life*.

6. Theodosius Dobzhansky, "Nothing in Biology Makes Sense Except in the Light of Evolution," *The American Biology Teacher* 35 (March 1973): 125–29.

7. Darwin, *Origin of Species*, 451.

8. Whether the variability of a species, says Darwin, "be taken advantage of by natural selection, and whether the variations be accumulated to a greater or lesser amount, thus causing a greater or lesser amount of modification in the varying species, depends on many complex contingencies—on the variability being of a beneficial nature, on the power of intercrossing, on the rate of breeding, on the slowly changing physical conditions of the country, and more especially on the nature of the other inhabitants with which the varying species comes into competition" (ibid., 649).

duction, but he admits that he is "ignorant of the cause of each particular variation."[9] Later biologists point to the role that genes play in species variations, but Darwin did not know about genes.

Darwin also speculated that "external conditions of life," such as climate and food, induce modifications and variations.[10] But "whatever the cause may be of each slight difference in the offspring from their parents—and a cause for each must exist," says Darwin, "it is the steady accumulation, through natural selection of such differences, when beneficial to the individual, that gives rise to all the more-important modifications of structure." By "natural selection," he means that "innumerable beings on the face of the earth are enabled to struggle with each other, and the best adapted to survive."[11]

Darwin titles chapter 3 "Struggle for Existence" in order to describe the fundamental urge for survival in all living things. His argument is that each creature strives to increase at a geometrical rate, but this striving inevitably requires some measure of destruction. Were all creatures somehow to avoid destruction, the world has neither enough resources to feed them nor enough space to hold them. Death is necessary. "As more individuals are produced than can possibly survive, there must in every case be a struggle for existence, either one individual with another of the same species, or with the individuals of distinct species, or with the physical conditions of life."[12] This struggle leads to "severe competition."[13]

Darwin's emphasis on severe competition provides a natural explanation for why overpopulation rarely occurs, but it also leads many today to wonder about the role of love and altruism in evolutionary theory. Darwin is clear that natural selection, which he considers the primary force in evolution, preserves favorable variations and rejects injurious ones. "Natural selection acts solely through the preservation of variations in some way advantageous," says Darwin, "which consequently endure."[14] But to put it negatively,

9. Ibid., 534.
10. Ibid., 557.
11. Ibid., 558.
12. Ibid., 490.
13. Ibid., 489.
14. Ibid., 519.

natural selection leads "to much extinction of the less improved and intermediate forms of life."[15]

The competition to survive turns on a variety of factors. Sometimes these factors are quite miniscule. "A grain in the balance will determine which individual shall live and which shall die," says Darwin. Even seemingly insignificant factors can determine which variety or species will increase in number, which will decrease, and which finally becomes extinct. Individuals compete with those of their own species, with those of similar species, and most often with those quite dissimilar. "The slightest advantage in one over those with which it comes into competition," concludes Darwin, "will turn the balance."[16]

We should note that the urge and struggle for "survival," "advantage," "profitability," "adaptation," and "improvement" Darwin describes are not essentially opposed to love. Desires for life are not opposed to love when we define love, as I have done, as the promotion of well-being. In fact, these words might be fitting descriptions of some intentional activity, done in response to others in one's environment, to promote well-being. To this extent, Darwin's theory of evolution is generally compatible with love.

Even the struggle to survive can be compatible with the promotion of well-being. In fact, contemporary environmental philosopher Holmes Rolston III argues that the struggle for survival is necessary for evolutionary advances in creaturely complexity, including sentience and the capacity to love. "Struggle is the dark side of creativity," says Rolston. "One cannot enjoy a world in which one cannot suffer, any more than one can succeed in a world in which one cannot fail."[17]

The evolution of sentience includes the possibility of both pain and pleasure. "Pain is eminently useful in survival, and it will be naturally selected, on average, as functional pain," Rolston observes. "Natural selection requires pain as much as pleasure in its construction of concern and caring . . . [but] any population whose members are constantly in counterproductive pain will be

15. Ibid., 532.
16. Ibid., 746.
17. Holmes Rolston III, *Genes, Genesis, and God: Values and Their Origins in Natural and Human History* (Cambridge: Cambridge University Press, 1999), 303–4.

selected against and go extinct or develop some capacities to mini-mize it."[18]

Not only is pain necessary; death is as well. All individuals in the struggle for existence eventually die. "Death can be meaning-fully integrated into the biological processes as a necessary coun-terpart to the advancing of life," says Rolston.[19] The death of a particular organism feeds into the nondeath of the species. Only when individuals are replaced by others, Rolston notes, "can the species track the changing environment; only by replacements can they evolve into something else."[20]

The world is a theater where life is learned and earned by labor. "This whole evolutionary upslope is a calling in which renewed life comes by blasting the old," says Rolston.[21] "Every organism is plunged into a struggle in which goodness is given only as it is fought for. . . . Since the beginning, the myriad creatures have been giving up their lives as a ransom for many."[22]

Rolston sees a connection between the suffering and renewal in biology and the teachings of some of the world's great religions. "The cruciform creation is, in the end, deiform," says Rolston. It is godly because of struggle, not in spite of it.[23] Although biology can document the struggle of survival, the sequence of life, death, and life renewed, Rolston argues, the redemption of suffering is a religious issue.[24] For Rolston, only humans can voluntarily self-sacrifice for others. This possibility transcends the strictly biological realm and moves into the realm of ethics and theology.[25]

Although Rolston argues that struggle and suffering are neces-sary for the evolutionary "upslope," the question remains open as to whether creatures, human and nonhuman, voluntarily act self-sacrificially for the good of the whole. Rolston questions whether a strictly biological basis exists for the possibility that creatures

18. Ibid., 304.
19. Holmes Rolston III, "Kenosis and Nature," in *The Work of Love: Creation as Kenosis*, ed. John Polkinghorne (Grand Rapids: Eerdmans, 2001), 59.
20. Rolston, *Genes, Genesis, and God*, 305.
21. Rolston, "Kenosis and Nature," 59.
22. Ibid., 60.
23. Rolston, *Genes, Genesis, and God*, 305.
24. Ibid., 307.
25. Rolston, "Kenosis and Nature," 64.

voluntarily undergo struggle and suffering for the good of others. According to him, biology requires additional information from religion and ethics to make sense of human love.

With this said, it is true that Darwin's own emphasis on individual competition and incessant struggle with others appears at odds with the cooperation at least sometimes appropriate for the promotion of overall well-being. The emphasis on competition and struggle pushed Darwin's readers to see evolution as antithetical to cooperation. Darwin famously said that natural selection cannot produce the formation of any part of the structure of any one species for the exclusive good of another.[26] After reading *On the Origin of Species*, Darwin's friend and "bulldog" Thomas Huxley wrote of evolution's moral conclusions:

> From the point of view of the moralist, the animal world is on about the same level as a gladiator's show. The creatures are fairly well treated, and set to fight; whereby the strongest, the swiftest and the cunningest live to fight another day. . . . The weakest and stupidest went to the wall, while the toughest and the shrewdest, those who were best fitted to cope with their circumstances, but not the best in any other sense, survived. Life was a continual free fight, and beyond the limited and temporary relations of the family, the Hobbesian war of each against all was the normal state of existence.[27]

Darwin's language in *On the Origin of Species* certainly tends toward portraying biological evolution as individual struggle for personal benefit at the expense of others. And this strikes many today, as it did Huxley, as eliminating a biological basis for love of others. Rolston is right to point out that pain and death may be necessary for evolutionary progress. However, the extent and severity of pain and death may not be necessary. On the face of it, *On the Origin of Species* suggests that Darwinian evolution does not allow for intentional action to benefit others at significant loss to oneself. Self-sacrificial love is absent. Jeffrey P. Schloss says it well: "If the struggle for existence is the engine of natural selection, and survival of the fittest is the direction of travel, then those

26. Darwin, *Origin of Species*, 578.
27. Thomas H. Huxley, "The Struggle for Existence: A Programme," *Nineteenth Century* 23 (1888): 163–65.

organisms that sacrifice their biological well-being for the good of another will be kicked off the train."[28]

Love and Common Descent

In his second-most significant book, Darwin introduces a way to account, at least partially, for love of others. He emphasizes relationship as a condition for love, an important element of love I identified earlier. In relationship, self-sacrificial love may have reason to emerge.

Darwin begins this book, *The Descent of Man*, by saying that his purpose is "to decide whether man is the modified descendant of some pre-existing form."[29] By this, Darwin intends to apply to humans the evolutionary principles he proposed earlier. At the outset, he affirms his general evolutionary principle: "At every stage in the process of modification, all the individuals which were in any way best fitted for their conditions of life, though in different degrees, would have survived in greater numbers than the less well fitted."[30]

An important part of the argument that humans are also subject to evolution is the claim that humans and nonhumans share much in common. Darwin assigns a large portion of *The Descent of Man* to surveying evidence that supports the view that continuity exists between humans and nonhumans. Much of this evidence comes from body shapes and features. But some evidence for continuity comes from mental and emotional similarities. "The close similarity between man and the lower animals," Darwin concludes, "cannot be disputed."[31]

Darwin's thoughts on morals in this book are of particular interest to contemporary love research. The fundamental basis for morals, says Darwin, is the social nature of existence. "The so-

28. Jeffrey P. Schloss, "Emerging Accounts of Altruism: 'Love Creation's Final Law'?" in Post et al., *Altruism and Altruistic Love*, 214.

29. Charles Darwin, *The Descent of Man, and Selection in Relation to Sex* (1871), reprinted in Wilson, *From So Simple a Beginning*, 783. Instead of the full title, in the main text I will use the shortened version, *The Descent of Man*.

30. Ibid., 1238.

31. Ibid., 1236.

called moral sense is aboriginally derived from the social instincts," he conjectures.[32] "Social instincts lead an animal to take pleasure in the society of its fellows, to feel a certain amount of sympathy with them, and to perform various services to them."[33] The impulse to help others may become habitual, and the community plays a key role in forming these habits. In fact, Darwin contends, the social instincts, along with the aid of the intellect and the effects of habit, lead naturally to the golden rule: Do to others as you would have them do to you.[34] In *The Descent of Man*, we find a more-developed biological basis for love.

Morality is not limited to humans, Darwin maintains. Moral continuity exists between humans and nonhumans, and all social animals have some sense of right and wrong.[35] For instance, Darwin notes that animals perform services for one another. Animals also sometimes warn one another of danger. Animals serve one another through parental and familial care. And creatures sometimes sympathize with each other's distress.

Darwin speculates that at least some nonhuman animals have something like a conscience. He says, "An inward monitor would tell the animal that it would have been better to have followed the one impulse rather than the other."[36] The differences between "man and the higher animals, great as it is, is certainly one of degree and not of kind." After all, says Darwin, "the senses and intuitions, the various emotions and faculties, such as love, memory, attention, curiosity, imitation, reason, etc., of which man boasts, may be found in an incipient, or even sometimes in a well-developed condition, in the lower animals."[37]

A number of contemporary scientists affirm Darwin's contention that continuity exists between humans and nonhumans with regard to morality.[38] Marc Bekoff, for instance, has made a strong case

32. Ibid., 832.
33. Ibid., 818.
34. Ibid., 837.
35. Ibid., 819.
36. Ibid.
37. Ibid., 837.
38. See a discussion of the moral continuities and discontinuities in Leonard D. Katz, ed., *Evolutionary Origins of Morality: Cross-Disciplinary Perspectives* (Bowling Green, OH: Imprint Academic, 2000).

for the existence of morality in nonhumans. For instance, animal morality is often evident in the fair play that dogs require of one another.[39] Bekoff argues that "we do not have to ascribe to animals far-fetched cognitive or emotional capacities to reach the conclusion that they can make moral decisions in certain circumstances."[40] He suggests that although moral similarities exist between humans and nonhumans, we must be careful to judge what is moral by what is appropriate for nonhumans and not necessarily by what is appropriate for humans.

Frans de Waal's work with chimpanzees, rhesus monkeys, and baboons also suggests moral continuities between humans and nonhumans. De Waal says that "a chimpanzee stroking or patting a victim of attack or sharing her food with a hungry companion shows attitudes that are hard to distinguish from those of a person picking up a crying child, or doing volunteer work at a soup kitchen. To classify a chimpanzee's behavior as based on instinct and the person's behavior as proof of moral decency is misleading, and probably incorrect."[41]

What Darwin calls social instincts, de Waal calls empathy toward others, relationship, or community concern. De Waal describes the role that community concern plays in the development of human morality from nonhuman morality. "The biggest step in the evolution of human morality was the move from interpersonal relations to a focus on the greater good," says de Waal. "In apes, we can see the beginnings of this when they smooth relations between others. Females may bring males together after a fight between them, thus brokering reconciliation, and high-ranking males often stop fights among others in an evenhanded manner, thus promoting peace in the group."[42] De Waal adds that humans "are not hypocritically

39. Marc Bekoff, *Minding Animals: Awareness, Emotions, and Heart* (New York: Oxford University Press, 2002), chap. 6.

40. Marc Bekoff, "Animal Passions and Beastly Virtues: Cognitive Ethology as the Unifying Science for Understanding the Subjective, Emotional, Empathetic, and Moral Lives of Animals," *Zygon: Journal of Religion and Science* 41, no. 1 (2006): 93.

41. Frans de Waal, *Good Natured: The Origins of Right and Wrong in Humans and Other Animals* (Cambridge, MA: Harvard University Press, 1996), 210.

42. Frans de Waal, *Primates and Philosophers: How Morality Evolved*, ed. Josiah Ober, Stephen Macedo, and Robert Wright (Princeton, NJ: Princeton University Press, 2006), 54.

fooling everyone when we act morally: we are making decisions that flow from the social instincts older than our species."[43]

Although the social nature of existence provides the conditions for the emergence of morality among nonhumans, this condition does not explain fully why some creatures might be self-sacrificial. Charles Darwin anticipates the question of how self-sacrifice for the good of others might arise in a world of severe competition. He speculates that self-sacrifice arose first in the parent-child relationship. Parents sometimes give sacrificially toward their children at a significant and sometimes even ultimate cost to themselves.[44]

From this extremely basic parental impulse to nurture children, says Darwin, a person retains "some degree of instinctive love and sympathy for his fellows."[45] The sacrificial love of parent for child arises as part of natural selection. We will see later in this chapter that contemporary biologists believe that the desire to promote a genetic heritage plays in important role in a parent's self-sacrificial behavior. The offspring of nurturing parents are more likely to survive and thrive than the offspring of uncaring ones. But Darwin did not know how genes might influence parental sacrifice, and a number of contemporary critics are skeptical that a parent's genes entirely determine nurturing.

The dynamics of community life can sustain the self-sacrificial love initiated in the parent-child relationship, says Darwin. Communities composed of those that aid and defend one another often succeed in competing against communities composed of selfish actors. "When two tribes of primeval man, living in the same country, came into competition," Darwin observes, and when the one tribe includes "a greater number of courageous, sympathetic, and faithful members, who were always ready to warn each other of danger, to aid and defend each other, this tribe would without doubt succeed best and conquer the other."[46] Communities that "included the greatest number of the most sympathetic members would flourish best and rear the greatest number of offspring."[47]

43. Ibid., 55.
44. Darwin, *Descent of Man*, 823.
45. Ibid., 825.
46. Ibid., 869.
47. Ibid., 824.

Contemporary researchers have documented the phenomenon of altruistic nonhuman species surviving and thriving in groups.[48] Here, again, is natural selection at work. But this is natural selection at the communal or group level.

In *Unto Others: The Evolution and Psychology of Unselfish Behavior*, philosopher Elliott Sober and biologist David Sloan Wilson revive for contemporary scholars Darwin's notion that groups of altruists can outcompete groups of egoists. Sober and Wilson call this evolutionary notion "group-selection theory." Their primary argument is that "the case for evolutionary altruism requires showing that group selection has been an important force in evolution."[49]

Group-selection theory says that individuals sometimes act altruistically toward members of their group so that the group as a whole survives and thrives. "Altruism can evolve to the extent that altruists and non-altruists become concentrated in different groups," report Sober and Wilson.[50] But "to be sufficient, the differential fitness of groups (the force favoring the altruist) must be strong enough to counter the differential fitness of individuals within groups (the force favoring the selfish types)."[51] Sober and Wilson provide data in the biological and anthropological sciences that substantiate group-selection theory.[52] They conclude, "The concept of human groups as adaptive units may be supported not only by evolutionary theory but by the bulk of empirical information on human social groups in all cultures around the world."[53]

Group-selection theory, however, does not lead Sober and Wilson to paint a rosy picture of universal benevolence. The theory only offers a way to account for why altruists can survive and thrive in a world of severe competition. Altruists in groups can have an evolutionary advantage. Sober and Wilson admit that "group selec-

---

48. See Bekoff, *Minding Animals*; de Waal, *Good Natured*.
49. Elliott Sober and David Sloan Wilson, *Unto Others: The Evolution and Psychology of Unselfish Behavior* (Cambridge, MA: Harvard University Press, 1998), 6.
50. Ibid., 26.
51. Ibid.
52. Ibid., chaps. 3–5.
53. Ibid., 193.

tion favors within group niceness and between group nastiness."[54] Altruism toward outsiders remains unexplained.

Charles Darwin thought there must be some reason, in addition to the parent-child care relationship, for unselfishness to first emerge in groups of nonrelated individuals. "It seems scarcely possible," says Darwin, that the number of people in a tribe who cooperate "could be increased through natural selection, that is by the survival of the fittest."[55]

Cooperation might arise, however, when a member of a group learns through personal experience that helping others provides personal benefits. "Each man would soon learn from experience that if he aided his fellow-men, he would commonly receive aid in return." Darwin adds that "from this low motive he might acquire the habit of aiding his fellows." Benevolence toward others would, in turn, "strengthen the feeling of sympathy, which gives the first impulse to benevolent actions."[56] Altruism toward nonkin could emerge through mutual cooperation.

The idea that creatures cooperate for their mutual benefit is found in Aristotle's work nearly three thousand years ago. But as Darwin's thought gained a foothold in the academy, his own affirmation of cooperation was largely silenced in favor of individual action for personal fitness.

A powerful biological voice in favor of cooperation emerging soon after Darwin's twin publications was biologist and political activist Petr Kropotkin. At the turn of the twentieth century, Kropotkin argued that cooperation was present in the natural world, an argument opposed to the idea that each creature acts only in the interest of its own survival. Kropotkin spent a great deal of time studying in Siberia, including taking five expeditions across the frozen ice. He summarizes what he observed by saying, "In all the scenes of animal lives which passed before my eyes, I saw mutual aid and mutual support carried on to an extent which made me suspect in it a feature of the greatest importance for the maintenance of life, the preservation of each species, and of its further evolution."[57]

54. Ibid., 9.

55. Darwin, *Descent of Man*, 870.

56. Ibid.

57. Petr Kropotkin, *Mutual Aid: A Factor of Evolution*, 3rd ed. (1902; repr., Montreal: Black Rose Books, 1989), xxxvii. For a similar argument with regard to

Significant biological research has been done on reciprocal altruism and cooperation in recent decades. In *Cooperation among Animals: An Evolutionary Perspective*, biologist Lee Alan Dugatkin brings together numerous studies of cooperation among fish, birds, nonprimate animals, nonhuman primates, and insects. For instance, Dugatkin reports on vampire bats who share food. Female vampire bats regurgitate blood meals to nest mates who otherwise would starve. Three factors are at play in this giving: there is a probability of future interaction, the blood meal is critical for the survival of the recipient, and those bats who have given in the past are more likely to receive in the future.[58]

After reporting numerous examples of reciprocal altruism, Dugatkin concludes that "while not ubiquitous, cooperation is certainly widespread in the animal kingdom." He reminds his readers, however, that "cooperation often takes place in the context of rather nasty situations; that is, competition, aggression, predation, and so on."[59] Dugatkin adds elsewhere that love often requires more than reciprocal altruism. "Reciprocal cooperation might be okay with friends, but in a spouse one might want a kind of cooperation that transcends [reciprocal altruism]."[60]

The notion that unselfish behavior arises when creatures discover that giving can benefit the giver is today called by scholars "reciprocal altruism" or "tit-for-tat altruism." Biologist Robert Trivers and political scientist Robert Axelrod have done much to establish reciprocal altruism as a central theory in biology.

In his oft-cited article "The Evolution of Reciprocal Altruism," Trivers reports that fish of different species act altruistically toward one another. Smaller fish provide a service to larger fish by cleaning them of debris. Larger fish do not eat the smaller fish, because the smaller fish provide this benefit. Trivers reports that various species of birds call out when predators near. Although

---

nonhuman primates, see Christopher Boehm, *Hierarchy in the Forest: The Evolution of Egalitarian Behavior* (Cambridge, MA: Harvard University Press, 1999).

58. Lee Alan Dugatkin, *Cooperation among Animals: An Evolutionary Perspective* (New York: Oxford University Press, 1997), 113–14.

59. Ibid., 164.

60. Lee Alan Dugatkin, *Cheating Monkeys and Citizen Bees: The Nature of Cooperation in Animals and Humans* (Cambridge, MA: Harvard University Press, 1999), 171.

calling out jeopardizes each caller, the cacophony of calls makes it difficult for predators to hone in on any one bird as potential prey. Cooperation among those of various species benefits each individually. Trivers also offers explanations for how organisms punish cheaters who do not reciprocate by giving gifts. Punishing cheaters is especially common in human interactions associated with reciprocal altruism.[61]

Robert Axelrod's contribution to the theory of reciprocal altruism is based largely on a computer-based competition he sponsored. Axelrod wanted to answer this question: When should a person cooperate and when should a person be selfish in an ongoing interaction with another person?[62] He devised a game that challenged participants to offer the best strategy for dealing with a prisoner's dilemma. Axelrod explains the game in this way: "In the Prisoner's Dilemma game, there are two players. Each has two choices, namely, cooperate or defect. Each must make the choice without knowing what the other will do. No matter what the other does, defection yields a higher payoff than cooperation. The dilemma is that if both defect, both do worse than if both had cooperated."[63]

The most advantageous strategy over the long run for Axelrod's computer game was for player A to cooperate in his or her first move. After that move, player A should do whatever player B does in response to player A's first move. If player B defects, player A should do likewise. But if player B cooperates, player A benefits from cooperating with player B's positive response. Axelrod calls this winning strategy to the prisoner's dilemma "tit for tat." It entails "the policy of cooperating on the first move and then doing whatever the other player did on the previous move."[64]

The game suggests that the best strategy for personal well-being is first to cooperate in a relationship that is likely to involve additional interactions. The best strategy suggests that cooperation is detrimental in ongoing relationships in which the giver's gift is not reciprocated. Axelrod's work has been the basis for many

61. Robert L. Trivers, "The Evolution of Reciprocal Altruism," *The Quarterly Review of Biology* 46, no. 1 (1971): 35–57.
62. Robert Axelrod, *The Evolution of Cooperation*, rev. ed. (1984; repr., New York: Basic Books, 2006), vii.
63. Ibid., 7–8.
64. Ibid., 13.

research projects on reciprocal altruism in disciplines within and outside biology.

Evolutionary psychologists John Tooby and Leda Cosmides propose that cooperative friendship can emerge in evolution such that humans deliver benefits to others without strict reciprocity. In human friendships, say the researchers, "explicit linkage between favors or insistence by a recipient that she be allowed to immediately repay is generally taken as a lack of friendship."[65] Humans have developed a variety of ways to identify and cultivate what Tooby and Cosmides call "deep engagement," which generates trust and overcomes barriers erected by the threat of being cheated. "Losing a valued friend, being able to spend less time with the friend, becoming less valued by the friend, or at the extreme, social isolation, may be more costly than being cheated," say Tooby and Cosmides. Instead of being cheated as the primary risk to the giver, "the primary risk is experiencing a world increasingly devoid of deeply engaged social partners, or sufficiently beneficial social partners, or both."[66]

Although Charles Darwin's speculation about reciprocal altruism and group altruism has been substantiated in recent research, contemporary scholars also explore a third reason why creatures, especially humans, might act unselfishly. We know that humans often desire praise and avoid blame. A human's "actions are largely determined by the expressed wishes and judgment of his fellowmen," says Darwin, "and unfortunately still oftener by his own strong selfish desires."[67] These social instincts "give the impulse to act for the good of the community, this impulse being strengthened, directed, and sometimes even deflected by public opinion."[68] In short, complex animals such as us may be self-sacrificial in hopes of receiving reputational gain.

According to Darwin, the instinct to desire praise or avoid blame "no doubt was originally acquired, like all other social instincts,

65. John Tooby and Leda Cosmides, "Friendship and the Banker's Paradox: Other Pathways to the Evolution of Adaptation for Altruism," in *Evolution of Social Behaviour Patterns in Primates and Man: A Joint Discussion Meeting of the Royal Society and the British Academy*, ed. W. G. Runciman, John Maynard Smith, and R. I. M. Dunbar (Oxford: Oxford University Press, 1996), 130.

66. Ibid., 122.

67. Darwin, *Descent of Man*, 826.

68. Ibid., 818.

through natural selection." For "it is obvious," he observes, "that the members of the same tribe would approve of conduct which appeared to them to be for the general good, and would reprobate that which appeared evil."[69] This suggests that the desire for reputational gain rests ultimately on the explanation that higher creatures give goods to others, because higher creatures originally or currently expected something good in return. Unselfishness arises out of prior selfishness.

In an important contemporary book on biology and morality, *The Biology of Moral Systems*, Richard D. Alexander champions the notion of reputational gain. Alexander suggests that reputational gain is based on indirect reciprocity. "I regard indirect reciprocity as a consequence of direct reciprocity occurring in the presence of interested audiences," he says. Interested audiences are "groups of individuals who continually evaluate the members of their society as possible future interactants from whom they would like to gain more than they lose."[70] In effect, says Alexander, "what goes on in such cases could be termed 'social hustling,' in which a 'player' more or less deliberately . . . loses in order to 'set up' the observer for a later overcompensating gain."[71] Even an actor's effort toward universal altruism "may raise status and multiply subsequent benefits so as to produce a net return to the actor."[72] Alexander's view on reputational gain is a less-convincing explanation, however, for why people act self-sacrificially when members of society are unlikely to notice. A better explanation seems required for self-giving love expressed when no one is looking.

Darwin thought that sometimes acting for the good of others might occur unconsciously. Conscious efforts to promote the well-being of others may emerge from a variety of motives. But such activity becomes firmly established in individuals, suggests Darwin, by habitual responses to social, survival, and reproductive pressures.[73] Over time, humans may even feel compelled, consciously or subconsciously, to love others.

69. Ibid., 871.
70. Richard D. Alexander, *The Biology of Moral Systems* (Hawthorne, NY: Aldine de Gruyter, 1987), 93–94.
71. Ibid., 94.
72. Ibid., 106.
73. Darwin, *Descent of Man*, 826.

As humans advance in civilization, small tribes unite into larger communities. This provides the opportunity for widening sympathies. Human sympathies may "extend to the men of all races, to the imbecile, the maimed, and other useless members of society, and finally to the lower animals."[74] But the aid "we feel impelled to give to the helpless," Darwin maintains, "is mainly an incidental result of the instinct of sympathy, which was originally acquired as a part of the social instincts."[75]

Richard Alexander echoes Darwin's thoughts here as well. Alexander frames the question of altruism toward larger groups in terms of what he calls "indiscriminate beneficence," which he defines as "willingness to risk relatively small expenses in certain kinds of social donations to whoever may be needy." Only in human systems of indirect reciprocity, says Alexander, "does a modicum of essentially indiscriminate beneficence or social investments exist in large groups."[76]

Acts of indiscriminate beneficence result in a more-unified society. Individuals often gain from living in this unity, but they also "gain from portraying themselves as indiscriminate altruists, and from thereby inducing indiscriminate beneficence in others." This means, Alexander continues, "that whether or not we know it when we speak favorably to our children about Good Samaritanism, we are telling them about a behavior that has a strong likelihood of being reproductively profitable."[77]

An individual who promotes the society-wide endorsement of altruism gains personally. It is to an individual's advantage, says Alexander, "to cause his neighbor, if possible, to be a little more moral than himself."[78] Societies honor individual models, mentors, and saints for their self-sacrifice, because the behavior of these altruists benefits those who honor them.

In fact, Alexander contends, each person has evolved keen abilities to appear more beneficent than is actually the case. Each person has evolved to encourage others to overinvest indiscriminately. "According to this view, individuals are expected to parade the idea

---

74. Ibid., 836.
75. Ibid., 873.
76. Alexander, *Biology of Moral Systems*, 97.
77. Ibid., 102.
78. Ibid.

of much beneficence, and even of indiscriminate altruism as beneficial, so as to encourage people in general to engage in increasing amounts of social investment whether or not it is beneficial to their interests."[79] Jeffrey P. Schloss summarizes Alexander's theory by saying it implies that "we're as unselfish as it pays to be; we're as selfish as we can get away with."[80]

Alexander's theories suggest a cynical explanation for the individual and social praise of universal beneficence. Not well accounted for in his theory, however, is the self-report of altruists who witness that their primary motives for giving do not include deceiving others into giving more in return. Alexander is forced to regard such self-reports as the product of delusion. As will be pointed out near the end of this chapter, the charge of unconscious self-delusion might just as easily be lodged against those who deny that some creatures act with the primary motive of benefiting others. The charge of self-delusion easily backfires.

Finally, Charles Darwin briefly explores the role he sees God playing for morality. At the conclusion of *The Descent of Man*, Darwin says, "With the more civilized races, the conviction of the existence of an all-seeing Deity has had a potent influence on the advancement of morality." Belief in God, however, is not "innate or instinctive in man," says Darwin. In fact, he speculates that "the idea of a universal and beneficent Creator of the universe does not seem to arise in the mind of man, until he has been elevated by long-continued culture."[81] Darwin's point seems to be that belief in God arises in highly civilized societies as the ultimate form of praise or blame. Praise and blame writ large guides natural selection's development of morals. This argument is an important one, but few contemporary theologians regard it as ultimately convincing. Darwin has no evidence that belief in God is not innate, instinctive, or written on the creaturely "heart."

Darwin's thoughts on the social nature in *The Descent of Man* are formative for contemporary love research. His construal of

79. Ibid., 103.
80. Jeffrey P. Schloss, "Hath Darwin Suffered a Prophet's Scorn? Evolutionary Theory and the Scandal of Unconditional Love," in *Spiritual Information: 100 Perspectives on Science and Religion*, ed. Charles L. Harper Jr. (Philadelphia: Templeton Foundation Press, 2005), 293.
81. Darwin, *Descent of Man*, 1242.

creaturely morality as fundamentally tied to social relationships fits nicely with the notion that love requires sympathetic responses to others. Because love requires relations, and Darwin's evolutionary theory suggests that morals are fundamentally grounded on social relations, Darwinian evolution provides a powerful framework for affirming at least some structural elements of love.

Darwin's speculation about the motives and mechanisms for loving others, however, are less helpful. It remains unclear how self-sacrificial love not ultimately tied to some version of prior or ultimate selfishness can ever be expressed. In Darwin's thought, giving sacrificially to others is at best a by-product of natural selection. At worst, Darwin and his followers say apparent self-sacrifice is selfishness in disguise. The case remains open.

Altruistic Genes

The contemporary story of biology and love cannot be told without exploring the role of genes. The views expressed thus far remain important for love research, but now they must be set in the context of theories about the nature and function of genetic forces. This context raises new possibilities and new challenges to love research.

Charles Darwin admitted in *On the Origin of Species* that he did not know the source of species variation. He was, in his own words, "ignorant of the cause of each particular variation."[82] Darwin observed that parents and offspring could possess important differences, but he did not have a strong reason for why offspring inherit particular advantages (or disadvantages) their parents do not possess.

A key explanation for this variation came from the work of the Augustinian monk Gregor Mendel. Mendel studied inheritance in pea plants during Darwin's time, observing that inherited traits were passed from one generation to the next in discrete units. Biologists eventually came to call these discrete units "genes" (derived from Darwin's word *pangenesis*) to signify the smallest particle representing an inherited characteristic. Mendel discovered that

82. Darwin, *Origin of Species*, 534.

variations in an organism's physical and behavior characteristics (its phenotype) emerge largely if not entirely from variations in that organism's set of genes (its genotype). His work and the work of others on genetics, however, went largely unnoticed until the twentieth century.

Research on genes in the early twentieth century confirmed Mendel's theory that mutations among genes lead to changes in the structures and behaviors of organisms. Chromosomes within cells were identified as the carriers of genetic material. James Watson and Francis Crick's famous discovery of the double helix molecular structure of DNA solidified the scientific importance genes play in the development of plants and animals. The mapping of the genome (i.e., the total complement of genes in a cell) at the beginning of the twenty-first century was an important step in the process of identifying which portions of the genome are directly reflected in an organism's physical features and behaviors.

The combination of Darwin's basic theories of evolution with the role of genes to produce species variation is now often called the "modern evolutionary synthesis." Evolutionary variation occurs largely through genetic mutation. Although gene replication typically is accurate from generation to generation, alterations occur in a gene's sequence. These alterations or mutations appear random. Most random mutations do not negatively or positively affect the organism. But other mutations enhance or diminish an organism's capacity to survive and thrive. Beneficial mutations passed to the next generation provide organisms with an evolutionary advantage.

The roles of genetics for explaining altruism increased throughout the twentieth century. During the middle decades, J. B. S. Haldane, R. A. Fisher, and Sewall Wright were pioneers in proposing that organisms are more altruistic toward those to whom they are most closely related genetically.[83]

Much of this early work on genetics was framed in terms of mathematics. Wright, for instance, introduced a variable to explain the penchant for altruistic action toward kin. He called this vari-

---

83. For a helpful summary of their work, see Lee Alan Dugatkin, *The Altruism Equation: Seven Scientists Search for the Origins of Goodness* (Princeton, NJ: Princeton University Press, 2006), chap. 4.

able the "coefficient of relationship." The relationship between an individual and its ancestors varies by the generations separating them. This coefficient gauges the likelihood that an individual might be self-sacrificial toward those to whom that individual is genetically related. Because of this work, biologists began to shift from understanding evolution primarily in terms of competition and struggle to the individual's aim to further its genetic heritage. Some biologists now consider furthering genetic heritage the ultimate explanation for any organism's behavior.

The research and theories of W. D. Hamilton solidified the theory that organisms act altruistically to sustain or expand an organism's genetic heritage. Hamilton showed that altruism more likely occurs the more individuals share genetic histories. Organisms sometimes give up the possibility of generating direct offspring if their self-sacrificial action toward kin could generate multiple offspring from those with whom they share many genetic similarities. Hamilton's theory on altruism has come to be called "kin selection."

Kin-selection theory suggests that to propagate their genetic lineage, organisms sometimes act in ways that undermine their own survival. This inclination to ensure the proliferation of one's genes, however, generates altruistic actions toward those whose genes are most like the altruist's. Hamilton offers a mathematical equation to account for the increased rate at which organisms may act altruistically toward relatives. Hamilton's equation says that the cost to the giver is less than the gain to the beneficiary, times the index of genetic relatedness ($C < B * R$). He called the sum of an individual's own fitness plus the sum of all its effects for the fitness of its relatives "inclusive fitness."[84] Agreeing with the theory, J. B. S. Haldane purportedly remarked that he would lay down his life to save two brothers or eight cousins.

The story of genes and kin altruism leads naturally to the seminal work of E. O. Wilson. He, more than anyone, made Hamilton's kin-selection theory widely known in the late twentieth and early

---

84. See Hamilton's essays, "The Evolution of Altruistic Behavior," *American Naturalist* 97, no. 896 (1963): 354–56; "The Genetical Evolution of Social Behavior I," *Journal of Theoretical Biology* 7, no. 1 (1964): 1–16; "The Genetical Evolution of Social Behavior II," *Journal of Theoretical Biology* 7, no. 1 (1964): 17–52; "Altruism and Related Phenomena, Mainly in Social Insects," *Annual Review of Ecology and Systematics* 3 (1972): 193–232.

twenty-first centuries. Wilson coined the label "sociobiology" to describe his systematic study of the biological basis for all social behavior. He considers Hamilton's idea of kin-selection altruism "a key organizing concept" in sociobiology.[85]

In *Sociobiology: The New Synthesis*, Wilson calls altruism "the central theoretical problem of sociobiology." The problem asks "How can altruism, which by definition reduces personal fitness, possibly evolve by natural selection?"[86] Wilson offers examples of organisms and animals that surrender "personal genetic fitness for the enhancement of personal genetic fitness in others."[87]

Wilson's own early observations of ant self-sacrifice influenced him to adopt Hamilton's theory of kin altruism.[88] He found that ants were more self-sacrificial toward those to whom they were most directly genetically related. And "if some of the individuals of the family are sterile and yet important to the welfare of fertile relatives, as in the case of insect colonies," says Wilson, "selection at the family level is inevitable. With the entire family as the unit of selection, it is the capacity to generate sterile but altruistic relatives that becomes subject to genetic evolution."[89]

In his Pulitzer Prize–winning book, *On Human Nature*, Wilson relates human kin altruism to the "self-sacrificing termite soldier [who] protects the rest of its colony, including the queen and king, its parents. As a result, the soldier's more fertile brothers and sisters flourish, and through them the altruistic genes are multiplied by a greater production of nephews and nieces."[90]

With Wilson's influential endorsement and evidence from various research projects, kin-selection theory has become the dominant biological explanation for altruism. Critics object, however, to the theory's inability to explain altruistic behavior toward nonkin. "For all its insights," say Elliott Sober and David Sloan Wilson, "kin se-

85. Edward O. Wilson, *Sociobiology: The New Synthesis* (Cambridge, MA: Harvard University Press, 1975), v.

86. Ibid., 3.

87. Ibid., 106.

88. Edward O. Wilson, *The Insect Societies* (Cambridge, MA: Harvard University Press, 1971).

89. Wilson, *Sociobiology*, 117–18.

90. Edward O. Wilson, *On Human Nature*, 25th anniversary ed. (1978; repr., Cambridge, MA: Harvard University Press, 2004), 153.

lection has led to the constricted view that genealogical relatedness is the one and only mechanism for the evolution of altruism."[91]

By contrast, Sober and Wilson propose that several mechanisms operating at several levels, what they call "multi-level selection," determine an organism's capacity for adaptation. "Altruism can be understood only in this context of broader framework," they conclude.[92] "Replacing kin selection theory with multilevel selection theory is like shutting off the spotlight and illuminating the entire stage."[93] Even when expanding the number of selection mechanisms, furthering one's genetic heritage is still considered a major force of biological altruism.

We noted earlier that Darwin emphasized the similarities between humans and nonhumans. The mapping of the human genome and the genomes of other creatures heightened the plausibility of this continuity. Completed in 2001 by separate research teams and their leaders, Francis Collins and Craig Venter, the genome offers compelling evidence for Darwin's contention that humans share great structural similarities with nonhumans.[94] For instance, the human genome has been found to be not significantly larger than the genome of a mouse or fruit fly. Venter reports that "if we showed you the mouse genome, you would not be able to tell its difference from the human genome."[95] The differences between human and chimpanzee genomes are indiscernible to the untrained eye.

The close continuity between humans and nonhumans at the genetic level adds credence to the notion that humans and nonhumans may share continuity at the moral level. Richard Dawkins probably has done more than anyone to argue that genetics have implications for understanding morals. In fact, he suggests that genes actually determine morality.

Dawkins argues that genes are the ultimate replicators in living organisms. Whereas Darwin and others refer to individuals and

91. Sober and Wilson, *Unto Others*, 158.
92. Ibid.
93. Ibid., 332.
94. See Francis S. Collins, *The Language of God: A Scientist Presents Evidence for Belief* (New York: Free Press, 2006), chap. 5.
95. Reported in Thomas Jay Oord, "The World in a Grain of Sand: Genome Project Center Stage at AAAS," *Research News and Opportunities in Science and Theology* 1, no. 8 (2001): 1–2.

groups as the locus of evolution, Dawkins offers a "gene's-eye view." "The fundamental unit of selection, and therefore of self-interest," says Dawkins, "is not the species, nor the group, nor even, strictly, the individual. It is the gene, the unit of heredity."[96]

In the opening pages of his widely influential book *The Selfish Gene*, Dawkins writes what causes some readers to wonder if gene-centered evolution renders self-sacrificial love impossible. "We are survival machines," Dawkins asserts, "robot vehicles blindly programmed to preserve the selfish molecules known as genes."[97] He continues:

> "The argument of this book is that we, and all other animals, are machines created by our genes. . . . A predominant quality to be expected in a successful gene is ruthless selfishness. This gene self-ishness will usually give rise to selfishness in individual behavior. However, as we shall see, there are special circumstances in which a gene can achieve its own selfish goals by fostering a limited form of altruism at the level of individual animals. . . . Much as we might wish to believe otherwise, universal love and the welfare of the species as a whole are concepts that simply do not make evolutionary sense."[98]

After this provocative beginning, Dawkins offers several qualifying statements. First, he does not advocate a morality based on gene selfishness. He deplores the thought of "a society based simply on the gene's law of universal ruthless selfishness," because it "would be a very nasty society in which to live." But Dawkins adds that "it does not stop it being true" that society might just be that way. "If you wish, as I do, to build a society in which individuals cooperate generously and unselfishly towards a common good," he says, "you can expect little help from biological nature."[99] In the end, this qualifying statement is only minimally qualifying.

Dawkins's second qualification of his opening comments on selfish genes is that despite being "genetically programmed" to be selfish, we "are not necessarily compelled" to obey our selfish genes.[100]

96. Richard Dawkins, *The Selfish Gene* (London: Granada, 1978), 11.
97. Ibid., x.
98. Ibid., 2.
99. Ibid., 3.
100. Ibid.

Here, as in the opening quotation above, Dawkins uses the language of "programmed." Apparently, however, being programmed does not mean being absolutely determined, in the sense of having no choice to act otherwise. We will return to this point.

The third qualification is that we should not disregard the possibility of human altruism, even if we find that all other animals are not genuinely altruistic. "We must expect that when we go and look at the behavior of baboons, humans, and all other living creatures, we shall find it to be selfish," says Dawkins. But "if we find that our expectation is wrong, if we observe that human behaviour is truly altruistic, then we shall be faced with something puzzling, something that needs explaining."[101] Dawkins does not answer, however, whether we can actually observe genuinely altruistic love in humans.

Fourth, Dawkins defines altruism in terms of a behavior's consequences. "I am not concerned with the psychology of motives," he says. "I do not mean that the underlying motives [of an altruistic act] are secretly selfish."[102] His definitions of altruism and egoism are behavioral, and they are "concerned only with whether the effect of an act is to lower or raise the survival prospects of the presumed altruist and the survival prospects of the presumed beneficiary."[103] This qualification corresponds with the general view that biological altruism should be judged on survival and genetic inheritance consequences, not intent and motives.

Each of these qualifying statements loses whatever strength they may have as Dawkins proceeds through the remainder of *The Selfish Gene*. He says that by accident, molecules he calls "replicators" emerged, and these replicators copied information to be passed to other replicators. Competition among the replicator molecules eliminated those not well-suited for survival. These "replicators began not merely to exist, but to construct for themselves containers, vehicles for their continued existence," says Dawkins. "The replicators that survived were the ones that built survival machines for themselves to live in."[104] Today these replicators

101. Ibid., 4.
102. Ibid., 4–5.
103. Ibid., 4.
104. Ibid., 19.

swarm in huge colonies, safe inside gigantic lumbering robots, sealed off from the outside world, communicating with it by tortuous indirect routes, manipulating it by remote control. They are in you and me; they created us, body and mind; and the preservation is the ultimate rationale for our existence. They have come a long way, those replicators. Now they go by the name of genes, and we are their survival machines.[105]

Although Dawkins says this passage does not imply that our genes absolutely determine us, it is difficult to regard his words as allowing a robust notion of human freedom.[106] The metaphors of machine and robot and the language of manipulation do not easily support the notion that we can choose anything other than what we have been "programmed" to do.

This point is important for interpreting Dawkins later in *The Selfish Gene*. He will not speculate whether a "unique quality of man is a capacity for genuine, disinterested, true altruism."[107] With our conscious foresight, however, we may be saved "from the worst selfish excesses of blind replicators," Dawkins says. "We have the power to defy the selfish genes of our birth. . . . We are built as gene machines and cultured as meme machines, but we have the power to turn against our creators. We, alone on earth, can rebel against the tyranny of the selfish replicators."[108]

Dawkins wants to emphasize the point that successful genes replicate themselves by acting for their future good. This action is, of course, not conscious or an action in any libertarian sense of self-determining. The bodies that carry these genes do not decide their own genetic makeup. They are "machines" useful for the replicating gene units that create them. Yet Dawkins contends that we as machines can act contrary to the "tyranny" of selfish replicators.

To the extent that Dawkins means for "selfishness" to describe only the consequences of a behavior for reproductive success and not a gene's or organism's motivation, his views are not directly contrary to love research. After all, love as I have defined it re-

105. Ibid., 19–20.
106. Ibid., 270–71.
107. Ibid., 200.
108. Ibid., 200–201.

quires intentionality. A biological view that ignores motives and intentions misses this crucial point. Dawkins's theories seriously undercut love only if they are understood to deny intentionality and freedom altogether.

To the extent that Dawkins sees genetically programmed behavior as beneficial only insofar as it benefits the gene or individual, however, his selfish-gene theory is incompatible with self-sacrificial love. Love sometimes requires acting for the good of those with whom an organism, human or otherwise, shares very little in common genetically. Love, as I have defined it, promotes *overall* well-being. Although this often includes promoting the well-being of the individual and of kin, love also sometimes requires self-sacrifice for the good of those beyond oneself or one's kin. This criticism applies to other biological accounts that define success entirely in terms of reproductive advantage.[109] In the end, Dawkins's theories do not well support research on love.

Richard Alexander extends the gene-centered approach to altruism that Dawkins, Wilson, and others advocate. Alexander says that "each person is programmed by the history of natural selection to maximize the likelihood of survival of his/her genetic materials."[110] We saw earlier that Alexander believes that altruism on a grand scale—what he calls "indiscriminate beneficence"—arises from actions based on the expectation of indirect reciprocal benefits from others. An altruist's status may be raised, and this reputational gain indirectly benefits the altruist. Furthermore, altruists have evolved keen abilities to appear more beneficent than is the case, and they have evolved to encourage others to overinvest.

Alexander offers four rules for giving that he believes arise from insights in biology. Give to others, first, if the benefit goes to a genetic relative and its return to the giver is the relative's improved reproduction (kin altruism). Give to others, second, when the giver is more likely to receive in return more than has been given (reciprocal altruism). Give to others, third, when failure to give will likely cause others to impose costs greater than the expense of giving (altruism to avoid punishment). And give to others, fourth, when the act is likely

109. For a strong criticism of Dawkins's work, see Alister McGrath, *Dawkins' God: Genes, Memes, and the Meaning of Life* (Oxford: Blackwell, 2004).
110. Alexander, *Biology of Moral Systems*, 108.

to cause a large number of people to regard this gift as indicating that the recipient will later return the gift (indirect altruism). "In all other situations," says Alexander, "do not give."[111]

A relatively easy criticism of Alexander's position is that many of us recall instances in which we gave to others and were not motivated by any of these four reasons. Our conscious decisions were for the good of others and not primarily ourselves. Alexander has a response for this criticism, however. Although we may *think* that we sometimes give to others without expecting personal benefit, we have actually been deceived. In fact, we all suffer from self-deception. "I expect any and all aspects of these strategies to be concealed—sometimes via self-deception as a means of deceiving others—whenever revealing them is likely to have adverse effects on inclusive-fitness maximizing."[112]

Although we have evolved finely tuned mechanisms for detecting deception in others, says Alexander, we have also evolved so that we remain largely unaware of our own deceptive practices.[113] It is to our evolutionary advantage to become unconscious of the fact that we are ultimately self-interested.[114] Evolutionary advantage goes to actors who can fool others into thinking that these actors are altruistic, all the while without these actors consciously knowing that they fool others to the actor's benefit. "We gain by thinking we are right, and by convincing both our allies and our enemies," says Alexander.[115] In sum, "social learning has been all about becoming better at self-interest—indeed, about becoming so good at it that we will be regarded as honest, kind, fair, impartial, reliable, and altruistic not only by our social interactants but also by our own conscious selves."[116]

The conclusion to Alexander's proposal is that our experience of believing ourselves primarily motivated for another's benefit is self-deception ultimately derived from our genes. The power of selection at the gene level surpasses and even undermines the trustworthiness of conscious motivation. "We will have to start

111. Ibid., 109.
112. Ibid., 109–10.
113. Ibid., 114.
114. Ibid., 121.
115. Ibid., 123.
116. Ibid., 139.

all over again," concludes Alexander, "to describe and understand ourselves, in terms alien to our intuitions, and in one way or another different from every discussion of this topic across the whole of human history."[117]

Alexander's hypotheses with regard to altruism do not seem to be any better news for biological research on love, at least as I have defined love, than Dawkins's. But Alexander's appeal to self-deception is the Achilles' heel of his challenge to self-sacrificial love. The issue also presents itself in the word "blindly" found in Dawkins's phrase "blindly programmed."

The problem with appeals to self-deception and blindness with regard to our motives is that self-deception and motive-blindness can also easily apply to theories critical of self-sacrificial love. One could say that the genes controlling the machines that are Richard Alexander and Richard Dawkins compel them to adopt evolutionary theories based on self-deception. The critic may argue that these same genes actually support the unconscious but real capacity for self-sacrificial love. Arguments relying on gene-controlled motive-blindness and inherent self-deception can be used either to support or deny love. They, therefore, are unconvincing.

Arguments that we do not express self-sacrificial love with the primary motive of helping others also fly in the face of scientific evidence we know best: our own personal experiences. Unfortunately, as Mary Midgley says, evolutionary theories that reject love are often presented as "reductive ideology requiring us to dismiss as illusions matters which our experience shows to be real and serious."[118] An essential aspect of adequate scientific epistemology is that what we know best—our own experience—should inform our theories about what the world is like. It cannot suffice to begin with what we know so very little, including the activity and influence of genes, and allow this meager knowledge to invalidate what we know best.[119] Although we should avoid at-

117. Ibid., 20.
118. Mary Midgley, *The Ethical Primate: Humans, Freedom, and Morality* (London: Routledge, 1994), 17.
119. See Thomas Jay Oord, "Morals, Love, and Relations in Evolutionary Theory," in *Evolution and Ethics: Human Morality in Biological and Religious Perspective*, ed. Philip Clayton and Jeffrey Schloss (Grand Rapids: Eerdmans, 2004), 287–301.

tributing all human characteristics to less-complex creatures (i.e., anthropomorphism), we must also avoid the assumption that we and other creatures are loveless machines, what Ian Barbour calls "mechanomorphism."[120]

Jeffrey P. Schloss sees the importance of our own experience and suggests that a biological account of altruism will be more adequate if we allow what he calls "the internal costs and benefits" of giving to others play a factor in our scientific explanations. Schloss points out that virtually all biological accounts of altruism are "undertaken at levels nonintegral, or external, to human organismal functioning." He suggests that robust biological theories must also "look at the internal costs and benefits of cooperating and not cooperating."[121]

Several studies have shown that negative internal experience and cognitive dysfunction contribute to lack of fitness. On the flip side, involvement in supportive personal relationships reduces depression and postpones mortality. "It is worth asking," says Schloss, "whether not only relational engagement but also the generous and other-regarding dispositions that facilitate them have internal physiological rewards."[122] An attitude of cooperation can lower the internal costs of giving to others. An altruistic agenda may allow individuals to process resources more efficiently.[123]

The possibility that other-regard provides internalized benefits, says Schloss, suggests a revision of the typical account of altruism in biology. Expanding adaptive advantage to include internal advantage provides "a biological substrate for other-regard that is genuinely uncoupled from direct or even indirect reciprocity. In some natural, nontranscendent sense, it really may be 'better to give than to receive.'"[124]

---

120. Ian G. Barbour, *Nature, Human Nature, and God* (Minneapolis: Fortress, 2002), 99.

121. Schloss, "Emerging Accounts of Altruism," 233.

122. Ibid., 234.

123. Jeffrey P. Schloss, "Sociobiological Explanations of Altruistic Ethics: Necessary, Sufficient, or Irrelevant to the Human Moral Quest?" in *Investigating the Biological Foundations of Human Morality*, ed. James P. Hurd (Lewiston, NY: Mellen, 1996), 107–45.

124. Schloss, "Emerging Accounts of Altruism," 235.

Schloss suggests that adding the evidence of internalized benefits to genuinely altruistic activity requires us to choose. Either we deny that humans act in ways that undermine their own reproductive success or we argue that humans can become unleashed from their genetic drive for reproductive success and thereby transcend biological conditions that constrain other organisms. "Just as enlargement of the forebrain both facilitated and was facilitated by language development," reasons Schloss, "so altruistic dispositions may have both given rise to and been extended by cultural values of altruism. . . . Altruism may be less a fulfillment of fixed human nature than a progressive realization of it."[125] Schloss does not speculate about the internal dispositions of nonhumans as they pertain to love and self-sacrifice, a possibility that scientists such as Frans de Waal and Marc Bekoff seem more willing to entertain.

In the end, Darwin's theories and speculations provide helpful biological tools for analyzing love. His work and the work of contemporary biologists account well for some of what we want to say about love. But he and like-minded biologists offer no strong theory for why someone might act for the good of others without some prior selfish motivation or genetic programming for personal benefit.[126] Darwin and contemporary biology offer no plausible explanation for why a creature might act self-sacrificially for an outsider, stranger, or enemy. Such self-sacrifice apparently occurs from time to time among humans. And if, as Darwin believes, moral continuities exist between humans and nonhumans, there seems to be no strong reason for why nonhumans might also act sacrificially toward outsiders and enemies.

125. Ibid., 236.
126. For a strong argument that evolution must play a role in understanding morality but that it cannot function as an ultimate explanation of morality as a naturalistic enterprise, see John F. Haught, *Is Nature Enough? Meaning and Truth in the Age of Science* (Cambridge: Cambridge University Press, 2006). For technical explorations of evolution and morality from the perspective of a moral philosopher, see Craig A. Boyd, *A Shared Morality: A Narrative Defense of Natural Law Ethics* (Grand Rapids: Brazos Press, 2007), chap. 3; Richard Joyce, *The Evolution of Morality* (Cambridge, MA: MIT Press, 2006); Neil Levy, *What Makes Us Moral? Crossing the Boundaries of Biology* (Oxford: Oneworld, 2004).

The Biology of Self-Organization and Freedom for Love

I earlier defined love in such a way as to require freedom as an essential aspect. I noted that freedom should not be understood as being without constraints and limitations. Unlimited freedom does not exist. But love that is coerced or unintentional is not love at all. I conclude this discussion of biological research pertaining to love and altruism with an examination of what biologists suggest concerning creaturely self-determination.

We have seen that contemporary theories in biology rely heavily on the role of genetics. Genetic-oriented theories tend toward describing organisms as programmed or controlled by genes. In light of this, Schloss reports that "current Darwinian approaches to morality tend to be ambivalent about or dismissive of moral agency or self-determination."[127] Biologists rarely attribute freedom and spontaneity to the organisms they study, in large part because biological theory is thought to be based on examining external results while ignoring internal experiences.

Biologist Sewall Wright summarizes this prevailing assumption in biology when he says that "science must restrict itself to the external aspect of things." Wright continues, saying that science is "concerned with the external and statistical aspect of events and incapable of dealing with the unique creative aspect of each individual event."[128] However, the practice of restricting scientific purview to observations of external behavior and refusing to infer what such behavior suggests about a creature's internal motivations is, as we have seen, not actually a restriction or refusal that biologists practice when offering explanations.[129]

Contemporary biology rejects questions of freedom and self-organization, in part because it rejects the view attributed to one of the earliest evolutionary biologists, Jean-Baptiste Lamarck.

127. Jeffrey Schloss, "Introduction: Evolutionary Ethics and Christian Morality," in Clayton and Schloss, *Evolution and Ethics*, 5.

128. Sewall Wright, "Biology and Philosophy of Science," in *Process and Divinity: Philosophical Essays Presented to Charles Hartshorne*, ed. William L. Reese and Eugene Freeman (LaSalle, IL: Open Court, 1964), 123–24.

129. For one of the better philosophical analyses of this problem, see Midgley, *Ethical Primate*.

Historians of science often credit Lamarck as being first to provide a general theoretical framework for organic evolution. Today, however, he is known mainly for the view that creatures can intentionally pass to their offspring the traits acquired through their own efforts, although some scholars suggest that Lamarck himself did not advocate this view.[130]

The giraffe is the Lamarckian's classic example of a creature that, through its own efforts, can change its own characteristics and pass those changes on to its children. As giraffes intentionally stretch to reach leaves residing high in trees, Lamarckians believe that they gradually lengthen their necks. Their offspring inherit longer necks as a result of their parents' efforts.

The vast majority of scientists today, however, reject the view that traits intentionally acquired during a creature's lifetime can be passed to offspring. They admit that offspring can learn beneficial behaviors from their parents, but each generation must learn these behaviors anew by imitating their elders. Beneficial behaviors, such as giraffes stretching for leaves atop trees, are not transmitted through genetic encoding.

An accepted view in contemporary biology, however, is the "Baldwin effect." Named after James Mark Baldwin and first proposed at the turn of the twenty-first century, this theory says that the sustained behavior of a species or group in response to its environment is gradually assimilated into the group's genetic structures.[131] Learned behaviors cannot be directly inherited, said Baldwin, but the initiatives of organisms can be a factor in the establishment of random genetic changes and thereby affect the direction of evolutionary change. The behavior of thriving organisms can be imitated by others and transmitted socially for a long enough period that random genetic mutations can support that beneficial behavior. The general propensity to act well in the organism's environment is supported by genetic mutations and becomes part of the offspring's genetic inheritance.[132]

130. See Stephen Jay Gould, *The Structure of Evolutionary Theory* (Cambridge, MA: Harvard University Press, 2002).

131. James Mark Baldwin, *Development and Evolution* (New York: Macmillan, 1902). For an examination of the importance of agency for morality, see Celia Deane-Drummond, *The Ethics of Nature* (Malden, MA: Blackwell, 2004), chap. 6.

132. For a contemporary positive reevaluation of Baldwin's thought, see Bruce Weber and David Depew, eds., *Evolution and Learning: The Baldwin Effect Reconsidered* (Cambridge, MA: MIT Press, 2003).

Science-and-religion scholar Ian Barbour uses bison and horses to illustrate how the Baldwin effect works. The common ancestors of bison and horses may have either charged or fled their enemies. The survival of those who charged would have been enhanced by strength, weight, strong skulls, and other bisonlike qualities. Those who survived by fleeing enemies would have benefited by speed, agility, and other abilities we see in horses. "The divergence of bison and horse," suggests Barbour, "may have arisen initially from different responses to danger, rather than from genetic mutations related to anatomy." Barbour concludes that "organisms participate actively in evolutionary history and are not simply passive products of genetic forces from within and environmental forces from without."[133]

The novelty of Baldwin's argument is that creaturely agency plays a role in evolution. Later biological research supports Baldwin's view. C. H. Waddington, for instance, found that a catastrophe or shock to an organism's environment produced phenotypical changes passed to later generations.[134] The radiation emitted from the Chernobyl nuclear disaster of 1986, for instance, caused changes both to the phenotypes and genotypes of those who survived. Biologist Francisco J. Ayala says that "the Baldwin effect has been generally involved in the origin of evolutionary novelties."[135]

Ian Barbour welcomes the renewed interest in the Baldwin effect, because it offers a way to account for "the initiatives of organisms to have significant long-term consequences."[136] Like Schloss, who emphasizes creaturely inward dispositions, Barbour speaks of creaturely "interiority" that evolves "starting from rudimentary memory, sentience, responsiveness, and anticipation in simple organisms, going on to consciousness with the advent of nervous systems, and then self-consciousness in the case of primates and

133. Barbour, *Nature, Human Nature, and God*, 33–34.
134. C. H. Waddington, *Organisers and Genes* (Cambridge: Cambridge University Press, 1940).
135. Francisco J. Ayala, "The Baldwin Effect," in *Back to Darwin: A Richer Account of Evolution*, ed. John B. Cobb Jr. (Grand Rapids: Eerdmans, 2008), 195. Ayala cites Mary Jane West-Eberhard, *Developmental Plasticity and Evolution* (Oxford: Oxford University Press, 2003).
136. Ian G. Barbour, "Evolution and Process Thought," in Cobb, *Back to Darwin*, 203.

human beings."[137] For the sake of metaphysical consistency and generality, Barbour argues that minimal interiority can be postulated even at the most basic levels of existence. "Our categories must also represent the continuity of developmental processes and of evolutionary history," argues Barbour, "and the impossibility of drawing any sharp lines between stages."[138]

Although it is not difficult to attribute self-determining agency to complex creatures such as humans, chimpanzees, canines, and dolphins, most biologists are reluctant to infer that less-complex creatures also possess a measure of self-determining agency. There are some, however, who believe that such inferences are appropriate.

Biochemist Ross Stein suggests that spontaneity arises in the evolutionary history at the molecular level, which is a degree of complexity preceding the emergence of autonomous cell-like structures. Stein argues that we should not think of molecular entities as mere objects. Rather, they "possess a subjective nature that allows them to experience and respond to their environment."[139] Stein says that "a molecule's interiority and ability to respond to its environment can account for seemingly diverse chemical phenomena including molecular change, molecular complexification, and, ultimately, the evolution of life."[140]

Stein believes that a fuller understanding of evolution must include an account of the internal states of creatures and their self-determination. "Evolution occurs by changes in the internal relations of the subject as they are influenced by the environment," he says. "The potentiality of self-transformation and self-transcendence that *is* evolution is actualized as teleological response, where . . . teleology is not the end determining the present, but the present, with the seeds of its future bound up in it, actualizing its potential."[141]

137. Ibid., 203–4.

138. Ibid., 213.

139. Ross L. Stein, "The Action of God in the World—A Synthesis of Process Thought in Science and Theology," *Theology and Science* 4, no. 1 (2006): 62. See also Ross L. Stein, "Enzymes as Ecosystems: A Panexperientialist Account of Biocatalytic Chemical Transformations," in *Applied Process Thought I: Initial Explorations in Theory and Research*, ed. Mark R. Dibben and Thomas Kelly (Frankfurt: Ontos-Verlag, 2008), 261–86.

140. Ross L. Stein, "Towards a Process Philosophy of Chemistry," *Hyle* 10, no. 1 (2004): 12.

141. Ibid., 19.

The scientist most well known for advocating scientific theories pertaining to self-organization is Stuart Kauffman. Kauffman argues that organized properties emerge from unorganized components of a system.[142] Dynamical systems can achieve new ordered states without any external selective pressures. This is true of aggregate entities, such as the emergent symmetry of snowflakes and the patterned movement of water. But order also emerges in biological organisms through self-organization and spontaneity. "Self-organization mingles with natural selection in barely understood ways to yield the magnificence of our teeming biosphere," says Kauffman.[143] Biological theory, he contends, must be expanded to include a greater role for self-organization.

To argue that organisms at varying levels of complexity exhibit self-organization, spontaneity, or self-determination does not require one also to argue that less-complex creatures are free to the same degree as more-complex creatures. Nor does it require one to deny the powerful influence of a creature's genes. Instead, one can appeal to the possibility that creatures of varying complexity possess varying degrees of freedom, interiority, or self-organization.

Biologist Charles Birch suggests that degrees of creaturely freedom are of great importance. "Determinism by genes is not an all-or-none affair," says Birch. "There can be different degrees of freedom. There is all the difference in the world between 100 percent determination and 99 percent determination. [One hundred percent determination] provides no room for choice and purpose. The other does."[144] The power of the genes may be more determinative for less-complex creatures, but it need not be considered all-determining.

Speculating that organisms at all levels of complexity possess some measure of spontaneity does not, of course, scientifically demonstrate that freedom is present throughout existence. "That entities at many levels seem to take account of their environment and to act in appropriately responsive ways," says Birch, "will

142. Stuart Kauffman, *At Home in the Universe: The Search for Laws of Self-Organization and Complexity* (New York: Oxford University Press, 1995).

143. Stuart Kauffman, *Investigations* (New York: Oxford University Press, 2000), 2.

144. Charles Birch, "Why Aren't We Zombies?" in Cobb, *Back to Darwin*, 260.

never prove that they are not in fact machines." But speculation that creatures are robots blindly programmed by their genes is not scientifically demonstrable either. Identifying apparently self-organizing activity at various levels of creaturely complexity, however, provides grounds for plausible inferences about self-determination at the biological level. Identifying apparent self-organizing activity will, as Birch puts it, "make clear that the reason for viewing [organisms] as machines, rather than as agents, is metaphysical, not empirical."[145]

It may be that the capacity to act freely as an agent is not a capacity present in nascent form at even the least-complex levels of existence. It could be that freedom and self-organization emerged at some point in the evolutionary process. Relatively simple organisms may not possess self-determination, but self-determination emerged as creatures increased in complexity. This view, often called "emergence," is attractive to those who wish to acknowledge the freedom apparent in human experience and apparently present in other complex creatures. This version of emergence also allows one to resist the claim that the least-complex entities of existence (e.g., atoms) are to some degree free.

Theologian and philosopher of science Philip Clayton advocates this emergent view of creaturely self-determination. Clayton speculates that "living systems first display purposive behavior not found in more-simple systems, and then gradually manifest higher degrees of self-monitoring and internal (neural) representation of their environment, until the internalized world of symbols and intentions that we associate with consciousness emerges." Clayton argues that human freedom should be "understood in terms of a developmental story that includes the role of physical laws, biological drives, and the increasing latitude of behavior in more-complex organisms—features both shared with other animals and distinguishing us from them."[146]

145. Ibid.
146. Philip Clayton, *Adventures in the Spirit: God, World, Divine Action* (Minneapolis: Fortress, 2008), 80. See also Philip Clayton, *Mind and Emergence: From Quantum to Consciousness* (Oxford: Oxford University Press, 2004); Philip Clayton and Paul Davies, eds., *The Re-Emergence of Emergence: The Emergentist Hypothesis from Science to Religion* (Oxford: Oxford University Press, 2006). Terrence Deacon's work on emergence is also noteworthy: "The Hierarchic Logic of

In contrast to Clayton, Ian Barbour argues for an emergent view that posits a minimum of interiority at even the most basic levels.[147] Barbour's argument is partly for the sake of metaphysical consistency and generality. "New phenomena and new properties emerge historically," says Barbour, "but we should seek fundamental categories that are as universal as possible." Barbour maintains that we ought to generalize from the human experience of freedom. "We are part of nature," he argues, and "even though human experience is an extreme case of an event in nature, it offers clues as to the character of other events."[148]

Which version of emergence—the one Clayton advocates or the one Barbour advocates—best accounts for biology is debatable. Resolving the question may be unnecessary for love research in the biological sciences. Even if molecules have the interiority and subjectivity that Stein postulates, for instance, few scholars are likely to feel comfortable describing the activity of molecules as loving. But as creatures increase in organizational and mental complexity through evolution, the importance of self-organization, freedom, and interiority arises. If humans share significant continuity with their nonhuman companions, it seems plausible that freedom and intentionality are present in earlier stages of evolutionary history.

Conclusion

The evidence and theories in biology provide important research for understanding the possibility and nature of love. Darwin and countless biologists in his wake have wrestled deeply with the issues of love and altruism, and their biological work offers essential insights for general love research.

Biologists suppose that existence is social and that creatures sometimes compete and at other times cooperate. They find ample

Emergence: Untangling the Interdependence of Evolution and Self Organization," in Weber and Depew, *Evolution and Learning*, 273–308.

147. For arguments for this position, sometimes called "panexperientialism," see Christian de Quincey, *Radical Nature: Rediscovering the Soul of Matter* (Montpelier, VT: Invisible Cities, 2002); David Ray Griffin, *Unsnarling the World-Knot: Consciousness, Freedom, and the Mind-Body Problem* (Berkeley: University of California Press, 1998).

148. Barbour, "Evolution and Process Thought," 212–13.

evidence that self-sacrificial action occurs. But biologists differ among themselves about how best to explain apparent altruistic action. Some believe that the genes control creaturely action in such a way that genuine altruism and actual freedom are illusory. Others find evidence that altruism and freedom are not illusory and propose theories to account for this evidence. The relative evolutionary continuity between humans and nonhumans raises questions about the extent to which the human experience of giving and receiving love exists also in nonhuman experience. If some nonhuman creatures can express love, accounting for the emergence of conditions necessary for and actual forms of such love remains a speculative venture.

5

Love and Cosmology

We conclude this investigation of love research in the natural and human sciences with an examination of cosmology. After reading previous chapters, one might be skeptical that cosmology has much to contribute to research on love. For the most part, this skepticism is warranted. Contemporary cosmologists, most of them physicists, are unlikely to include love in their scientific hypotheses. However, the data and theories of cosmology have wide-ranging applications. When cosmology blurs the boundaries of metaphysics, as it almost inevitably does, it offers valuable material for love research.

Scholars understand cosmology in several ways. In the broad sense, cosmology encompasses all the natural and human sciences, philosophy, and even religion. This sense of cosmology might be better called "metacosmology." It attempts to account for all relevant facts and phenomena in the universe,[1] which includes, of course, the facts and phenomena of love. A metacosmology

---

1. Alfred North Whitehead proposed one of the twentieth century's most powerful cosmologies, in this broad sense. Whitehead's most complete account of this cosmology appears in his magnum opus, *Process and Reality: An Essay in Cosmology*, ed. David Ray Griffin and Donald W. Sherburne, corrected ed. (1929; repr., New York: Free Press, 1978).

amounts to what physicists call "a theory of everything." Unfortunately, however, most contemporary attempts to offer a theory of everything overlook large amounts of data from human experience, including love.[2]

To distinguish between cosmology and metaphysics and to avoid the need to account for less-concrete aspects of reality, contemporary cosmology typically is called "physical cosmology." Physical cosmology is concerned with both the macrolevels and the microlevels of existence. Macrocosmology considers the structures of space, the laws governing galaxies, stars, and planets, and the origin of existence as we know it. Some refer to this as "astrophysics." Macrocosmology relies heavily on observations from optical, infrared, X-ray, radio, and ultraviolet telescopes.

Microcosmology is concerned with the smallest units that exist. Microcosmology research is often subdivided into atomic physics, nuclear physics, elementary particle physics, and other subdisciplines. Some refer to microcosmology as the realm of quantum physics. Most cosmologists believe that some relationship exists between the laws and characteristics evident at the smallest level of existence and the laws and characteristics of other levels of existence, including the wider universe. The exact nature and degree of this relationship is widely discussed and of great consequence for attempts to formulate a grand theory of everything. No consensus exists among cosmologists, however, as to the specific details of this much sought-after theory of everything.

---

2. A twentieth-century exception to this rule is Pierre Teilhard de Chardin. The basis for Teilhard's work is philosophical, religious, scientific, even mystical, and his claims about love are understandably expansive. Among his books, see especially *Human Energy*, trans. J. M. Cohen (New York: Harcourt Brace Jovanovich, 1969); *The Human Phenomenon* (Brighton: Sussex Academic, 1999); *Toward the Future* (London: Collins, 1975). For extensive comment on Teilhard's understanding of love, see Kathleen Duffy, "The Evolution of Love in Teilhard de Chardin" (paper presented at the conference "Works of Love: Scientific and Religious Perspectives on Altruism," Villanova University, June 2003); Ursula King, "Love—A Higher Form of Human Energy in the Work of Teilhard de Chardin and Sorokin," *Zygon* 39, no. 1 (2004): 77–102; Mathias Trennert-Hellwig, *Die Urkraft des Kosmos: Dimensionen der Liebe im Werk Pierre Teilhards de Chardin* (Freiburg: Heder, 1993).

A Universe Fine-Tuned

We begin by considering the work of philosopher and theologian Nancey Murphy and physicist and mathematician George Ellis. Their work not only considers issues of altruism and love, but it does so by incorporating leading theories in cosmology. Murphy and Ellis set the stage for an important question in cosmology: How do we best account for the origin of the universe? This question, as we will see, has implications for love research.

It is no exaggeration to say that *The Moral Nature of the Universe: Theology, Cosmology, and Ethics*, the groundbreaking and critically acclaimed book by Murphy and Ellis, is the best contemporary attempt to address issues in cosmology and love. The authors' arguments require a wide-ranging examination of topics. Murphy and Ellis believe and demonstrate that an adequate overall account of existence must include research in physical cosmology alongside other research disciplines.[3]

Early on in their work, Murphy and Ellis address the general relationship between science and morality. They believe that ethicists and theologians must take science into account when constructing adequate ethical theories. "Ethical judgments should be affected by developments in scientific knowledge," say Murphy and Ellis, "but cannot be determined by scientific knowledge alone."[4] One feature of reality as humans know it is the sense of moral obligation. Although science can contribute to understanding this obligation, science cannot fully explain it. Yet any complete account of reality—a metacosmology or cosmology in the broad sense—must adequately account for moral obligation. Hence the book's name, *The Moral Nature of the Universe*.

Murphy and Ellis assume the truth of major theories in physics that attempt to describe both the macro- and microlevels of

3. Nancey Murphy and George F. R. Ellis, *On the Moral Nature of the Universe: Theology, Cosmology, and Ethics* (Minneapolis: Fortress, 1996). See also George F. R. Ellis, "The Theology of the Anthropic Principle," in *Quantum Cosmology and the Laws of Nature: Scientific Perspectives on Divine Action*, ed. Robert J. Russell, Nancey C. Murphy, and C. J. Isham, 2nd ed. (Vatican City State: Vatican Observatory; Berkeley, CA: Center for Theology and the Natural Sciences, 1996), 367–406.
4. Murphy and Ellis, *Moral Nature of the Universe*, 6.

existence. They note the role that elemental constituents play in the formation of the universe and the four fundamental forces. In particular, they affirm the "hot big bang theory" of the origin of the universe. Hubble telescope observations in the mid-twentieth century show that the rate at which distant galaxies recede from our planet is proportional to the distance that these galaxies are from us. The red shift observed in star movement is the primary basis for speaking of our universe as expanding. The expansion of the universe was likely much more rapid in its very early stages.

Because big bang theory plays a central role in physical cosmology and in the work of Murphy and Ellis, a brief explanation of the theory is in order here. In the mid-twentieth century, Arno Penzias and Robert Wilson first noted, and others have since confirmed, that cosmic microwave background radiation is present in the universe. This radiation provides strong evidence that the universe began with a very hot explosion. In 1989, NASA sent the Cosmic Background Explorer (COBE) satellite into orbit to investigate the cosmic microwave background in detail, and in 2001 the Wilkinson Microwave Anisotropy Probe (WMAP) was sent into space. These satellites have discovered further evidence of a big bang's cosmic afterglow. This evidence confirms the discovery by Penzias and Wilson and has solidified big bang theory as a central notion in contemporary physical cosmology. The details of the big bang, however, are disputed by cosmologists.

The basic idea of big bang theory is that our universe exploded into existence some ten to twenty billion years ago. Within the first second after that explosion, basic physical forces and fundamental particles of matter emerged. Over time, fundamental elements of existence were drawn together by gravity and other forces. From this emerged the basic and the massive structures of existence, including nuclei, atoms, molecules, dust, rocks, planets, stars, galaxies, galaxy clusters, and superclusters. The formation of more-complex entities gives reason to speak of the universe's development in evolutionary terms.

Cosmology combines with metaphysics to speculate about the initial conditions required for the big bang. This speculation pertains not only to the laws, constraints, and substance required for the initial burst but also to the evolution of the universe in general and to the existence of the life-sustaining planet we call "Earth."

Physicists have offered a number of proposals as to the nature of these initial conditions.[5] However, there are obvious limitations for testing these proposals.

Scientists call the question of why life is possible at all "the anthropic question."[6] The "anthropic principle," a phrase coined by physicist Brandon Carter,[7] states that life as we know it required very specific laws and conditions in the beginning of the universe. If these laws and conditions had been altered ever so slightly, the evolution of life would have been impossible. Only very particular laws of physics and very specific initial conditions allow the existence of intelligent life.[8] Physicist Paul Davies refers to the anthropic principle as "the Goldilocks factor" because the evidence suggests that our universe is "just right" for life.[9] It is common for physicists to offer various mathematical calculations to quantify the precise initial parameters required for the later emergence of life.

Among the conditions required for life were the right supply and balance of various chemicals, especially carbon, oxygen, nitrogen, and sulfur. A stable environment was also necessary. This environment needed plenty of water and an energy source like the sun. The universe in which life emerged had to be a particular temperature (neither too hot nor too cold) and orderly enough that galaxies and stars could form and not collide too often. The right sort of forces had to have been present at the big bang and have to remain at work in the life of the universe. Any slight difference would have made life impossible. Stephen Hawking describes the situation this way:

5. Among the texts explaining these issues in accessible ways, see Lee Smolin, *The Life of the Cosmos* (New York: Oxford University Press, 1997).

6. Key texts explaining the anthropic principle, fine-tuning, and their various forms and features include John Barrow and Frank Tipler, *The Anthropic Cosmological Principle* (Oxford: Oxford University Press, 1986); John D. Barrow et al., eds., *Fitness of the Cosmos for Life: Biochemistry and Fine-Tuning* (Cambridge: Cambridge University Press, 2008), esp. parts 1 and 2; Paul Davies, *The Accidental Universe* (Cambridge: Cambridge University Press, 1982).

7. See Brandon Carter, "Large Number Coincidences and the Anthropic Principle in Cosmology," in *Modern Cosmology and Philosophy*, ed. John Leslie (Amherst, NY: Prometheus Books, 1998), 131–39.

8. Ibid., 52.

9. Paul Davies, *Cosmic Jackpot: Why Our Universe Is Just Right for Life* (Boston: Houghton Mifflin, 2007), 3.

Why is the universe so close to the dividing line between collapsing again and expanding indefinitely? In order to be as close as we are now, the rate of expansion early on had to be chosen fantastically accurately. If the rate of expansion one second after the big bang had been less by one part in 10 to the tenth power, the universe would have collapsed after a few million years. If it had been greater by one part in 10 to the tenth power, the universe would have been empty after a few million years. In neither case would it have lasted long enough for life to develop.[10]

The anthropic principle is often categorized as having both a weak and a strong form. The weak anthropic principle states that life *might* occur in restricted regions and times. The constants of physics cannot deviate too much and still allow life to function. The strong anthropic principle, proposed by John Barrow and Frank Tipler, states that life *must* exist in the universe.[11] The laws of physics and the evolution of the universe in some way destined the emergence of life and mind. Life in general and conscious beings in particular are active selective mechanisms.[12] Physicist Freeman Dyson puts it this way: "As we look out into the universe and identify the many accidents of physics and astronomy that have worked together to our benefit, it almost seems as if the universe must in some sense have known we were coming."[13]

Neither the weak nor the strong anthropic principle provides a scientific answer to the even more basic question of why life exists at all. These principles only affirm that specific laws, constraints, and conditions are required for life. Murphy and Ellis join the majority of cosmologists when they say that "if we take seriously the issue of why life exists, the purely scientific approach fails to give a satisfactory answer. We end without a resolution of the issue, essentially because science attains reasonable certainty by limiting its considerations to restricted aspects of reality."[14] Sci-

10. Stephen Hawking, "Quantum Cosmology," in *The Nature of Space and Time*, ed. Stephen Hawking and Roger Penrose (Princeton, NJ: Princeton University Press, 1996), 89–90.

11. Barrow and Tipler, *Anthropic Cosmological Principle*.

12. See especially Davies, *Cosmic Jackpot*.

13. Freeman Dyson, *Disturbing the Universe* (New York: Harper & Row, 1979), 250.

14. Murphy and Ellis, *Moral Nature of the Universe*, 53–54.

ence alone cannot answer the question of ultimate causation for the entire universe.

Murphy and Ellis note that, theoretically, the universe could have emerged by (1) pure chance, (2) necessity, (3) high probability, or (4) because everything possible will happen. Each of these possibilities has inherent weaknesses, however. Murphy and Ellis think that a general theory of design best accounts for the fine-tuning of the universe: "The symmetries and delicate balances we observe in the universe require an extraordinary coherence of conditions and cooperation of laws and effects, suggesting that in some sense they have been purposefully designed."[15] They are aware that the claim of purpose and design slips into the domains of metaphysics and theology. "The design concept is one of the most satisfying overall approaches," they argue, but it necessarily takes one "outside the strictly scientific arena."[16]

Speculation about the ultimate cause and design of a unique universe would be seriously hampered, say Murphy and Ellis, if one were to restrict data to confirmable scientific laws alone. Such speculation requires metaphysical judgment that extends beyond physical cosmology. Major metaphysical questions, such as why there is a universe at all and why this universe has these specific laws, lay outside the domain of purely scientific cosmology. After all, no experimentation can show why the universe has the particular laws it does or prove why the universe exists at all. In short, speculation on these larger questions requires the superstructure of metaphysics.

Murphy and Ellis defend the metaphysical move beyond physical cosmology as essential to providing an adequate overall account of existence. "Physicists can simply claim that there is no need for this extra layer of explanation in order to understand the physical world, and they will be right," they say. This simple claim only carries weight, however, "provided we attempt to explain only physical reality, accept without question the given nature of physical laws, and ignore the question of the ontological status of those laws, *as well as* all the issues raised by the existence of a moral or ethical order, by religious experience, and, indeed,

15. Ibid., 57.
16. Ibid., 59.

also by the aesthetic dimension of life encompassed in great art and drama." This places too many limitations on the attempt to provide an overall explanation for existence. "When we try to make sense of these extra dimensions of existence," Murphy and Ellis argue, "the simple physical explanation is woefully lacking; something like [our own proposal] is much more profound and satisfying."[17]

Murphy and Ellis believe that cosmology in general and the apparent fine-tuning of our universe in particular "add important evidence to some theories of ultimate reality."[18] Fine-tuning alone does not provide the ultimate ground for a grand theory about ultimate reality, but it can give weight to some theories and not others. Murphy and Ellis also acknowledge that "fine-tuning alone does not provide a great deal of support for any particular designer hypothesis."[19] They suggest that extra evidence is required to distinguish which designer hypothesis among the many possible ones is most adequate.

A Universe Fine-Tuned for Love

A central claim that makes Murphy and Ellis's work important for research on love is this: a noncoercive, self-renunciation ethic of love fits well with the fine-tuning that cosmologists have discovered is necessary for life to emerge.[20] To support this claim, Murphy and Ellis explain and defend the general features of the self-renunciation ethic in relation to theology.

The self-renunciation ethic is in direct conflict with what Murphy and Ellis call "the ontology of violence," versions of which we encountered in the previous chapter on biology. The ontology of violence "implies that selfishness and violent coercion are basic to human nature."[21] The authors contend, by contrast, that creatures, at least humans, are capable of self-sacrifice and nonviolence. The core of their ethic theory is stated this way: "self-renunciation for

17. Ibid., 218.
18. Ibid., 63.
19. Ibid., 202.
20. Ibid., 249.
21. Ibid., 17.

the sake of the other is humankind's highest good."[22] Genuine self-sacrifice for the good of the other opens us to a greater good. Those who make generosity the order of the day find their lives transformed, because a life of generosity transcends the miserly ethic of nicely calculated debts and duties. "This way of 'giving up' one's own interests," argue Murphy and Ellis, "is the true way to self-fulfillment."[23]

Murphy and Ellis consider theology a science, and theological science plays a key role in their argument. In particular, they draw on the Christian theology of kenosis. The word *kenosis* comes from the Greek verb *kenoō* ("to empty") and is used by the apostle Paul in the well-known passage Philippians 2:5–11. It is often defined as "self-giving," "self-renunciation," or "self-denying." A Christian theology of kenosis suggests that God and at least some creatures are capable of self-renunciation. In fact, Murphy and Ellis suggest the kenotic ethic reflects the moral character of God, and divine kenosis is the basis for creaturely kenosis. "Only if kenosis is somehow in harmony with the ultimate character of reality," say Murphy and Ellis, "should it be regarded as expected to be anything but foolishness."[24]

Kenosis is not only a feature of God's moral character; it also reflects the nature of God's initial creative and ongoing activity. God's purpose for creating the universe may be reflected in the structures and characteristics of the universe itself. This is especially evident in the fine-tuning of the universe. "While the fine-tuning does not logically require the assumption of a designer," say Murphy and Ellis, the existence of a God provides a suitable explanation of fine-tuning.[25] The universe was created by kenosis.

Murphy and Ellis suggest that the anthropic features of the universe can be interpreted as the necessary conditions not only for

22. Ibid., 118.
23. Ibid., 121. Murphy and Ellis note in various segments of the book some of the implications that an ethic of self-renunciation or kenosis has in economic, legal, and political realms. They argue that the nonviolence of kenosis will be more effective in the long run in bringing about the common good, in part because the habitual practice of kenosis transforms the moral character of those who act nonviolently.
24. Ibid., 174.
25. Ibid., 208.

life but also for intelligence, freedom, and morality. "The anthropic universe is . . . a moral universe," they maintain. And "once the universe is seen as a moral universe, it becomes possible to explain added cosmological features that other (nontheistic) accounts of the anthropic features cannot explain: Why is there a universe at all? and, Why is it lawlike?" This suggests that "while the purpose of creating free creatures cannot be 'read off' from cosmology alone, both life and lawlike behavior of the nonhuman universe are necessary conditions for freedom."[26]

If the ultimate purpose of the universe is to make possible free and moral responses, the universe needs to have been created in such a way that ordered patterns of events occur. Without this order, free will is meaningless.[27] "We envisage the creator at all times maintaining the nature and processes of the physical world so that a chosen set of laws of physics *describe* its evolution," say Murphy and Ellis. They also "assume freedom of action, albeit constrained by many biological, psychological, and social factors, for without this the concept of morality is meaningless."[28] After all, "any moral response requires an ordered and predictable universe, as well as creatures with free will."[29]

Indeterminacy at the quantum level of existence—the microlevel—plays an important part in the moral universe hypothesis that Murphy and Ellis propose. Contemporary research in quantum physics grounds this proposal. Indeterminacy at the quantum level makes possible scientific denial of an entirely deterministic universe.

Prior to the twentieth century, most physical cosmologists claimed that the basic units of existence are entirely determined, and these units entirely determine all higher levels of existence. If the smallest entities were entirely controlled by their environments or natures, complex creatures, such as humans, were also entirely controlled and not genuinely free. Those who affirmed genuine human freedom typically appealed to special divine action that "inserted" freedom into the human species. The basic units of existence and those creatures that evolved from these units were

26. Ibid., 203.
27. Ibid., 206.
28. Ibid., 207.
29. Ibid., 208.

fully determined, but humans were a cosmological exception. The powerful force of evolutionary theory, however, suggests to many scholars today that humans should not be an exception to the hypothesis that all things are entirely determined. Evolved humans must be entirely determined, they conclude, and therefore not genuinely free.

Research in quantum physics in the twentieth century seriously undermined the view that the most fundamental units of existence are entirely determined by their environment or natures. The specifics of this research, including major contributions from people such as David Bohm, Niels Bohr, Max Born, Paul Dirac, Richard Feynman, Werner Heisenberg, and Erwin Schrödinger, are beyond the scope of this chapter and can be found in various physics books.[30] The results of the research, however, indicate that descriptions of the activity of the most basic units of existence are necessarily incomplete. The best that physicists can do is make probable predictions about activity at the quantum level. What occurs at any particular moment cannot be entirely predicted—a conclusion encapsulated in what became known as Heisenberg's Uncertainty Principle.

Physicists call this inability to offer complete descriptions of causation at the microlevel "quantum indeterminacy." Scientists debate whether this inability actually refers to the ontological status of these entities or merely expresses the epistemological notion that outside observers cannot fully know how these entities are determined.[31] If the latter is correct, then the microworld may be fully determined, but we remain ignorant of it. If the former correctly describes the quantum level, the basic constituents of existence should not be said to fully determine creatures. The universe is neither preordained nor mechanistically programmed.

30. See, for instance, John Polkinghorne, *Quantum Theory: A Very Short Introduction* (Oxford: Oxford University Press, 2002).

31. For a physicist's argument that freedom exists ontologically at the smallest levels of existence, see Geoffrey F. Chew, "A Historical Reality That Includes Big Bang, Free Will, and Elementary Particles," in *Physics and Whitehead: Quantum, Process, and Experience*, ed. Timothy E. Eastman and Hank Keeton (Albany, NY: State University of New York Press, 2004), 84–91. See also John A. Jungerman, *World in Process: Creativity and Interconnection in the New Physics* (Albany, NY: State University of New York Press, 2000).

Actual indeterminacy, at the least, would be an essential part of the microworld of physics. Many cosmologists affirm the notion that indeterminacy is the ontological character of entities at the microlevel, because to claim indeterminacy is merely an epistemological issue undermines claims about the ontological status of other phenomena scientists examine.

Murphy and Ellis make a claim that moves beyond affirming indeterminacy at the quantum level. They argue that genuine freedom—self-determination—is present among at least some creatures in the universe. They offer no explanation as to how freedom emerged from indeterminacy.[32] But this contention about freedom has direct implications for love research. To say that creatures are not entirely determined at the microlevel and that freedom is present at least among humans fits well with what I said earlier about the necessity of freedom for love. Freedom plays a key role in love, if love is defined as acting intentionally, in sympathetic response to others (including God), to promote overall well-being. Intentionality, as argued in chapter 1, entails some form of genuine freedom.

Murphy and Ellis's affirmation of indeterminacy has important implications for their suggestion about how a self-renunciatory God acts in the world. God's noncoercive activity at the quantum level, they argue, provides an explanation for indeterminacy at the lowest levels of existence. They speculate that God's communication to creatures may occur at a person's quantum level as God stimulates "visions and other religious experience described in religious literature."[33] In short, physical reality at the macrolevel of fine-tuning and the microlevel of quantum indeterminacy shapes the context and needs of moral behavior.

Murphy and Ellis take their argument a step further by making particular claims about the relevance of Christian theology for their enterprise. They note that the Christian paradigm for divine activity is the revelation of God found best in Jesus Christ. This means that "the relevant feature of God's action is its self-sacrificial

32. Some of Nancey Murphy's thoughts on the subject are found in a book she coauthored with Warren Brown, *Did My Neurons Make Me Do It? Philosophical and Neurobiological Perspectives on Moral Responsibility and Free Will* (Oxford: Oxford University Press, 2007).

33. Murphy and Ellis, *Moral Nature of the Universe*, 217.

and noncoercive character."[34] After all, Jesus was self-sacrificial and noncoercive.

God does not overrule or dominate creatures. Murphy and Ellis argue that such action would be necessary for divine intervention in the world, and they reject such intervention. God acts consistently at all times throughout all creation. Cosmology supports this view, they maintain, because "fine-tuning suggests a 'uniformitarian' and noninterventionist pattern of divine action—God achieves the divine purposes within the carefully planned system rather than by overriding the natural system."[35] But God can manipulate indeterminate quantum events somewhat, Murphy and Ellis believe, because such events have no freedom, strictly speaking. "Openness is needed at the bottom level of the hierarchical structuring," they argue, "to enable noninterventionist divine action."[36]

Murphy and Ellis conclude with a brief look at what many believe is the chief obstacle to believing that God loves perfectly, if not also the chief obstacle to believing that God exists at all. That obstacle is the problem of evil, and this problem relates directly to important questions in love research. An engagement with the problem of evil provides Murphy and Ellis an opportunity to bring together many of their orienting themes.

The regularities in nature, Murphy and Ellis claim, are necessary to have a cosmos, and these regularities are necessary for meaningful human action. "Yet, as by-products of those inexorable laws," they say, "both humans and animals suffer through illness, starvation, and natural disasters." The problem of evil as they see it amounts to why God does not occasionally intervene in the natural order, "overruling natural processes when greater good will come from the exception than from following the rule."[37]

Murphy and Ellis believe it best to conceive of God's action as voluntarily noninterventionist. "God voluntarily withholds divine power," they speculate, "out of respect for the freedom and integrity of the creatures."[38] God has decided not to violate the rights of created entities to be what they are. "This mode of action

34. Ibid., 214.
35. Ibid., 230.
36. Ibid., 215.
37. Ibid., 246.
38. Ibid.

is a voluntary choice on the part of the Creator," writes Ellis in a summary article, "made because it is the only mode of attaining the goal of eliciting a free response of love and sacrifice from individuals endowed with free will. It implies total restraint in the use of God's omnipotent power, for otherwise a free response to God's actions is not possible."[39]

Voluntarily deciding not to violate the freedom and integrity of creatures entails divine risks and potential costs. After all, some creatures violate or fail to measure up to God's purposes. God accepts these risks and costs, however, "in order to achieve a higher goal: the free and intelligent cooperation of the creature in divine activity."[40]

Murphy and Ellis speculate that "at the human level, God's action is limited by human limitations but also by free choices in rebellion against God. At the lower levels of complexity, the issue is not sin, but simply the limitations imposed by the fact that the creature is only what it is, and is not God."[41] Suffering and evil occur because of free humans who sin and because of the long, noncoercive creative process that aims at developing free and intelligent beings.

This cooperative, noncoercive activity of God fits well with an evolutionary picture of existence. The process of creating creatures from recalcitrant matter is slow, indirect, and sometimes painful. But this process reflects God's "noncoercive, persuasive, painstaking love all the way from the beginning to the end, from the least of God's creatures to the most splendid."[42] In fact, the universe's "fine-tuning can be taken up into a theology that sees God's noncoercive respect for the freedom and integrity of creatures go all the way back to the initial design of an anthropic (intelligence- and freedom-producing) universe." For "the freedom of the creature is central to God's eighteen-billion-year project."[43]

39. George F. R. Ellis, "Kenosis as a Unifying Theme for Life and Cosmology," in *The Work of Love: Creation as Kenosis*, ed. John Polkinghorne (Grand Rapids: Eerdmans, 2001), 114.

40. Murphy and Ellis, *Moral Nature of the Universe*, 246.

41. Ibid., 247.

42. Ibid.

43. Ibid., 249.

Murphy and Ellis seek not just to provide an explanation for cosmology and ethics in the wide-ranging array of disciplines they explore; they also believe that this explanation suggests to humans a way to live lives of love. Their proposal suggests an ethic: "If freedom from coercion is absolutely central to God's purposes, going all the way back to the beginning, then who are we, God's creatures, to attempt to coerce one another?"[44] Divine self-renunciation is a model that humans ought to follow.

The Universe from Nothing

We have seen that twentieth-century cosmology strongly suggests that the universe is expanding. This expansion began with a big bang ten to twenty billion years ago. Contemporary cosmology suggests a limited number of viable overarching theories to account for the beginning and expansion of the universe.[45] Cosmologist Paul Davies identifies six such theories:[46]

1. an absolute beginning to the universe and subsequent everlasting expansion;
2. an absolute beginning to the universe followed by the termination of the universe after a period of expansion;
3. an absolute beginning to the universe, expansion to a maximum state, and a return to a state identical to the absolute beginning;
4. an everlastingly cyclic universe, in which expansion and contraction is followed by a "big bounce" into another cycle of expansion and contraction;
5. a steady-state universe with no beginning or end but everlasting expansion;

44. Ibid.
45. For a clever and accessible taxonomy of possible explanations for why the universe exists at all, see Robert Lawrence Kuhn, "Why This Universe?" *Skeptic* 13, no. 2 (2007): 28–39.
46. Paul Davies, "Eternity: Who Needs It?" in *The Far-Future Universe: Eschatology from a Cosmic Perspective*, ed. George F. R. Ellis (Philadelphia: Templeton Foundation Press, 2002), 42–44.

6. an everlasting multiverse in which our universe is one among others.[47]

Each of these theories supports various emotional, theological, and metaphysical preferences. For instance, some theists prefer the steady-state model because it eliminates the big bang theory. They regard the big bang theory as a naturalistic hypothesis meant to eliminate the need for divine action. Other theists prefer big bang models that emphasize the absolute beginning of our universe, because they believe the big bang fits better with the notion that God created from absolutely nothing (*creatio ex nihilo*). Some atheists prefer the multiverse model, because it seems to weaken the fine-tuning argument and thus cosmology's vulnerability to hypotheses about a creative role for God. In this segment, we examine what is at stake in speculation about before, during, and after the initiation and expansion of our universe.

The notion that there was no "before" the big bang—at least no creaturely "before"—has played an important part in Christian, Jewish, and Muslim creation narratives. Many identify the idea with the Latin phrase *creatio ex nihilo* and suggest that God is the sole cause of the universe. Advocates of *creatio ex nihilo* typically believe that these first verses of Hebrew Scripture affirm the doctrine:

> In the beginning when God created the heavens and the earth, the earth was a formless void and darkness covered the face of the deep, while a wind from God swept over the face of the waters. (Gen. 1:1–2)

Although other relevant creation texts exist in Hebrew and Christian Scriptures, theologians return time after time to these verses for inspiration on how best to think of God's initial creative activity.

John Polkinghorne, a Cambridge University physicist who later became an Anglican priest and an important voice on issues of science and religion, affirms *creatio ex nihilo*. He believes that the doctrine and its implication that there was no "before" the big bang

---

47. For a well-written explanation of the multiverse possibility, see Alex Vilenkin, *Many Worlds in One: The Search for Other Universes* (New York: Hill & Wang, 2006).

remains relevant for contemporary reflections in cosmology and theology. His best defense of this view is his Gifford Lectures, *The Faith of a Physicist: Reflections of a Bottom-Up Thinker.*[48]

Polkinghorne begins his discussion of the origin of the universe by affirming the dominant view of cosmology: "In the beginning was the big bang."[49] After a brief description of the big bang story's features, Polkinghorne turns to theology to answer the question of the universe's ontological origin. Christian theology should draw from research in physical cosmology, he says, but it "sees the world as the consequence of a free act of divine decision and as separate from deity. The universe's inherent contingency is conventionally and vividly expressed in the idea of creation *ex nihilo*."[50] The doctrine that God creates from absolutely nothing implies that "the divine will alone is the source of created being."[51]

Creatio ex nihilo is important, asserts Polkinghorne, for what it says about science. The doctrine implies "both that the world was rational and also that the nature of its rationality depended on the choice of its Creator, so that one must look to see what actual form it had taken."[52] Polkinghorne rejects the claim that physical cosmologists have provided a nondivine version of *creatio ex nihilo*. Physics may be able to show that a universe will appear, "given quantum mechanics and a certain gauge field theory of matter." However, science cannot give an adequate explanation for why there is something rather than nothing. This is the domain of theology, because "theology is concerned with the Giver of those laws which are the basis of any form of physical reality."[53]

Crucial to Polkinghorne's view of creation from nothing is the idea that no conditions bind God's free and omnipotent decision to create. "To hold a doctrine of creation *ex nihilo* is to hold that all that is depends, now and always, on the freely exercised will of

48. John Polkinghorne, *The Faith of a Physicist: Reflections of a Bottom-Up Thinker* (Minneapolis: Fortress, 1996).
49. Ibid., 71.
50. Ibid., 73.
51. Ibid., 74.
52. Ibid.
53. Ibid., 75.

God. It is certainly not to believe that God started things off by manipulating a curious kind of stuff called 'nothing.'"[54]

Like Murphy and Ellis, Polkinghorne affirms that creatures, humans at least, are not entirely determined. The chance and necessity present in the universe "should be seen as reflections of the twin gifts of freedom and reliability," says Polkinghorne, "bestowed on his creation by One who is both loving and faithful."[55] The intrinsic unpredictability of chaotic systems at the microlevel can be interpreted as leaving room for the insertion of information from organizing principles and agents. Organizing principles in nature might be interpreted theologically as expressions of God's creative will.[56] In any case, these principles affect both animate and inanimate entities:

> God's gift of "freedom" to his creation is conveyed by his respect of the integrity of [the natural] processes. In the case of inanimate creation, the outworking of these principles will not be overruled, though their effects may be reinforced in positively fruitful ways. . . . In the case of animate creatures, there is a much greater degree of autonomy to be respected, and I believe that God will interact with them in ways that are appropriate to their natures.[57]

This scheme proposes that God is now active in the universe without absolutely determining everything.

Polkinghorne appeals to kenosis theology to account for existence. "God interacts with the world but is not in total control of all its process," he says. This involves a "curtailment of divine power" that comes through self-limitation. "It arises from the logic of love," says Polkinghorne, "which requires the freedom of the beloved."[58] It includes the notion that "God remains omnipotent in the sense that he can do whatever he wills, but it is not in accordance with his will and nature to insist on total control."[59]

54. Ibid.
55. Ibid., 77. See also John C. Polkinghorne, *Science and Creation: The Search for Understanding* (London: SPCK, 1988), chap. 4.
56. Polkinghorne, *Faith of a Physicist*, 78.
57. Ibid., 79.
58. Ibid., 81.
59. Ibid. Polkinghorne realizes that these issues inevitably lead many to wonder about the problem of evil. I will return to this issue and use Polkinghorne's thought

Polkinghorne admits that Genesis 1 need not be interpreted as supporting the view that the universe was created from absolute nothingness, but he thinks that Genesis is best interpreted as implying the doctrine. This implication has to do with what the text implies about divine power. In the next segment, I address the issue of God's power. But given the relative importance that Polkinghorne and others place on Genesis 1, however, I must briefly examine that text and the doctrine of *creatio ex nihilo*.

Although advocates of *creatio ex nihilo* often cite the opening verses of Genesis, these verses do not contain any reference to an absolute nothingness from which God created. Many contemporary biblical scholars do not believe that Genesis 1, or other biblical texts for that matter, supports *creatio ex nihilo*.[60] Perhaps the most eloquent of biblical scholars on this issue is Jon D. Levenson, author of *Creation and the Persistence of Evil: The Jewish Drama of Divine Omnipotence*.[61]

Levenson notes that biblical scholars from Rashi to Ephraim Speiser have argued that readers best interpret Genesis 1:1 as a temporal clause: "When God *began to create* the heaven and the earth."[62] This temporal clause does not suggest an absolute beginning of time. Furthermore, the phrase in Genesis 1:2 typically translated "formless void" (*tōhû wābōhû*), says Levenson, is best translated as "primordial chaos."[63] Following the biblical reference

---

in the final chapter. I should note here that Polkinghorne offers what he calls a free-will defense: "despite the many disastrous choices . . . , a world of freely choosing beings is better than a world of perfectly programmed automata." This defense has a parallel for nonmoral evil: "God allows the whole universe to be itself. Each created entity is allowed to behave in accordance with its nature, including the due regularities which may be part of that nature" (ibid., 83). Others have suggested theological schemes similar to Polkinghorne's. In particular, see Denis Edwards, *The God of Evolution: A Trinitarian Theology* (New York: Paulist Press, 1999).

60. Of course, there are still some Hebrew Bible scholars who argue that Genesis 1 should be interpreted as affirming *creatio ex nihilo*, but they are in the small minority. See Paul Copan and William Lane Craig, *Creation Out of Nothing: A Biblical, Philosophical, and Scientific Exploration* (Grand Rapids: Baker Academic, 2004).

61. Jon D. Levenson, *Creation and the Persistence of Evil: The Jewish Drama of Divine Omnipotence* (1988; repr., Princeton, NJ: Princeton University Press, 1994).

62. Ibid., 121; emphasis mine.

63. Ibid., xx. Levenson also notes that nowhere in the seven-day creation scheme does God create the waters; they are also most likely primordial (ibid., 5).

to the Spirit hovering over this primordial chaos, the author of Genesis speaks of darkness on the "face of the deep." The "deep" in this last phrase, which is *tĕhôm* in Hebrew, refers to something nondivine and primordially present when God began to create. Biblical scholar Brevard Childs says that "the *tehom* signifies here the primeval waters which were also uncreated."[64]

Levenson joins other biblical authors in arguing that Genesis 1 suggests that even in the first moments of creation God encounters other forces. These forces oppose, at least partially, God's creative will. Therefore, says Levenson, the concern of creation theology in Hebrew Scripture is not *creatio ex nihilo* but rather the establishment of a benevolent and life-sustaining order founded on God's demonstrated authority and triumphs over all rivals.[65] "We can capture the essence of the idea of creation in the Hebrew Bible with the word 'mastery,'" argues Levenson.[66] In that mastery, God is the victor in combat, but God's foes continue to survive.[67] "Properly understood," says Levenson in summary, Genesis 1:1–2:3 "cannot be invoked in support of the developed Jewish, Christian, and Muslim doctrine of *creatio ex nihilo*."[68]

Other Genesis scholars agree with Levenson. Claus Westermann argues, for instance, that *creatio ex nihilo* "is foreign to both the language and thought of P [the unknown author of Genesis 1]. . . . It is clear here that there can be no question of a *creatio ex nihilo*; our query about the origin of matter is not answered"; the idea of an initial chaos goes back to "mythical and pre-mythical primitive thinking."[69] Terence Fretheim remarks, "God's creating in Genesis 1 . . . includes ordering that which already exists. . . . God works creatively with already existing reality to bring about newness."[70] Theologian Catherine Keller summarizes recent biblical scholarship: "Among biblical scholars there has existed on this matter a

64. Brevard S. Childs, *Myth and Reality in the Old Testament* (London: SCM Press, 1960), 33.
65. Levenson, *Creation and the Persistence of Evil*, 47.
66. Ibid., 3.
67. Ibid., 17–18.
68. Ibid., 121.
69. Claus Westermann, *Genesis 1–11: A Commentary*, trans. John J. Scullion (London: SPCK, 1984), 110, 121.
70. Terence E. Fretheim, *God and World in the Old Testament: A Relational Theology of Creation* (Nashville: Abingdon, 2005), 5.

near, if nervous, consensus for decades. The Bible knows only of the divine formation of the world out of a chaotic something."[71]

If *creatio ex nihilo* is not found in Scripture,[72] one wonders why it would have arisen and taken root in Christianity and other theistic traditions. Gerhard May seeks to answer that question in *Creatio Ex Nihilo: The Doctrine of "Creation out of Nothing" in Early Christian Thought*.[73] Hellenistic Jews could talk of a creation by God "out of nothing," says May, but the formula was not meant in an ontological sense. To speak of creation out of nothing in no way excluded an eternal material for the world.[74] Instead, early theologians used the phrase rhetorically to compare the goodness of God to that which opposed God's creative activity.

The question of initial creation arose specifically in connection with the gnostic rejection of matter and the world. Most gnostics believed the world to be the creation of heavenly beings of lesser rank who were either ignorant of God or in rebellion. Early theists adopted *creatio ex nihilo* to combat the gnostic notion that the world was inherently evil. May contends that for most gnostics, "the origin of the cosmos is conceived as a disturbance of the original plan, caused by the self-exaltation of the demiurgical powers, and the process of salvation has as its first goal the destruction of the material world."[75]

Although early theists championed the notion of *creatio ex nihilo* as a way to reject Gnosticism, the introduction of the doctrine of *creatio ex nihilo* is, ironically, credited to two gnostics: Basilides and Valentinus. Basilides was the first to advance the theory. His second-century version was that the supreme God created in a single act what would come potentially into being in the unfolding of space and time.[76] From this one act, utterly unimaginable, ineffable, and disanalogous to any historical activity, all being proceeds

71. Catherine Keller, *The Face of the Deep: A Theology of Becoming* (New York: Routledge, 2003), 4.

72. Some cite 2 Macc. 7:28 as biblical warrant for *creatio ex nihilo*, but this text does not support this claim well.

73. Gerhard May, *Creatio Ex Nihilo: The Doctrine of "Creation out of Nothing" in Early Christian Thought*, trans. A. S. Worrall (Edinburgh: T&T Clark, 1994).

74. Ibid., xi.

75. Ibid., 40.

76. Ibid., 70.

automatically. The primary presupposition for Basilides's theory of *creatio ex nihilo* was that God does not act in the history of the evil world. Gnostic theists originally invent the theory of God creating from absolute nothingness, then, in order to support a strong form of gnostic monism in which a sovereign and exterior God unilaterally generates an other. Christians later came to treat the doctrine of *creatio ex nihilo* as a kind of orthodoxy as a way to reject the gnostic view that the world is inherently evil.

May identifies leading early Christian theologians who embraced the world-formation hypothesis rather than creation from absolute nothingness. Philo, for instance, postulated a preexistent matter alongside God.[77] Justin, Athenagoras, Hermogenes, and Clement of Alexandria, notes May, "show that Christians educated in Platonism could hold that acceptance of an unformed matter was entirely reconcilable with biblical monotheism and the omnipotence of God."[78] But accepting divine creation from unformed chaos eventually became the minority report.

The first Christian theologian to use unambiguously the substance and the terminology of the doctrine of *creatio ex nihilo* was Theophilus of Antioch. It would be Irenaeus, however, who solidified *creatio ex nihilo* in the theology of the church. The doctrine fit well with the Neoplatonic doctrine of God that was gaining influence in early Christianity. Neoplatonism taught that God is eternal, self-sufficient, simple, impassible, omnipotent, immutable, and commands the world through the divine will.[79] The all-sovereignty of God was an especially important element in *creatio ex nihilo*.[80] "The will of God must rule and dominate in everything," Irenaeus argued, "but everything else must give way to it, be subordinated to it and be a servant to it."[81]

After the first and second centuries, leading theologians in Christianity and in other theistic traditions affirmed *creatio ex nihilo*.[82]

77. Ibid., xiii.
78. Ibid., 74.
79. Ibid., 164–74.
80. Ibid., 169, 172, 174, 175, 177.
81. Irenaeus, *Adversus haereses* 2.34.4 cited in ibid., 174.
82. See James Noel Hubler, "Creatio ex Nihilo: Matter, Creation, and the Body in Classical and Christian Philosophy through Aquinas" (PhD diss., University of Pennsylvania, 1995).

Theologian Catherine Keller has argued that *creatio ex nihilo* dominated in the Christian tradition as a polemic against what leaders deemed heresies.[83] The idea that God could have created this universe from something rather than nothing did not disappear altogether, however. Thomas Aquinas, for instance, affirmed that creation from something was a logical possibility. But he affirmed *creatio ex nihilo* instead, citing Genesis 1 and claiming that the doctrine was divinely revealed.

The fact that Genesis 1 does not support *creatio ex nihilo* is not lost on many contemporary physicists. Some cosmologists recognize the implications that creation out of absolute nothing has for conceiving of divine power and natural law. Paul Davies, for instance, notes that *creatio ex nihilo* is the preferred doctrine among contemporary and ancient Christians, "even though the doctrine of creation *ex nihilo* was never intended to invest huge significance into the originating cosmic event as such."[84] Davies argues that "those who invoke God as an explanation of cosmic organization usually have in mind *a super-natural* agency, acting on the world in defiance of natural laws. But it is perfectly possible for much, if not all, of what we encounter in the universe to be the product of intelligent manipulation of a purely natural kind: within the laws of physics."[85]

Some contemporary physicists offer theories about the origin of the universe that conform to the laws of physics and do not require belief that something came from absolute nothingness. Before looking at one such theory, we need to examine contemporary theologies that affirm contemporary cosmology but deny *creatio ex nihilo*. A significant issue at play is the nature and degree of God's power as Creator of the cosmos. The issues of divine power and love are important for the problem of evil.

83. Keller, *Face of the Deep*, 43.

84. Davies, "Eternity: Who Needs It?" 44.

85. Paul Davies, *God and the New Physics* (London: Dent, 1983), 208. Davies opts for the expression "natural God" to describe the intelligent creator or manipulator. He says that this natural God "would not be omnipotent for he could not act outside the laws of nature. He would be the creator of everything we see, having made matter from pre-existing energy, organized it appropriately, set up the conditions necessary for life to develop and so on, but he would not be capable of creation out of nothing (*ex nihilo*) as the Christ doctrine requires" (ibid., 209).

Creatio ex Chaosmos

If God created the fine-tuned universe in which we live billions of years ago out of absolutely nothing, God must have a particular kind of power. As we have seen, some theologians defend *creatio ex nihilo* because of what it implies about God's sovereignty. Murphy, Ellis, and Polkinghorne argue that a central issue in the problem of evil is how best to conceive of God's power in light of creaturely freedom. An adequate view of the origin of the universe seems to require a theory of divine power that accounts both for the big bang and for why a loving God fails to prevent the occurrence of genuine evil.

Theologian David Ray Griffin has addressed the issues of initial creation, evil, and divine power in several writings. Griffin affirms that God loves perfectly and that God created the universe. He argues, however, that the classic Christian doctrine of *creatio ex nihilo* (understood as creation from absolutely nothing) implies that God has the kind of power that makes God culpable for failing to prevent genuinely evil occurrences. A God who can single-handedly create from absolutely nothing could also single-handedly prevent any genuine evil. Because evil occurs, God must not have that kind of power.

The main implication of the doctrine of *creatio ex nihilo*, says Griffin, "is that the world has no inherent power, no power of its own, with which it could resist the divine will." This means that God can totally control or unilaterally determine creatures, and God can arbitrarily suspend the laws of nature.[86] But a God with the power to control creatures entirely seems culpable for making evil possible in the first place and for failing to prevent genuine evil that subsequently occurs. "If God is said to have created the world out of absolute nothingness," says Griffin, "the origin of evil cannot be explained, at least without implying that God's goodness is less than perfect."[87]

Griffin draws from and expands basic notions that philosopher of science and cosmologist Alfred North Whitehead proposed

86. David Ray Griffin, *Reenchantment without Supernaturalism: A Process Philosophy of Religion* (Ithaca, NY: Cornell University Press, 2001), 137.

87. David Ray Griffin, "Creation Out of Nothing, Creation Out of Chaos, and the Problem of Evil," in *Encountering Evil: Live Options in Theodicy*, ed. Stephen T. Davis (Louisville: Westminster John Knox, 2001), 114.

about God's relation to the world. Whitehead speculated that the beginning of our universe was "not the beginning of [finite] matter of fact, but the incoming of a certain type of order."[88] In one sense, a world/universe exists necessarily alongside God. "Whitehead does not mean that our particular world, with its particular forms of order—such as its electrons, protons, and neutrons and its inverse square law of gravitation—is necessary to the divine experience," Griffin explains. Rather, Whitehead "means that beneath the contingent order of our cosmic epoch there is a more fundamental order, a *metaphysical* order, which is necessarily embodied in some world or other."[89] The metaphysical principles "belong to the very essence of God," says Griffin, which means that "it makes no sense to speak of God as interrupting them."[90]

Griffin speculates that our universe began from the relative chaos—what might be called a "chaosmos"—of a previous universe. We can suppose, says Griffin, "that between the decay of the previous cosmic epoch and the beginning of the present one . . . there would have been no social order, no societies—no electrons, protons, photons, or even quarks."[91] All finite occasions would have been extremely trivial. "The first stage of the creation of our cosmic epoch," suggests Griffin, "would have involved the formation of very low-grade serially ordered societies (perhaps quarks) out of such a chaotic state. Later stages would have involved the creation of more complex societies out of these simpler ones."[92]

Griffin's alternative creation proposal is important for what it means for divine power. "There was no stage at which God could unilaterally determine the states of affairs. . . . Divine creativity can never obliterate or override the creativity of the creatures."[93] The God unable to obliterate or override the creativity of creatures even at the creation of the universe cannot be held culpable for failing to override creaturely creativity to prevent genuine evil any time in the history of the universe.

88. Whitehead, *Process and Reality*, 96.
89. Griffin, *Reenchantment without Supernaturalism*, 138.
90. Ibid., 140.
91. Ibid., 143.
92. Ibid.
93. Ibid.

Griffin argues that his proposal fits with central notions of fine-tuning that most contemporary cosmologists affirm. According to Griffin's view, God can set the laws and constraints for a particular universe in its initial moments and yet not have the capacity to control others entirely at any time before, during, or after. Divine coercion, even at the big bang, is not necessary to regard God as Creator.

Although God always interacts with others with some power of their own, the competition between God's power and creaturely powers prior to the big bang is different in degree than competition thereafter. "Prior to the beginning of our particular cosmic epoch . . . the realm of finite actualities was (by hypothesis) in a state of chaos, in the sense that there were no societies, not even extremely simple serially ordered societies such as photos and quarks." There was "a multiplicity of finite actual occasions," says Griffin, "but they were extremely brief events . . . happening at random."[94] In the first instant of our particular universe, God's noncoercive power could be almost coercive, given the simplicity of occasions that existed in the chaosmos with which God related. "A divine spirit, brooding over the chaos, would only have had to think, 'Let there be X!' (with X standing for the complex interconnected set of contingent principles embodied in our world at the outset, constituting its fine tuning)."[95]

Subsequent to the instantiation of these laws and principles typically identified as the fine-tuning of our universe, God would relate to entities and individuals that embody those laws and principles. But the emergent and emerging creation would possess a heightened sense of order and individuals with increasingly complex freedom. Before the big bang, during it, and thereafter, God's power is always and necessarily persuasive.[96]

Griffin is careful to point out that although entities predated the big bang of our universe, his hypothesis does not require any particular world to exist necessarily. "What exists necessarily," he maintains, "is God-with-a-realm-of-finite-existents." Although God is the only being who exists necessarily, God is necessarily

94. Ibid., 217.
95. Ibid., 217–18.
96. Ibid., 218.

related to some world or another. "The necessary existence of God," Griffin says summarily, "implies the necessary existence of a world—not of *our* world, of course, and not even a world in the sense of an ordered cosmos, but simply a realm of finite existents, which can exist either in an ordered or a chaotic state."[97]

Theologian Catherine Keller's work in *The Face of the Deep: A Theology of Becoming* is similar to Griffin's in its denial of *creatio ex nihilo*. Keller offers, however, perhaps the fullest creation theology available built on the notion that God as Creator does not create out of absolutely nothing.[98] Her work engages a wide spectrum of literature as she weaves together affirmations and criticisms of scientific cosmology, biblical materials, chaos theory, literature, and complexity theory. She examines the work of theologians such as Augustine, Karl Barth, and Jürgen Moltmann, literature such as Herman Melville's *Moby Dick*, feminist and gender studies, and philosophies inspired by Jacques Derrida, Gilles Deleuze, Luce Irigaray, and Alfred North Whitehead.

Keller begins *The Face of the Deep* by addressing biblical and historical scholarship pertaining to *creatio ex nihilo*. "The author of Genesis," says Keller, "assumed that the universe was created from a primal chaos: something uncreated, something Other, something that a creator could mold, form, or call to order."[99] This assumption was suppressed in early Christian history, however. "The Christian theology that early came to dominate the church," Keller observes, "could not tolerate this constraint upon God's power: for why should 'He' have had to reckon with an Other? This prevenient chaos cramped the growing Christian imagery of mastery—what we may call its *dominology*, its logos of lordship."[100] In fact, Keller charges the early church fathers with "deliberately conceal[ing] the chaos of scripture."[101] This allowed for "the triumphant orthodox

97. Griffin, "Creation Out of Nothing," 122.

98. See also Sjoerd L. Bonting, *Chaos Theology: A Revised Creation Theology* (Ottawa: Novalis, 2002); James Edward Huchingson, *Pandemonium Tremendum: Chaos and Mystery in the Life of God* (Cleveland: Pilgrim Press, 2001); Michael E. Lodahl, "Creation Out of Nothing? Or Is *Next* to Nothing Enough?" in *Thy Nature and Name Is Love: Wesleyan and Process Theologies in Dialogue*, ed. Bryan P. Stone and Thomas Jay Oord (Nashville: Kingswood Books, 2001), 217–38.

99. Keller, *Face of the Deep*, xvii.

100. Ibid.

101. Ibid., 58.

synthesis of omnipotence with ontology." This synthesis "made possible the *ex nihilo* even as it founded the discourse of the Christian *imperium*."[102] Contemporary theology, argues Keller, has largely disregarded the biblical case against the *ex nihilo*, and it is still coming to grips with the negative realities of union with empires.[103]

Keller calls her alternative to *creatio ex nihilo* a "tehomic" theology of *creatio ex profundis*. The word *tehomic* is a derivative of the Hebrew word *tĕhôm*, found in Genesis 1:2 and typically translated "the deep." *Profundis* refers to the chaos from which God creates. Keller's creation theology explores and expands the Genesis motif of God creating from the watery depths.

The tehomic theology that Keller proposes is relational at its core. Its relational God "remains enmeshed in the vulnerabilities and potentialities of an indeterminate creativity."[104] This indeterminate creativity, says Keller, is never before or outside time and space.[105] God's essential relatedness to others means that God is never immune from response to creatures, including creaturely suffering.[106] This integral relationship between Creator and creation makes tehomic theology "a theological alternative to the dangerously unavowed amorality of omnipotence."[107]

To say that God always relates to or enmeshes in the creativity of others undermines the idea that creation is entirely independent of God. A God related to creation also undermines the idea that the *tĕhôm* of Scripture is inherently evil. *Creatio ex profundis* does not require one to say that the chaos from which God creates is ab-

---

102. Ibid., 160.

103. Ibid., 103. Keller briefly notes Jürgen Moltmann's dizzying array of comments on *creatio ex nihilo*. Sometimes Moltmann denies the doctrine; mostly he affirms it. A key concept for him is the Jewish mystical *zimsum*, which involves divine contraction. God creates "by letting be, by making room, and by withdrawing himself" (Jürgen Moltmann, *God in Creation: A New Theology of Creation and the Spirit of God*, trans. Margaret Kohl [New York: Harper & Row, 1985], 88). See also Moltmann, *The Trinity and the Kingdom: The Doctrine of God*, trans. Margaret Kohl (London: SCM Press, 1981). I join Keller in criticizing Moltmann's use of *zimsum*, as it seems to deny divine omnipresence and is unable to deal effectively with the issue of God's essential power.

104. Keller, *Face of the Deep*, 226.

105. Ibid., 157.

106. Ibid., 226.

107. Ibid., 49.

solutely autonomous or essentially evil. Instead, Keller affirms that the chaosmic other from which God creates intimately relates to and depends on God. "If beginning takes place in the interplay between the possible future and the given past," she argues, "it presupposes always a tangled complexity of relations. These relations remain largely unconscious, dim, unformed. Thus the nexus of relations may be felt as chaos. . . . Chaos is not just prevenient; it is also . . . created."[108] In fact, Keller asserts, the interaction between God and the *těhôm* might be labeled in Latin as *creatio cooperationis*.[109] The creativity with which God relates is "the active potentiality for both good and evil."[110]

Keller draws from a number of sources, including the natural sciences, to compose her tehomic theology of *creatio ex profundis*. Drawing from science is natural, says Keller, because "theology, like science, wonders about the complex and relatively stable systems in which we move, live, and get to be." Scientific work in self-organization theory, especially as proposed by Ilya Prigogine and Stuart Kauffman, is especially helpful. Keller suggests that self-organization in science is "a transcoded theological equivalent to the 'order' of creation." Order maintains itself *within* instability. "Fluctuation signifies both the repetitions comprising a chaotic process and the genesis of order," Keller remarks.[111]

In light of contemporary cosmology, Keller refers to the Genesis 1 narrative of creation as "seven days of self-organization." Keller notes that scientific autocatalysis makes no such presumption of creation from absolutely nothing: "On the contrary, it signifies emergence as creation from the chaos of prevenient conditions."[112] But this self-organization requires divine influence. Although God does not unilaterally order a world into existence, God does attract multitiered cooperation. "Creation takes place as invitation and cooperation," suggests Keller.[113] She asks, "Could what scientists call 'self-organizing complexity' now be read as an articulation of divine creativity?"[114]

108. Ibid., 161.
109. Ibid., 117.
110. Ibid., 91.
111. Ibid., 188.
112. Ibid., 196.
113. Ibid., 195.
114. Ibid., 117.

Keller draws from scientific theory, but her proposal involves an essential role for a creator. God plays the role of attractor to the chaos. "Within the chaoplexity of endless fluctuations, an order *emerges*," says Keller. "It reinforces certain differences amidst the endless possible ones. The strange attractor of chaos theory can serve as another figure of the natural law, logos or Torah, that permits genesis at the edge of chaos." Conceiving of God as attractor, suggests Keller, can "also shed light on divine love." But this is divine *eros*, and it does not control or guarantee in its attraction-based love.[115] In fact, Keller states, "to love is to bear with the chaos."[116]

It is important to note that the creative God envisioned by Griffin and Keller is different from the evolving God proposed by some others, including some eminent scientists.[117] God's creation out of chaosmos differs from the speculation of cosmologist Edward Harrison, for instance, who suggests that a superintelligence, born in some previous universe and having developed such power and intelligence as to be responsible for our existence, is responsible for the big bang.[118] God's creation from chaosmos differs from the theory Heinz Pagels proposes, in which an impersonal demiurge created the universe and encoded hidden messages for us to discover.[119] Unlike these alternative visions, Griffin and Keller affirm ancient theist affirmations that God necessarily and everlastingly exists.

An Endless Universe

The work of Griffin and of Keller suggests that the general picture offered by Murphy, Ellis, and Polkinghorne would be more plausible if God were thought to have created our universe from

115. Ibid., 198–99.
116. Ibid., 29.
117. It is not clear whether Sjoerd L. Bonting realizes this when he distinguishes his chaos theology from process thought: "The fact that process theologians also happen to reject *creatio ex nihilo* does not make me one of them, because I firmly reject their notion of an evolving Creator" (*Chaos Theology*, 26).
118. E. W. Harrison, "The Natural Selection of Universes Containing Intelligent Life," *Quarterly Journal of the Royal Astronomical Society* 36, no. 3 (1995): 193.
119. Heinz Pagels, *The Dreams of Reason: The Computer and the Rise of the Sciences of Complexity* (New York: Bantam Books, 1983).

chaos billions of years ago. God always relates to some universe or another, and God is the persuasive Creator of all that exists. This essentially persuasive God is powerful enough to initiate the big bang of our universe and every universe before and after. Yet this God is not culpable for failing to prevent the evils caused by free or indeterminate creatures. God works persuasively, never coercively, and therefore is not indictable for evil.

The notion that there has always been some universe or another is not new. In fact, some contemporary cosmologists consider the idea that our universe emerged from the chaos of a previous universe a superior overall cosmological hypothesis.

Physicist John Barrow, for instance, finds attractive the idea that the universe had no absolute beginning. "A persistently compelling picture," says Barrow, "is one in which the universe undergoes a cyclic history, periodically disappearing in a great conflagration before reappearing phoenix-like from the ashes."[120] This picture can be harmonized with a model in which the universe expands to a maximum and then contracts back to almost nothing. "We could imagine an infinite number of past oscillations and a similar number to come in the future," says Barrow.[121] Our universe would be a singularity, although one singularity in an everlasting succession of singularities. "It is possible for any particular domain to have a history that has a definite beginning in an inflationary quantum event, but the process as a whole could just go on in a steady fashion for all eternity, past and present."[122]

Other cosmologists find the theory of an endless universe attractive. Physicist Alan Guth contends, "It seems far more plausible that our universe was the result of universe reproduction than that it was created by a unique cosmic event."[123] The notion of successive universes, sometimes called a "cyclic universe," is plausible to physi-

120. John D. Barrow, "The Far, Far Future," in Ellis, ed., *Far-Future Universe*, 28.

121. Ibid. See also John D. Barrow, *The Infinite Book: A Short Guide to the Boundless, Timeless, and Endless* (New York: Pantheon Books, 2005).

122. Barrow, "The Far, Far Future," 30.

123. Alan Guth, quoted in Paul J. Steinhardt and Neil Turok, *Endless Universe: Beyond the Big Bang* (New York: Doubleday, 2007), 226. See Alan Guth, *The Inflationary Universe: The Quest for a New Theory of Cosmic Origins* (Reading, MA: Addison-Wesley, 1997).

cist Paul Davies. Davies argues that we should make a distinction between cyclic models that suggest time is a closed circle in which we are doomed to repeat the same events endlessly and models in which the most basic metaphysical features are passed from one universe to a succeeding one. The cyclic model, in other words, can involve the emergence of genuine novelty while maintaining some metaphysical continuity.[124]

Physicists Paul J. Steinhardt and Neil Turok, in their book *Endless Universe: Beyond the Big Bang*, offer perhaps the most complete cyclic universe proposal. They consider the creation of our universe part of an infinite cycle of collisions. According to them, the big bang was not the beginning of time. The "big bang might not be the 'beginning' of the universe after all," say Steinhardt and Turok, "but instead a physically explicable event with a 'before' and an 'after.'"[125] The big bang is part of an endless cycle of emerging new universes, each with new materials and new entities. "The cyclic tale pictures a universe in which galaxies, stars, and life have been formed over and over again long before the most recent big bang, and will be remade cycle after cycle far into the future."[126]

Steinhardt and Turok refer to the dominant cosmological view based on the emergence of space and time as "the inflationary model." They note that cosmologists have needed to add auxiliary theories to the inflationary model to account for new scientific findings. The standard inflationary theory now appears contrived. For instance, argue Steinhardt and Turok, the standard inflationary model has no elegant answer for why, if the initial bang relied on inflationary energy alone, so much dark energy exists. The standard inflationary view provides no explanation for the energy needed for the big bang.

Even more objectionable, Steinhardt and Turok insist, is that the inflationary theory has no answer to one of the most fundamental questions of existence: How did the universe begin if there was nothing existing before it?[127] The standard inflationary theory implies that space and time were created from absolutely nothing, or it at least provides no ultimate explanation for its origin. This is

124. Davies, "Eternity: Who Needs It?" 45.
125. Steinhardt and Turok, *Endless Universe*, 15.
126. Ibid., 61.
127. Ibid., 11.

problematic, Steinhardt and Turok observe, because "there are no rigorous physical principles that dictate how to go from 'nothing' to 'something.'" Cosmologies based on the standard inflationary theories are incomplete because they offer "no compelling reason for the universe to emerge in an inflating state."[128]

Steinhardt and Turok state that their cyclic model builds on several key elements. From string theory and M theory come the ideas of branes and extra dimensions. These theories allow for a big bang where the density of matter and radiation is finite. Furthermore, observations of the present universe indicate the existence of dark energy, and dark energy is ideal for smoothing and flattening the universe. Steinhardt and Turok speculate that the same dark energy acting before the big bang could explain why the universe is smooth and flat on large scales today. Finally, the decay of the dark energy leads to a buildup of energy sufficient to power the big bang. Yet this dark energy can simultaneously generate density variations that can give rise to galaxies after the bang.[129] "A combination of branes and an extra dimension, with regular assists from gravity and dark energy," suggest Steinhardt and Turok, "can cause the universe to repeatedly replenish itself with galaxies, stars, and life at regular intervals while always obeying the second law of thermodynamics."[130]

The cyclic model offers several advantages over the standard inflationary model. First, instead of the big bang being the absolute beginning of space and time, the cyclic model suggests that our universe began with a collision of materials that predate the big bang. According to the cyclic theory, say Steinhardt and Turok, "the big bang was triggered by the decay of dark energy that existed before the big bang."[131]

Second, the cyclic model suggests that big bangs occur at intervals of about one every trillion years, with many big bangs occurring before ours and many yet to come. "Each bang creates new matter and radiation and initiates a new period of cosmic expansion," say Steinhardt and Turok, "leading to the formation of new galaxies, stars, planets and life. Space naturally smoothes

128. Ibid., 226.
129. Ibid., 164.
130. Ibid., 193.
131. Ibid., 60.

and flattens itself after each cycle of galaxy formation and before the next big bang."[132]

Third, some features of our current universe were present in and influenced by previous universes. "All the physical properties of the universe are the same, on average, from cycle to cycle," Steinhardt and Turok remark. "Some properties thought to be constants, like the masses of elementary particles, the strengths of the various forces, and the cosmological constant, could actually vary over very long periods."[133]

Steinhardt and Turok's proposal can be told in narrative form. The narrative begins with a big bang. But "unlike the inflationary, the cyclic model does not include a moment when the temperature and density become infinite. Instead the big bang is an event that can, in principle, be fully described using the laws of physics."[134]

At the bang, Steinhardt and Turok suggest, some energy from the previous universe "is transformed into smoothly distributed matter and radiation at a very high temperature, high enough to evaporate ordinary matter into its constituent quarks and electrons and to produce many other exotic particles through high-energy collisions. But from *before* to *after* the bang, the fabric of space remains intact, the energy is always finite, and time proceeds smoothly."[135]

After the big bang, the standard inflationary model and the cyclic model tell the same basic story of the early and middle stages of the universe's evolution. However, dark energy plays a more important role in the cyclic universe the older the universe becomes. According to Steinhardt and Turok, "A key assumption in the cyclic universe is that the dark energy can decay: after a period of perhaps a trillion years, the physical properties of dark energy undergo a transformation that causes the expansion to slow down and eventually halt, leading to a phase of very gentle contraction."[136]

The role of dark energy in the cyclic model Steinhardt and Turok propose differs from the standard model. They explain by saying that "to achieve agreement with astronomical observations,

132. Ibid., 61.
133. Ibid., 166.
134. Ibid., 61.
135. Ibid., 61–62.
136. Ibid., 63.

the inflationary picture requires two forms of gravitationally self-repulsive energy, inflationary energy and dark energy, differing in density by a googol (10 to the 100th power) in magnitude. Although dark energy is the predominant form of energy in the universe today and it will determine the future, it has no connection to inflation."[137] In the cyclic model, by contrast, dark energy explains the current accelerated expansion and regulates the cycling.[138]

The conclusion of each universe involves a big crunch as the universe completes its contraction. But in the cyclic model, a new big bang follows this crunch. Some features from the previous universe persist, but "every cycle is different in fine details because the quantum jumps are random and governed by the laws of chance," say Steinhardt and Turok. The average properties of each universe remain the same. Galaxies, stars, and planets like Earth, on which intelligent forms of life may develop, will be created anew in each universe.[139]

Steinhardt and Turok hint that their cyclic model offers a directionality missing in either the standard inflationary model or the cyclic models supposing an eternal recurrence of the same. A universe with an absolute beginning and headed for an uninhabitable everlasting state sounds ultimately misanthropic. But multiple universes arising successively, with each possessing the possibility for something new and new life forms, is more hopeful. They do not address, however, the problem of evil, which Griffin and Keller believe *creatio ex nihilo* and its requisite notion of divine coercion render insoluble.

Although many theoretical theorists do research in the hypothesis of a cyclic universe and in string theory, not all physicists find the hypothesis attractive. Lee Smolin, for instance, points out that some aspects of string theory have not been tested experimentally, and some seem, in principle, incapable of being tested. These objections are important. They push us to be cautious on the one hand and to ask questions of metaphysics on the other. But they may not be pertinent to the general idea that there has always been something with which God relates and has created. In other words, a model of

137. Ibid., 67.
138. Ibid., 68.
139. Ibid., 65.

an endless universe may not need string theory. All models asking the question of ultimate origins and the possibility of divine agency require further research and theories in metacosmology.

Conclusion

Cosmology, in its various forms, provides valuable data and theories pertaining to love. The origin of our universe from a big bang leads to ultimate questions about the forces at play before and after the initiation of our universe. We explored standard features of contemporary cosmology, including big bang theory, the anthropic principle, quantum indeterminacy, string theory, and the inflationary universe. These issues were linked to issues in metacosmology and theology, including the classic doctrine of *creatio ex nihilo*, divine power, kenosis, creaturely freedom, and the problem of evil. All of these issues play a role in the wide-ranging contemporary research in cosmology and love.

6

A Theology of Love
Informed by the Sciences

I have argued that love is best defined as acting intentionally, in sympathetic response to others (including God), to promote overall well-being. I suggest that scientific research on love might be sufficiently grounded and the love research program expanded if scientists, theologians, and philosophers employed this definition.

Love comes in many forms, and creatures express love in many ways. Scholars typically identify *agape*, *eros*, and *philia* as three main love forms. As I define them, these three forms are distinct and yet share the same quality that all forms of love should share: they are intentional responses to promote overall well-being. Full-orbed love often characterizes a life that increases the common good, because complex creatures typically express each love form at various times and in various circumstances.

The social sciences provide hypotheses and empirical data to establish and advance studies in love. Psychologists typically offer theories that understand love to require a relationship with some positive quality or consequence. Research in positive psychology, attachment theory, emergency intervention, prosocial behavior, social-psychological altruism, empathy, personality theory, virtues,

173

and character formation provides valuable information for describing human love. An increasing number of social scientists affirm that humans love in the sense of acting intentionally to promote well-being. We should reject on empirical grounds the claim that humans always intend to act self-beneficially.

The biological sciences have been at the fore of controversy about the creaturely capacity for love and altruism. Charles Darwin's thoughts on love and morality emphasize the social and relational character of creatureliness. Darwin also identifies well-being, typically understood as fitness, as the criterion for evolutionary success. His characterization of existence as fraught with competition, however, does not always correspond well with love and, as it turns out, does not accurately describe all creaturely interaction.

The Mendelian turn toward genetics in biology reframed the issues of love and altruism for contemporary biology. Biologists have largely regarded a creature's fitness as pertaining to its ability to pass on its genetic inheritance. The genetic turn in biology also has implications for explaining the altruistic actions of creatures. We examined theories in cooperation, kin selection, reciprocal altruism, reputational gain, group selection, parental self-sacrifice, and cost-benefit analyses. Although some prominent biologists use language suggesting that creatures are blindly programmed and therefore not genuinely free, we explored issues in self-organization, molecular spontaneity, and the Baldwin effect suggesting otherwise. Biological research provides both confirmation and challenges to widely and deeply held convictions about the nature of love.

Studies in cosmology give important clues and offer hypotheses concerning love. The big bang and expansion of the universe billions of years ago suggest that the conditions for life were present in the beginning. A theory of origins that acknowledges that the universe has been finely tuned and affirms that a loving Creator endows creation with freedom provides a powerful cosmological grounding for love. Whether the universe had an absolute beginning—*creatio ex nihilo*—plays an indirect but important role in how divine power and love might be understood in light of the problem of evil. The loving Creator who cannot coerce creatures should not be considered culpable for failing to prevent genuinely evil events.

In this concluding chapter, I address contributions that theology might make to love research in light of the definition of love offered and scientific research examined. The chapter does not contain, however, a general survey of theological love research currently available. Rather, this chapter provides the general structures of my own theology of love in light of research and theories in the social and natural sciences.

I begin with a brief look at the relationship between theology and science. This look sketches methodological issues significant for some of my later proposals. Following that, I propose a doctrine of divine love intended to be scientifically informed and theologically coherent. I show the importance of the parenthetical phrase "including God" found in the definition of love that I have proposed and explore the role that God plays in the creaturely promotion of overall well-being. I conclude the chapter by proposing a solution to the problem of evil. I argue that this solution is crucial for a robust theory of love that takes into account the social, natural, and theological sciences.

Can Research in the Social and Natural Sciences Inform Theology?

What does the science of love have to do with theology? For some religious traditions, the connection is obvious: theology requires sustained and serious reflection on love. Christian traditions, for instance, argue that God is love, and God wants creatures to love in some way analogous to how God loves. By this they typically mean that God's chief attribute is love, God loves creation, and creatures ought to love God, others, and themselves. Other religious traditions also emphasize love, whether divine, creaturely, or both. One of the most fundamental religious intuitions is that love resides at the heart of ultimate reality.[1]

Two related methodological issues are at stake in the connection between the science of love and theology. The first concerns

1. See Jacob Neusner and Bruce Chilton, eds., *Altruism in World Religions* (Washington, DC: Georgetown University Press, 2005); Thomas Jay Oord, *Science of Love: The Wisdom of Well-Being* (West Conshohocken, PA: Templeton Foundation Press, 2004), chap. 1.

the general relation of science to theology. The second concerns the adequacy of language to describe both Creator and creation. Getting clear about these methodological issues will help us when theological proposals are developed later in the chapter.

In recent decades, an increasing number of scholars have rejected the popular belief that science and theology are essentially at odds or entirely unrelated. This new wave of scholars differs from scientists who promote the view that science and theology are inherently irreconcilable, scientists such as Albert Einstein, Francis Crick, Richard Dawkins, Stephen Jay Gould, Stephen Hawking, Fred Hoyle, and Carl Sagan. Often overlooked is the fact that none of these scientists qualifies as an expert in theology.[2] In their relative theological ignorance, they promote what Ian Barbour calls "conflict" and "independence" as the correct ways to consider the connection between science and religion.[3] These approaches assume that science and theology are essentially at war or the two are entirely separate domains with nothing essentially in common.[4]

A close examination of theology, however, reveals that many theological traditions and doctrines are compatible with the general themes and structures of science.[5] Because scholars today are discovering this compatibility, a contemporary revolution is occurring

2. See Karl Giberson and Mariano Artigas, *Oracles of Science: Celebrity Scientists versus God and Religion* (Oxford: Oxford University Press, 2007).

3. Ian Barbour, *Religion in an Age of Science*, vol. 1 (San Francisco: HarperSanFrancisco, 1990), chap. 1.

4. For a particularly good attempt to show the compatibility between evolution and theology, see John F. Haught, *God after Darwin: A Theology of Evolution* (Boulder, CO: Westview Press, 2000).

5. John Hedley Brooke, for instance, has argued extensively that theology has not been predominantly antagonistic to science. "Serious scholarship in the history of science has revealed so extraordinarily rich and complex a relationship between science and religion," notes Brooke. "Conflicts allegedly between science and religion may turn out to be between rival scientific interests, or conversely between rival theological factions" (*Science and Religion: Some Historical Perspectives* [Cambridge: Cambridge University Press, 1991], 5). See also Karl W. Giberson and Donald A. Yerxa, *Species of Origins: America's Search for a Creation Story* (Lanham, MD: Rowman & Littlefield, 2002); Leslie A. Muray, *Liberal Protestantism and Science* (Westport, CT: Greenwood Press, 2008); and an authoritative rendering of the Galileo story in William R. Shea and Mariano Artigas, *Galileo in Rome: The Rise and Fall of a Troublesome Genius* (Oxford: Oxford University Press, 2003).

as scholars ask questions about God within the orbit of science and questions about science within the orbit of theology.[6]

Those at the fore of this revolution suggest various labels to describe the ways that science and theology are compatible. Barbour identifies two as "dialogue" and "integration."[7] Ted Peters and Ernan McMullin call the relation that science and theology best enjoy "consonance."[8] David Ray Griffin uses the word "harmony" to argue that science and theology can work together peacefully.[9] These labels suggest that science and theology can relate positively, although the two domains are not identical.[10] I join this revolution and assume that science and theology can relate positively.[11]

The second methodological issue at stake relates to the first. This is the question of whether language and theories derived from the creaturely world refer accurately to God. At its heart is the issue of whether creaturely categories or language correspond in a true way to the Creator. Theologians have debated the subtleties of the issue for centuries.[12]

Many contemporary scholars of science and theology meet this second methodological challenge by adopting a critical realist stance with regard to theological language and hypotheses. Critical realism rejects the notion that we can know with certainty that our language corresponds fully with the nature and activity of God. Critical realists suggest, however, that what creatures say

6. Ted Peters, "Theology and Science: Where Are We?" *Zygon* 31, no. 2 (1996): 323–43. See also Ted Peters and Martinez Hewlett, *Evolution from Creation to New Creation: Conflict, Conversation, and Convergence* (Nashville: Abingdon, 2003).

7. Barbour, *Religion in an Age of Science*, chap. 1.

8. Peters, "Theology and Science"; Ernan McMullin, "How Should Cosmology Relate to Theology?" in *The Sciences and Theology in the Twentieth Century*, ed. Arthur Peacocke (Notre Dame, IN: University of Notre Dame Press, 1981), 17–57.

9. David Ray Griffin, *Religion and Scientific Naturalism: Overcoming the Conflicts* (Albany: State University of New York Press, 2000), chap. 1.

10. Alan Padgett suggests a mutuality model in *Science and the Study of God: A Mutuality Model for Theology and Science* (Grand Rapids: Eerdmans, 2003).

11. One of the best overviews of various issues in science and religion is Philip Clayton, ed., *The Oxford Handbook of Religion and Science* (Oxford: Oxford University Press, 2006).

12. For a strong argument for the role of analogy, see Philip Rolnick, *Analogical Possibilities: How Words Refer to God* (Atlanta: Scholars Press, 1993).

about the Creator and creation may be at least partially correct. Models, analogies, hypotheses, and metaphors may refer truthfully to God and to the world. Just as critical realists in science adopt hypotheses to account for what seems true about the created world, so critical realists in theology adopt hypotheses for what seems true about God.[13]

Critical realism is important for proposing a theology of love informed by the social and natural sciences. What science, including our personal experiences, suggests about the nature of existence offers clues about how we should think of divine existence in general and divine love in particular. While allowing for differences between God and creatures, the critical realist can rightfully assume that important similarities also exist. What we consider loving in the creaturely realm we should also consider analogous, at least as a hypothesis, to loving in the divine realm. Theological instructions, such as "Be merciful, just as your Father is merciful" or "Be imitators of God . . . and live in love" (Luke 6:36; Eph. 5:1–2), can have meaning only if creaturely love corresponds in some way with God's love. In fact, love should be the primary analogy for language and categories comparing God and creatures.[14]

My own definition of love applies to what I believe should be regarded, generally speaking, as the love that both God and creatures express. Both divine and creaturely love entails intentionally responding to others to promote overall well-being. Love is the same in kind for both the Creator and the creatures. When we apply a

13. On these issues, see Paul Allen, *Ernan McMullin and Critical Realism in the Science-Theology Dialogue* (Burlington, VT: Ashgate, 2006); Ian Barbour, *Issues in Science and Religion* (Englewood Cliffs, NJ: Prentice-Hall, 1966); Philip Clayton, *Explanation from Physics to Theology: An Essay in Rationality and Religion* (New Haven: Yale University Press, 1989); Alister McGrath, *A Scientific Theology*, 3 vols. (Edinburgh: T&T Clark, 2001–2003); Nancey Murphy, *Theology in the Age of Scientific Reasoning* (Ithaca, NY: Cornell University Press, 1990); Arthur Peacocke, *Intimations of Reality: Critical Realism in Science and Religion* (Notre Dame, IN: University of Notre Dame Press, 1984); John Polkinghorne, *Reason and Reality: The Relationship between Science and Theology* (Philadelphia: Trinity Press International, 1991); Wentzel J. van Huyssteen, *Theology and the Justification of Faith: Constructing Theories in Systematic Theology* (Grand Rapids: Eerdmans, 1989).

14. For a strong argument on this, see Gary William Chartier, *The Analogy of Love: Divine and Human Love at the Center of Christian Theology* (Charlottesville, VA: Imprint Academic, 2007).

common definition both to creaturely and divine love, theological instructions pertaining to the *imitatio Dei* become meaningful. The possibility of imitating God makes sense.

One ancient and one contemporary theological tradition provide conceptual resources for the claim that an adequate definition of love applies both to creatures and to God. The ancient tradition derives from Hebrew Scripture but today typically takes the Latin label *imago Dei.* "Let us make humankind in our image," Genesis records God saying (Gen. 1:26). Theologians throughout the centuries have debated exactly how God created humans in the divine image and to what extent that image remains intact.[15] Some suggest that cognition is the link that God and humans share. Others say that the human ability to create is the *imago Dei.* We are created cocreators.[16] Still others suggest that the capacity for moral decisions is the way God created creatures in the divine image.[17] Some say that relationality is the image of God. Theologians suggest diverse proposals concerning the precise content of the *imago Dei.*

Some who consider love to be God's primary attribute also propose that we best understand the *imago Dei* in terms of love. "To be created in God's image," says Stephen Post, "means that we are created *for* love *by* love."[18] Michael Lodahl argues that the image of God is the capacity to love, and God renews this image in fallen humans. The restored image of God allows us, says Lodahl, "to

15. For an examination of original sin that takes into account evolution and sociobiology, see Jerry D. Korsmeyer, *Evolution and Eden: Balancing Original Sin and Contemporary Science* (New York: Paulist Press, 1998); Patricia A. Williams, *Doing without Adam and Eve: Sociobiology and Original Sin* (Minneapolis: Fortress, 2001).

16. Philip Hefner, *The Human Factor: Evolution, Culture, and Religion* (Minneapolis: Fortress, 1993).

17. Anna Case-Winters considers the *imago Dei* a "common calling" (*Reconstructing a Christian Theology of Nature: Down to Earth* [Aldershot: Ashgate, 2007]). H. Ray Dunning considers the image of God to be a relational category by which we are related to God, others, the church, the earth, and ourselves (*Reflecting the Divine Image: Christian Ethics in Wesleyan Perspective* [Downers Grove, IL: InterVarsity Press, 1998]). Ian A. McFarland considers the divine image in humans to be their identification as the body of Christ (*The Divine Image: Envisioning the Invisible God* [Minneapolis: Fortress, 2005]).

18. Stephen G. Post, *Unlimited Love: Altruism, Compassion, and Service* (Philadelphia: Templeton Foundation Press, 2003), 20.

care for all of God's creatures and to labor also to renew the face of the ground."[19]

Over the centuries, some theologians have suggested that the *imago Dei* represents the human distinctive. The image distinguishes humans from other creatures. "According to Scripture," argues Louis Berkhof, "the essence of man consists in this, that he is the image of God. As such he is distinguished from all other creatures and stands supreme as the head and crown of the entire creation."[20]

Given the increasing evidence that humans share much in common with nonhumans due to a common evolutionary history, however, we should question the notion that the *imago Dei* is the absolute dividing line between humans and nonhumans. "The anthropocentrism of the concept of the image of God requires revision today," argues Philip Hefner. "Whatever we say about humans applies, at least in potentiality, to all of nature. . . . Because the human is made up of the basic stuff of the planet, the image of God in that human being indicates that the world itself is capable of that special relationship to which the image of God points."[21] Of course, affirming *imago Dei* in this way does not mean that humans and nonhumans are identical. Profound differences exist. It remains an open question, however, whether these differences are ultimately matters of degree or of kind.

Although the questions of what the image of God entails and whether nonhumans share with humans the possibility of being made in the image of God are worth pursuing, my present purposes do not require any specific position on them. My present purpose is methodological. I simply claim that theistic traditions have sometimes affirmed the belief that at least some creatures bear the image of God. The *imago Dei* in creatures provides an important basis for establishing a definition of love that applies both to creatures and to the Creator. This connection makes possible the use of love language to describe that which creaturely and divine love share in common.

19. Michael Lodahl, *God of Nature and of Grace: Reading the World in a Wesleyan Way* (Nashville: Kingswood Books, 2003), 205.

20. Louis Berkhof, *Systematic Theology* (Grand Rapids: Eerdmans, 1953), 205.

21. Hefner, *Human Factor*, 239.

The contemporary tradition that provides a conceptual framework for a love definition applicable to both God and creatures derives from Alfred North Whitehead. It was Whitehead who wrote famously, "You cannot shelter theology from science, or science from theology; nor can you shelter either of them from metaphysics, or metaphysics from either of them. There is no short cut to truth."[22] Whitehead, Charles Hartshorne, David Ray Griffin, and others in the process tradition argue that we need a grand vision of how things work—a metaphysics—if we are to harmonize theology and the social and natural sciences. Only if we harmonize science and theology can the two make sense in relation to each other and to experience as we know it.[23]

Whitehead offers helpful technical language to account for the general features of existence, including divine existence. A key aspect in Whitehead's enterprise is his insight that "God is not to be treated as an exception to all metaphysical principles, invoked to save their collapse. He is their chief exemplification."[24] This insight is important, because theologians often attribute to God categories of being that make God different from creatures in *all* ways. When theologians consider God utterly different from creatures, key religious instructions such as "Be merciful, just as your Father is merciful" and "Be imitators of God . . . and live in love" become unintelligible.

Theologian Daniel Day Williams illustrates the importance of considering God's existence as metaphysically analogous to creaturely existence. Williams does so by noting the inadequacy of Paul Tillich's view that God is Being itself rather than a being sharing similarities with other beings. "'Being itself' is either the absolutely alone ONE, utterly beyond all categories," says Williams, "or it is the synthesis of all structures and beings. But can a synthesis of all structures be a loving being?"[25] The absolutely alone one

22. Alfred North Whitehead, *Religion in the Making: Lowell Lectures 1926* (1926; repr., New York: Fordham University Press, 1996), 79.

23. See Griffin, *Religion and Scientific Naturalism*.

24. Alfred North Whitehead, *Process and Reality: An Essay in Cosmology*, ed. David Ray Griffin and Donald W. Sherburne, corrected ed. (1929; repr., New York: Free Press, 1978), 343.

25. Daniel Day Williams, *The Spirit and the Forms of Love* (New York: Harper & Row, 1968), 126.

cannot have the relations with others that love requires. Instead, we should regard the divine being as a relational and purposive agent, says Williams, rather than existence itself.[26] If we consider God an agent metaphysically similar to other agents, what we say about love—for example, love involves responsive relations to others—can apply both to God and to creatures.

When the basic structures of God's existence comply with the metaphysical principles applying to all beings, we render claims about divine love intelligible. These words can make sense: "See what love the Father has given us, that we should be called the children of God; and that is what we are" (1 John 3:1). In this instance, divine love is analogous to parental love. If such analogies exist, scientific and theological research can help us better understand divine and creaturely love in terms of parental activity that promotes well-being. The social sciences can aid our ascertaining the character of parental love, and this makes it possible for us to grasp something of what divine love entails. Theology can help us better gauge what divine love looks like, and in this we identify what good parental love should entail. Rather than science and theology being sheltered from each other, each contributes to the truth about the love God and creatures express. Theology and science relate positively and become complementary.

God and the Turn to Love

Recent scientific research provides evidence that at least some humans, and apparently some nonhumans, express love. We have seen that creatures act in ways that promote well-being, and sometimes their primary motive is to enhance the well-being of others. However, at least three questions remain unanswered.

The first has to do with the breadth or extensivity of creaturely love. Can creatures respond intentionally to promote overall well-being, which may sometimes include promoting the well-being of outsiders and enemies? We encountered this question in the discussions of biology in chapter 4, but it is also a central concern

26. See also John B. Cobb Jr. "Being Itself and the Existence of God," in *The Existence of God: Essays from the Basic Issues Forum*, ed. John R. Jacobson and Robert Lloyd Mitchell (Lewiston, NY: Mellen, 1988), 5–19.

for the moral systems of various religious traditions. Can we love the other who is immensely different from ourselves?

The second question has to do with the role that God plays in promoting overall well-being. The majority of theological traditions argue that creaturely love requires divine action in some way. The definition of love that I proposed contains the parenthetical phrase "including God." This parenthetical insertion should not be interpreted as suggesting that God is an afterthought or secondary condition for love. Rather, as I will show in this chapter, God is the source, inspiration, and model of love. The insertion of "including God" in my definition of love is meant to propose that love is impossible without divine action. In light of this claim, we need to answer the question "Why does an adequate definition of love refer to the divine?" The answers to this question and the first interrelate.

The third question is one that has plagued believers for millennia. Many believe this question has become more important in the last century than in any previous one. It is reportedly the primary obstacle to faith for atheists and a source of great confusion for theists. We typically call this question the "problem of evil," and we might best frame it in this way: Why does the powerful God of love not prevent genuine evils from occurring? I addressed the problem of evil to some extent in chapter 5, but I conclude the book with my own concise answer to the theoretical aspect of this vital question.

We begin with the first question, which pertains to love's breadth in terms of loving enemies and outsiders. We saw in chapter 4 that contemporary biologists argue that kin selection, reciprocal altruism, and other theories generally explain altruistic action insofar as organisms act for the good of those near and dear. Other scientific disciplines have adopted versions of these hypotheses as well. These theories propose that the only candidates for receiving love are those expected to reciprocate love or those creatures genetically similar to the actor. These theories offer a general account for love of friends and family.

We also saw that group-selection advocates such as Elliott Sober and David Sloan Wilson suggest that altruists may assist those with a different genetic lineage and those unable to reciprocate the altruist's love. Altruists may offer such loving assistance in their own groups. Evolution favors groups whose members act for the good of fellow members. Groups composed of altruists flourish when competing with groups composed of egoists. Creatures may love colleagues, their communities, and fellow tribal members.

Prominent theories in biology cannot account well, however, for instances in which individuals act altruistically for the good of outsiders and opposition groups. Sober and Wilson admit that "group selection favors within group niceness and between group nastiness."[27] No good theory exists to account for the love expressed for strangers and enemies. The love of the good Samaritan remains unexplained.

David Sloan Wilson extends the group-selection hypothesis as an explanation for religion. Religious groups are "rapidly evolving entities adapting to their current environments," he says.[28] These entities have moral systems that define appropriate behaviors for their members and prevent subversion from within. In particular, he observes, "a religion instructs believers to behave for the benefit of their group."[29] Jews, early Christians, and Calvinists are examples of religious groups whose beliefs and rules benefit members. These member-benefiting beliefs and rules allow these groups to outcompete other religious groups. Religions that promote intramember cooperation survive and reproduce better than competitors whose members do not cooperate. However, religious groups do not promote well what Wilson calls "universal brotherhood."[30] Religions, says Wilson, seek only to benefit the faithful.

A glance at world history reveals instances of war between those avowing allegiances to differing religious traditions. Contemporary conflicts between Christians, Jews, and Muslims serve as painful illustrations of interreligious hostility. However, sometimes even groups within one religious tradition war among themselves. "Endless religious wars of Christian denominations and nations with one another, and a multitude of bloody revolutions and civil wars

27. Elliott Sober and David Sloan Wilson, *Unto Others: The Evolution and Psychology of Unselfish Behavior* (Cambridge, MA: Harvard University Press, 1998), 9.

28. David Sloan Wilson, *Darwin's Cathedral: Evolution, Religion, and the Nature of Society* (Chicago: University of Chicago Press, 2002), 35.

29. Ibid., 96.

30. Ibid., 217.

of one Christian faction with others," says Pitirim Sorokin, "glaringly testify to the enormous chasm between the Sermon on the Mount which the Christians preached and their fratricidal, most selfish, and un-Christian conduct."[31] Wilson's group-selection hypothesis seems verified at least in some cases.

Despite evidence of hatred or indifference toward enemies and outsiders, however, abundant evidence also exists that creatures at least sometimes love enemies and outsiders. We noted in previous chapters actual cases in which overall well-being has been promoted to the detriment of the individual or group. Theories in sociobiology do not account well for this drive and occasional practice of promoting overall well-being.

Loving all others is an ethic commanded by at least some religious traditions and apparently put into practice at least some of the time. Some religious traditions urge their members to promote overall well-being as a means to overcome interpersonal, intertribal, and interreligious hostilities. Religious people, many of them believing they are responding to the call of God, act self-sacrificially for the good of adversaries, outcasts, the marginalized, and even nonhumans.

We need a theory to account both for the truth that altruism can benefit those near and dear and in one's group and for the truth that sometimes creatures act to benefit outsiders and enemies.[32] The social and natural sciences we examined earlier do not account for unlimited love.

One theory for why at least some humans can love all others says that God provides unnatural, or supernatural, power to enable humans to love outsiders and enemies. In their natural state, says this theory, humans promote only their own good and the well-being of those near and dear. Proponents of this theory say that science explains natural love, but God supernaturally empowers at least some to go above and beyond nature. Often part of this theory is

---

31. Pitirim A. Sorokin, *The Ways and Power of Love: Types, Factors, and Techniques of Moral Transformation* (1954; repr., Philadelphia: Templeton Foundation Press, 2002), 179–80.

32. For a strong argument for a universal ethic based on divine love, see Frank G. Kirkpatrick, *A Moral Ontology for a Theistic Ethic: Gathering the Nations in Love and Justice* (Burlington, VT: Ashgate, 2003).

the notion that creatures naturally express *eros* but require divine action to express *agape*.

Theologian Martin C. D'Arcy advocates the theory that creatures naturally love those near and dear but need supernatural help to love outsiders and enemies. "We can advance a high theory of love by making full use of natural love," says D'Arcy, "but the keynote of it will always be possessiveness. Our neighbours will be loved like to ourselves; they will be as it were another self."[33] D'Arcy argues that the solution to loving outsiders and enemies is *agape*. "In Christian Agape the complete revelation of love is given," he says. "Here the finite is lifted to a new degree of being, whose limit is measured only by the necessity of its remaining a human person. This new life which is thus set going is a pure gift and beyond the natural capacity of the finite human person."[34]

The natural/supernatural scheme that D'Arcy and like-minded theologians advocate presents conceptual problems. It implies, for instance, that we can adequately understand important aspects of creaturely love without reference to God. Divine inspiration is necessary only when nature proves insufficient to empower us to love those whom we consider difficult. This view is unsatisfactory to theists who want to affirm that God is the source and inspiration of all love, not just some.

The natural/supernatural scheme is also vulnerable to the God-of-the-gaps problem, whereby science is believed to explain fully all but a few occurrences. These unexplained events, says the God-of-the-gaps theory, require an appeal to the mysterious workings of deity. When science eventually provides hypotheses to explain fully what previously was inexplicable, however, divine action provides no explanatory role either ontologically or epistemologically. The progress of science eliminates any function for the supernatural, and the gap closes.

Instead of adopting the natural/supernatural scheme in which we try to explain creaturely love without reference to God, I suggest that an adequate explanation of all creaturely love must include a

33. Martin C. D'Arcy, *The Mind and Heart of Love: Lion and Unicorn; A Study in Eros and Agape* (New York: Meridian, 1956), 363.
34. Ibid., 370. This quotation does not represent D'Arcy's only view on the relation of nature and grace. He presents a kaleidoscope of opinions on the relation, with no coherent explanation of the differences.

necessary role for divine action. Love for oneself, love for those near and dear, and love for outsiders and enemies require God's activity. To put it another way, we require a God hypothesis to account for how limited creatures can express both limited and unlimited love. This hypothesis must include a robust role for incessant divine action rather than seeing God's influence as an occasional add-on. Further, this hypothesis incorporates rather than ignores the scientific work on love that we explored earlier.

In contrast to the natural/supernatural scheme, another theory suggests that only God expresses authentic love. This theory, which I call "divine unilateralism," contends that creatures cannot love at all. Any expression of genuine love is entirely an act of God, and creatures contribute nothing. Only God loves.

Anders Nygren, perhaps the twentieth century's most influential love theologian, advocates divine unilateralism. Nygren says that the only authentic love is *agape*, and God is the only agent who expresses this authentic love. "The Christian has nothing of his own to give," he says. "The love which he shows his neighbor is the love which God has infused in him."[35] Nygren likens creatures to tubes that pass genuine love received from above to others below. The tubes/creatures do not contribute to the character or shape of this love.[36] "It is God's own Agape which seeks to make its way out into the world through the Christian as its channel," Nygren asserts.[37] "What we have here is a purely theocentric love, in which all choice on man's part is excluded."[38]

There are many reasons to reject divine unilateralism. For centuries, theologians have noted that it implies absolute determinism, divine predestination, and lack of intrinsic creaturely value. Divine unilateralism entails the notion that God acts single-handedly to secure any good that occurs, because inherently evil creatures are incapable of promoting well-being. We should reject divine unilateralism for its understanding of divine causation.

We should also reject divine unilateralism for what it implies about science. It denies that science tells us anything important

35. Anders Nygren, *Agape and Eros*, trans. Philip S. Watson (1930; repr., New York: Harper & Row, 1953), 129.
36. Ibid., 735, 741.
37. Ibid., 218.
38. Ibid., 213.

about creaturely love. Science is superfluous; all the scientific love research that I have explored in this book ultimately amounts to nothing. Theology is not only queen of the sciences if divine unilateralism is correct, but also the only science describing what actually occurs in creation.

Divine unilateralism also permits sidestepping any responsibility to love, because all responsibility rests on God. When God is believed to be the sole cause and finisher of all that is good, creatures should not consider themselves liable or accountable for promoting well-being. Divine unilateralism undercuts our motivation to love.

Instead of adopting divine unilateralism, an adequate explanation of love must include a necessary role for both God and creatures. Creaturely love is not the work of God alone. Creatures should not be considered tubes, channels, or conduits through which God unilaterally promotes well-being. Instead, we should claim that creatures also love when responding appropriately to divine love. Creatures play a role in love. An adequate hypothesis for how creatures express limited and unlimited love must include reference to creaturely contributions.

Previous chapters offered evidence that creatures sometimes act to promote well-being. I assume that this evidence tells us something true about existence in general and creaturely love in particular. We need a God hypothesis that affirms the scientific evidence while making theological sense.[39] It must be a God hypothesis that avoids the natural/supernatural scheme, which proposes that divine action is an occasional add-on and only sometimes necessary for love.[40] And this hypothesis must reject divine unilateralism, which says that God is the only loving agent and that scientific research on love is ultimately pointless.

39. For important contributions to a theology of love, see George M. Newlands, *Theology of the Love of God* (Atlanta: John Knox, 1980); Williams, *Spirit and the Forms of Love*; Kevin J. Vanhoozer, ed., *Nothing Greater, Nothing Better: Theological Essays on the Love of God* (Grand Rapids: Eerdmans, 2001); Mildred Bangs Wynkoop, *A Theology of Love: The Dynamic of Wesleyanism* (Kansas City, MO: Beacon Hill Press, 1972).

40. F. LeRon Shults combines the notions of divine love and divine power into a category he calls "omnipotent love" (*Reforming the Doctrine of God: After the Philosophical Turn to Relationality* [Grand Rapids: Eerdmans, 2005]).

An adequate God hypothesis would be especially helpful if it accounted well for why creatures sometimes love those near and dear but also sometimes love outsiders and enemies. If this hypothesis about God included an empirically oriented explanation of how limited creatures express both limited and unlimited love, we would have a proposal that could ultimately marry theology and science in the name of love. Such matrimony could bear significant fruit.

Full-Orbed Divine Love

Obviously, the attributes and activity that we postulate of God are central to an adequate hypothesis about God's action in the world of science. I now turn to propose a doctrine of God adequate both to science and to a theology of love.

My own proposal of an adequate doctrine of God begins with the claim that love is an essential divine attribute.[41] It is necessarily the case that God acts intentionally, in sympathetic response to others (which includes past divine actions), to promote overall well-being. Loving others is not an arbitrary divine decision but rather an aspect of God's eternal, unchanging nature. To put it negatively: God cannot not love.[42] With the writer of 1 John, I affirm that "God is love" (1 John 4:8).

In suggesting that love is an essential aspect of the divine nature, however, I am not suggesting that God has no choice whatsoever with regard to love.[43] *That* God will love others is necessarily the

41. Instead of "essential," some philosophers prefer "superessential" to refer to divine attributes. The latter term implies that a particular attribute applies to God in all possible worlds. I mean for "essential" to imply the same.

42. Here I affirm both the theology of Jürgen Moltmann and some of the philosophical conclusions of William L. Rowe. Moltmann argues that divine freedom does not include the freedom not to love (*The Trinity and the Kingdom: The Doctrine of God* [San Francisco: Harper & Row, 1981], 52–56). Rowe argues that God is not free to do some things. For example, God is not free to make something less than the best of all possible worlds (*Can God Be Free?* [Oxford: Clarendon Press, 2004]). As I point out in the text, though, I do think that God is free in other ways.

43. For a stimulating discussion of the relation between the divine will and divine nature with regard to love, see various essays in John Polkinghorne, ed., *The Work of Love: Creation as Kenosis* (Grand Rapids: Eerdmans, 2001), especially

case; *how* God loves others is a free choice on God's part.[44] This distinction requires further explanation.

In ongoing love relations, we can rest assured that God will always act intentionally, in sympathetic response to others (including God's own past actions), to promote overall well-being. This relentless, steadfast love is a necessary aspect of what it means to be divine. The fact that God loves others, therefore, is an aspect of God's eternal essence.[45]

The manner in which God chooses to promote overall well-being, however, arises from how God sympathetically responds to others. There is neither a formula nor circumstances exterior to God that entirely determine what these divine choices will be. How God loves others, therefore, is a matter of the divine will. How God loves is a free choice on God's part, and in this sense, God freely chooses love.

The issue of how God loves involves more than questions of divine freedom. It also involves questions of the forms that divine love takes. Just as creaturely love sometimes takes the form of *agape, eros,* or *philia,* and these forms can mix, I propose that God also expresses *agape, eros,* and *philia,* and sometimes these forms mix. In *agape,* God intentionally responds to ill-being by promoting overall well-being. God repays evil with good. God's *eros* appreciates the value of others and seeks to enhance that value. God calls creation good and desires to increase its beauty. God expresses *philia* by working cooperatively with creatures to increase the common good. We are God's fellow workers. God's love is full-orbed.

The notion that God's love is full-orbed presupposes that God is a relational being. As relational, God is affected by those with whom God relates. For some time, relational theologians have rejected the idea that God is an aloof and distant monarch un-

---

Ian Barbour, "God's Power: A Process View" (1–20); Keith Ward, "Cosmos and Kenosis" (152–66); Paul S. Fiddes, "Creation out of Love" (167–91).

44. On this, see Thomas Jay Oord, "Divine Love," in *Philosophy of Religion: Introductory Essays,* ed. Thomas Jay Oord (Kansas City, MO: Beacon Hill Press, 2003), 93–107.

45. For a scholarly analysis of the notion that love is an essential divine attribute, see Mark Lloyd Taylor, *God Is Love: A Study in the Theology of Karl Rahner* (Atlanta: Scholars Press, 1986).

influenced by others.[46] Instead, relational theologians affirm that God suffers and is passible, to use the classic language. This means that God is influenced by the ups and downs, joys and sorrows, sins and loves of others. God truly cares. God is the best and most moved mover.[47]

46. Ronald Goetz notes that "the rejection of the ancient doctrine of divine impassibility has become theological commonplace" ("The Suffering God: The Rise of a New Orthodoxy," *Christian Century* 103, no. 13 [1986]: 385). The list of those who deny divine immutability and affirm divine suffering, at least in some way, is long. Works on that list, in addition to works by process theologians and philosophers, include the following: Marcus J. Borg, *The God We Never Knew: Beyond Dogmatic Religion to a More Authentic Contemporary Faith* (San Francisco: HarperSanFrancisco, 1997); Barry L. Callen, *God as Loving Grace: The Biblically Revealed Nature and Work of God* (Nappanee, IN: Evangel, 1996); Wendy Farley, *Tragic Vision and Divine Compassion: A Contemporary Theodicy* (Louisville: Westminster John Knox, 1990); Paul S. Fiddes, *The Creative Suffering of God* (Oxford: Clarendon Press, 1988); Peter Forrest, *Developmental Theism: From Pure Will to Unbounded Love* (Oxford: Oxford University Press, 2007); Elizabeth A. Johnson, *She Who Is: The Mystery of God in Feminist Theological Discourse* (New York: Crossroad, 1996); Catherine Mowry LaCugna, *God for Us: The Trinity and Christian Life* (San Francisco: HarperSanFrancisco, 1991); Jung Young Lee, *God Suffers for Us: A Systematic Inquiry into a Concept of Divine Passibility* (The Hague: Marinus Nijhoff, 1974); Geddes MacGregor, *He Who Lets Us Be: A Theology of Love* (New York: Seabury, 1975); John Macquarrie, *Principles of Christian Theology* (London: SCM Press, 1977); Warren McWilliams, *The Passion of God: Divine Suffering in Contemporary Protestant Theology* (Macon, GA: Mercer University Press, 1985); Jürgen Moltmann, *The Crucified God: The Cross of Christ as the Foundation and Criticism of Christian Theology*, trans. R. A. Wilson and John Bowden (New York: Harper & Row, 1974); idem, *God in Creation: An Ecological Doctrine of Creation* (London, SCM Press, 1985); Moltmann, *Trinity and the Kingdom*, 42–47; Thomas V. Morris, *Our Idea of God: An Introduction to Philosophical Theology* (Downers Grove, IL: InterVarsity Press, 1991); Clark H. Pinnock et al., *The Openness of God: A Biblical Challenge to the Traditional Understanding of God* (Downers Grove, IL: InterVarsity Press, 1994); John Sanders, *The God Who Risks: A Theology of Divine Providence*, rev. ed. (Downers Grove, IL: InterVarsity Press, 2007); S. Paul Schilling, *God and Human Anguish* (Nashville: Abingdon, 1977); Dorothee Sölle, *Suffering*, trans. Everett R. Kalin (London: Darton, Longman & Todd, 1975); Richard Swinburne, *The Coherence of Theism* (Oxford: Clarendon Press, 1977); Keith Ward, *Rational Theology and the Creativity of God* (Oxford: Blackwell, 1982).

47. The notion that God is the most moved mover, rather than the unmoved mover, derives from Abraham Heschel. Various process theologians employ the phrase as well. Clark Pinnock titles a book that promotes the idea that creatures affect God *Most Moved Mover: A Theology of God's Openness* (Grand Rapids: Baker Academic, 2001).

Although creatures affect this relational God, God's nature as love remains unchanging. God's eternal nature is fixed. God's nature is love, and that nature never alters. Creaturely conditions and responses influence the particular way—*agape, eros, philia*—God chooses to love others. We have seen that science suggests that a creature's own characteristics and its relations with others influence the form and extent of that creature's love. Similarly, the theology I propose suggests that God's own characteristics and God's relations with others influence the forms and extent of divine love.

God is always present to all creatures, and God's loving omnipresence plays a crucial role for understanding divine action in relation to creation. Divine omnipresence pertains directly to love's breadth. Because God is present to all creatures and because God loves perfectly, all creatures are directly loved.

After divine love, omnipresence may be the divine attribute that classical theologians least emphasize. By omnipresence, I mean that God is present to all things. Nothing exists that is not graced by the presence of deity.[48] We might say that God is omni-immanent, as long as we do not regard omni-immanence as negating divine transcendence altogether. To say that God is omnipresent does not require one to say that all things are divine, however. Distinctions between creation and Creator remain, and these important distinctions are the basis for divine transcendence.

Some philosophers and theologians have called God "the Soul of the universe" to describe God's all pervasiveness.[49] If one understands a soul to be present to and influencing all parts of one's body, the label is appropriate. Instead of referring to God as the Soul of the universe, however, some today adopt the label "panentheism" to emphasize God's immanent omnipresence without denying divine transcendence.[50] God penetrates the entire created

48. For a Wesleyan reading of divine omnipresence, see Michael Lodahl, *God of Nature and of Grace: Reading the World in a Wesleyan Way* (Nashville: Kingswood Books, 2003), especially chaps. 4, 6.

49. See Michael Lodahl's examination of John Wesley's rendering of God as the "Soul of the universe" in ibid., chap. 4.

50. A number of scholars have embraced panentheism in recent years. One of the better accounts of the diverse meanings that this label carries is the collection of

realm, but the divine being is neither identical to nor exhausted by the universe. God is distinct from others, having divine essence, constitution, and agency. Elsewhere, I have also suggested that "theocosmocentrism" might be a helpful label to identify God as the one intimately and everlastingly present to all that exists in our cosmos or any other.[51]

The love of an omnipresent God is all pervasive, optimally sensitive, and perfectly influential. We have seen that God is present to all things as the all-pervasive one. God enters moment by moment into give-and-receive interaction with others. In this interaction, God is omnirelational. God acts as both the ideal recipient and the ideal contributor. As the ideal recipient, God takes in the experiences of all others.

God does not look at creation from a distance, as a spectator on the sidelines who occasionally gets in the game. Rather, God is present to all creatures and all creation at all times, and God experiences the experiences of others immediately upon their occurrence. Because God is the all-embracing one who sympathizes fully with all others, God possesses the capacity to assess flawlessly what the promotion of overall well-being requires at any particular moment in any particular place.

God not only loves incessantly and by virtue of divine omnipresence loves all others; God also calls creatures, both human and nonhuman, to promote overall well-being. In this activity of calling creatures, God is the ideal contributor. This contributory call entails empowering and inspiring creatures to love given the

---

essays *In Whom We Live and Move and Have Our Being: Panentheistic Reflections on God's Presence in a Scientific World*, ed. Philip Clayton and Arthur R. Peacocke (Grand Rapids: Eerdmans, 2004), especially Michael W. Brierley, "Naming a Quiet Revolution: The Pantheistic Turn in Modern Theology" (1–15); David Ray Griffin, "Panentheism: A Postmodern Revelation" (36–47); Philip Clayton, "Pantheism Today: A Constructive Systematic Evaluation" (249–64).

51. I use the word *theocosmocentrism* to distinguish my own view from the variety of panentheisms that scholars have adopted (for these varieties, see Clayton and Peacocke, *In Whom We Live*). By it, I mean that God has always been related to some universe or another, and God did not create the universe from absolutely nothing (*creatio ex nihilo*) (see Thomas Jay Oord, *The Nature of Love: A Theology* [St. Louis: Chalice Press, 2010]). Some panentheists, by contrast, affirm *creatio ex nihilo* and the notion that God existed alone prior to God's creation of this universe.

capacities of each individual.[52] The God hypothesis I propose suggests that all creatures feel God's direct, causal call.

God's loving omnipresence provides empirical grounds for hypotheses about divine action in relation to creaturely love.[53] The call to love that God gives each creature is, in one sense, no different from the causal influence that other creatures exert. In a universe of cause and effect, divine efficient causation is a direct objective cause of the same metaphysical kind as creaturely causes. No appeal to mysterious divine action is necessary; special pleas to inexplicable supernaturalism are not required. God's influence on creatures breaks no theoretical principles pertaining to the metaphysical laws that apply to all existents. Whitehead's plea that we not treat God as an exception to the metaphysical principles is heeded.[54]

52. The Christian doctrine of prevenient grace, as understood in the Wesleyan tradition, offers a similar concept of love as entailing divine call and creaturely response. Prevenient grace might best be described as God acting in each moment to empower creatures to respond freely and then wooing them to choose responses that increase overall well-being. Creatures who respond appropriately to the specific calls of an omnipresent, omnirelational God will act in ways that promote overall well-being. See Randy L. Maddox, *Responsible Grace: John Wesley's Practical Theology* (Nashville: Kingswood Books, 1994); Wynkoop, *Theology of Love*. For the importance of prevenient grace in religious pluralism, see Al Truesdale, with Keri Mitchell, *With Cords of Love: A Wesleyan Response to Religious Pluralism* (Kansas City, MO: Beacon Hill Press, 2006).

53. For a proposal of how psychological perspectives on love can inform theology, see Alan C. Tjeltveit, "God's Love Encountering Human Love: Psychological Perspectives Informing (and Informed by) Theology," in *Visions of Agapé: Problems and Possibilities in Human and Divine Love*, ed. Craig A. Boyd (Burlington, VT: Ashgate, 2008), 103–22.

54. If God exerts causal influence as an efficient cause and relationally assesses the states of all others, God must possess both physical and mental aspects. To say that God has a physical aspect that exerts causal influence, however, need not conflict with the claim made by most theistic religions that God is a spirit. It does conflict, however, with the positivistic claim that the physical aspects of all beings must be perceptible by a human's five senses. But positivism so understood cannot account for inevitable aspects of existence, let alone justify its own agenda. I propose that (1) a spiritual entity exists (and perhaps there are more), (2) spiritual entity exerts efficient causation, and (3) we perceive the influence of this entity nonsensorily. God is a spirit whose invisible physicality affects others in a way analogous to the physical influence, whether sensory or nonsensory, that other beings exert. For a similar view of divine action, see Keith Ward, *Divine Action: Examining God's Role in an Open and Emergent Universe* (Philadelphia: Templeton Foundation Press, 2007).

God's call to love differs in some ways, however, from the influence that creatures exert, although these ways do not treat God as an exception to the metaphysical principles pertaining to all beings. God's call differs from the causation of creatures, first, in that God always influences creatures to act in ways that optimize overall well-being. God's essence is love, and this means that God loves relentlessly. God's power invariably urges but does not coerce all things toward the common good. By contrast, creatures sometimes influence others to choose ill-being. Whereas creaturely love is more or less sporadic, God's love is steadfast and never fails.

God's causal action in our cause-and-effect universe differs from other creatures, second, in that only God is a necessary cause in every creature's love. Without divine influence, no creature can love. Divine action is required for creatures to live, and move, and have their being. Creatures are, to use the words of theologian Friedrich Schleiermacher, "utterly dependent" on God to be empowered and inspired to love.[55] By contrast, any particular creature is a contingent cause for the love that creatures express. No creature requires the influence of another specific creature to promote overall well-being, although all creatures relate to other creatures.

Third, God's causal call differs from creaturely causation in that God takes into account the influence of others and persuades each creature to respond in a way that promotes overall well-being. God presents the possible actions to creatures, and those options arise from past creaturely and divine actions. God inspires creatures to love, given what is possible in the particular circumstances that each creature faces.[56] God's call is situation-specific.

55. Friedrich Schleiermacher, *The Christian Faith*, 2nd ed. (1830; repr., Edinburgh: T&T Clark, 1989). The translation of *schlechthinig* as "utter" is my own, but this translation is not unique to me.

56. The notion that God offers possible options for action to creatures is perhaps best articulated in the writing of many process theologians. See, for instance, John B. Cobb Jr., *A Christian Natural Theology, Based on the Thought of Alfred North Whitehead* (Philadelphia: Westminster, 1965); David Ray Griffin, *Reenchantment without Supernaturalism: A Process Philosophy of Religion* (Ithaca, NY: Cornell University Press, 2001); Marjorie Hewett Suchocki, *God-Christ-Church: A Practical Guide to Process Theology* (New York: Crossroad, 1982); Whitehead, *Process and Reality*.

Process theologians in the tradition of Whitehead have called this presentation of possible actions a creature's "initial aim."[57] I claim that this aim includes God's call to a particular creature to love in a particular moment and in a particular way. God takes into account the influence of all others when presenting this call. God knows creatures even better than they know themselves, and God offers each creature options for how each may come to be.

Given that God's causal agency is required for creaturely love, the parenthetical insertion in my love definition of the phrase "including God" should be clearer. God always acts to promote overall well-being, and every creature begins each moment of existence "feeling" or "hearing" that call. God is the only necessary cause among the many causes that each creature experiences. The omnipresent God knows all and can lovingly provide opportunities for love to creatures, given the diversity of the past and the present environment. In short, God's role in love is not parenthetical, in the sense of less important. Without God, love is impossible.

The similarities and differences between the divine agent and creaturely agents provide the basis for overcoming problems inherent in the natural/supernatural and divine unilateralism schemes. Divine causation is neither an occasional add-on nor an eclipse of creaturely causation. Creaturely love requires God's empowering and inspiring call, and yet God does not interrupt the natural causal relations that creatures require to love. When creatures love, they synergistically respond to the divine call to promote overall well-being.

God's causal influence in the divine-creaturely relationship that I advocate is not the same in content and effectiveness for all creatures.[58] Rather, God exerts oscillating and diverse causal efficacy.[59]

---

57. For a constructive doctrine of election drawing from Karl Barth and process thought, see Donna Bowman, *The Divine Decision: A Process Doctrine of Election* (Louisville: Westminster John Knox, 2002).

58. See my essay, "Love as a Methodological and Metaphysical Source for Science and Theology," *Wesleyan Theological Journal* 45, no. 1 (Spring 2010).

59. This is similar to what David Ray Griffin calls "variable divine influence." God's influence on others, says Griffin, is always formally the same but variable in content (*Reenchantment without Supernaturalism*, 147).

The content of God's call to love depends on the particularities of each creature in each moment. Science shows us that creatures are diverse, and they dwell in diverse environments. God's diverse causation depends on what possibilities for the future are genuinely available for instantiation in the present moment. God's specific influence on an electron, for instance, will be different in content from God's influence on a worm. God's specific causal call for a child will be different in content from God's call for an adult. God's omniscient assessment of all conditions provides God with the resources to tailor perfectly the call to love for each creature. The diversity of the divine vision and the diversity of creation generate the diversity of divine causation. How God loves is pluriform.

The variability of a particular divine call's effectiveness, however, is not based on God's decision to exert either maximal or minimal influence. God consistently exerts maximal creative causality. God's desire for overall well-being prompts utmost divine effort to enhance the common good, given what is possible in each moment. God never rests passively, never waits uninterested, and never needs prayerful prompting to love. Prayer can affect the particular ways that God exerts maximal loving influence, but it is never a question whether God will love at all. Although divine love is diverse, it is also relentless. God never takes a holiday from love.

Divine causation oscillates in its effectiveness. This oscillation is neither random nor routine. Instead, creatures respond in various ways to God's causal calls, and these responses may be appropriate or inappropriate in varying degrees. When creatures respond well, God's activity to promote overall well-being is most effective. God's activity is least clearly expressed when an event profoundly undercuts overall well-being.

Some creatures are highly complex and possess a greater degree of freedom and information richness. God presents to them a vast array of possibilities in each moment. God empowers complex creatures to choose among these possibilities and inspires them to choose that which promotes overall well-being. When creatures respond appropriately to God's call to love, the common good heightens. Righteousness rains like rivers when mercy reigns supreme.

To say that God's causal influence oscillates, however, does not mean that God is inconsistent. God acts uniformly when inspiring and empowering each creature in each moment of life. The fact that God loves all creation is unwavering and uniform. By "uniform," I mean that God calls each creature to act to promote overall well-being. In this, all creatures feel divine causation in the same formal way. To say that divine causation oscillates does not mean that God chooses sometimes to be more influential and other times to remain relatively uninfluential. Instead, God's nature as love prompts God to exert the most influence possible in any situation. God does not love at half-throttle. The uniformity aspect of God's call is God's call to promote the common good. "Oscillation" refers to the way creatures respond appropriately or inappropriately to God's steadfast, yet form-varying, love.

Given this hypothesis of what God might be like and how God might act, I am now ready to suggest how limited creatures might express unlimited love. While the extensivity of localized creatures is necessarily limited, the one whose awareness is universal constantly influences them. This omnipresent being assesses in each moment what each creature should do to promote the common good. Only an omnipresent and omniscient being knows what each local creature should do to promote overall well-being at any one time.

Creatures can express unlimited love because they have access to the one with an unlimited perspective. Pitirim Sorokin might say that unlimited love requires maximal extensivity.[60] In the scheme I propose, finitude, intrinsically narrow sympathies, and restricted extensivity do not prevent creatures from contributing to the common good. Our maximally extensive God envisions the good of the whole and communicates what contribution each creature might make. The communication not only involves the possibility for how each creature might love, but also provides the power that each creature requires to live and move and have its being.

Most of the time, the best way a particular creature might promote overall well-being is to act in ways that simultaneously promote the creature's own well-being and the well-being of those near and dear. In an interrelated universe, actors often enjoy mutual benefits as they relate. Sometimes, however, promoting overall well-being requires self-sacrifice for the good of those near and dear. Scientific studies verify that creatures sometimes act self-sacrificially

60. Sorokin, *Ways and Power of Love*, 16.

for the good of those genetically similar to themselves or for the good of fellow group members. Other times, love involves acting for one's own well-being at the expense of some others. This self-affirming action can enhance overall well-being, despite loss to some others. Self-love that deprives resources from some others can sometimes be appropriate.

My hypothesis that God's love is all pervasive, optimally sensitive, and perfectly influential provides grounds to affirm that creatures sometimes act for the good of outsiders and enemies. A universal, maximally extensive God inspires and empowers confined creatures to promote universal brother- and sisterhood. Limited creatures express unlimited love if they respond appropriately to the call of the omnipresent one who knows what the common good requires and assesses perfectly what each creature can contribute. Because of God, good Samaritans are possible.

When we do regard the omnipresent God as acting in accordance with the universal laws of cause and effect, we find empirical grounds to hypothesize that God causally influences creatures in ways that encourage the enhancement of overall well-being. This causal efficacy oscillates and its content varies, depending on the situation and its agents. When we regard God as a necessary cause for all creaturely existence, it is plausible to speculate that all creatures rely on God when choosing to love outsiders and enemies, those near and dear, and even themselves. God is an objective though invisible agent, and creatures perceive divine causality. God's causal activity serves as the ground and inspiration for all creaturely love. We love, because God first loves us.

We should not think that creatures know with absolute certainty the specificity of God's calls, however. We can affirm that all creatures have access to the universal agent who calls them to promote the common good, but we need not also affirm that creatures always "hear" that call clearly. Creaturely limitations remain. Ambiguity, to varying degrees, characterizes reality. Habitual or momentary sin can hinder our ability to perceive God's call as clearly as we otherwise might. We discern God's moment-by-moment calls in the context of a wide variety of relations, emotions, and obligations. God's influence is part of a multilateral array of influences. Our ultimate justification for choosing one way to express love rather than another is the imprecise intuition that God calls us to act in such a way.

Tools, practices, insights, and wisdom are available to help creatures better discern God's call to love. Over the millennia, religious people have discovered means by which they can assess with greater accuracy, but rarely if ever with absolute certainty, God's leading. Religious people improve their skills at discernment when they engage in activities such as contemplation, living in loving communities, confession, worship practices, education, meditation on sacred Scriptures, and following exemplars and saints. Some ways of living enhance our ability to detect divine appeals.

Science also has a role to play in improving the discerning capacity of creatures. Research can help refine our expectations for what love might require. Science can serve as a means to help us focus on the real limits and possibilities that each creature faces as it determines how best to express love. The science of love is essential to improving discernment.[61]

Essential Kenosis and the Evil in the World

Having answered the first two questions posed at the outset, I conclude with the third. It would be strange to offer a theology of love informed by the sciences without noting and then removing what is widely regarded the single greatest obstacle to believing that a loving deity exists at all.[62] That obstacle is the problem of evil. I conclude, therefore, with an answer to the third question noted earlier in this chapter: Why does this God of love not prevent genuine evil from occurring?

Before addressing this problem, I should respond to those who would question the brashness of the claim that I can resolve the problem of evil. For some, an adequate answer is inherently impos-

61. See Oord, *Science of Love*.
62. For arguments from scientists for the compatibility between belief in God and contemporary science, see Francis S. Collins, *The Language of God: A Scientist Presents Evidence for Belief* (New York: Free Press, 2006); Darrel R. Falk, *Coming to Peace with Science: Bridging the Worlds between Faith and Biology* (Downers Grove, IL: InterVarsity Press, 2004); Karl Giberson, *Saving Darwin: How to Be a Christian and Believe in Evolution* (New York: HarperOne, 2008).

sible. It strikes these critics as hubris that someone should claim to have solved the problem of evil.

My response to this worry is both to qualify what I mean by an adequate answer and to respond boldly that my answer really does solve the problem of evil. To the qualifying point: I offer a solution to the theoretical aspect of the problem of evil. A theoretical solution answers the question of why God does not prevent genuinely evil occurrences. I am not offering an answer for how precisely we are to deal with the various events of actual evil in the world. I do not have all the specific answers to how we can prevent all evil, and I do not offer comprehensive counseling for those who suffer from pain. The answer I offer removes the theoretical barriers that plague both those who choose not to believe that God exists on these grounds and those who believe in God but remain puzzled by the occurrence of evil.

Although the problem of evil has been an obstacle to faith for millennia, the emergence of evolutionary theory has raised the issue in a new way.[63] The poet Alfred Tennyson ponders the impact of evolutionary theory on our understanding of evil and the apparent purposelessness of life in his masterful poem "In Memoriam." Here are a few especially pertinent lines:

> Are God and Nature then at strife,
>   That Nature lends such evil dreams?
>   So careful of the type she seems,
>   So careless of the single life;
> That I, considering everywhere
>   Her secret meaning in her deeds,
>   And finding that of fifty seeds
>   She often brings but one to bear,
>
> . . . .
> "So careful of the type?" but no.
>   From scarped cliff and quarried stone
>   She cries, "A thousand types are gone:
>   I care for nothing, all shall go.

63. Important work in tackling the problem of evil while taking Christian theology of love and evolutionary theory seriously includes Sjoerd L. Bonting, *Creation and Double Chaos: Science and Theology in Discussion* (Philadelphia: Fortress, 2005); Christopher Southgate, *The Groaning of Creation: God, Evolution, and the Problem of Evil* (Louisville: Westminster John Knox, 2008).

> "Thou makest thine appeal to me:
>   I bring to life, I bring to death:
>   The spirit does but mean the breath:
>   I know no more." And he, shall he,
> Man, her last work, who seem'd so fair,
>   Such splendid purpose in his eyes,
>   Who roll'd the psalm to wintry skies,
>   Who built him fanes of fruitless prayer,
> Who trusted God was love indeed
>   And love Creation's final law—
>   Tho' Nature, red in tooth and claw
>   With ravine, shriek'd against his creed—
> Who loved, who suffer'd countless ills,
>   Who battled for the True, the Just,
>   Be blown about the desert dust,
>   Or seal'd within the iron hills?[64]

Tennyson says that evil and suffering are at odds with the idea that God loves the world and all its creatures. He wonders why we should consider God loving if evolution, "red in tooth and claw," apparently does not care whether single individuals or even entire species go extinct as fossils and dust. Tennyson raises in poetic form the problem of evil in light of the evolutionary story. The problem emerges just as intensely in our own personal losses, tragedies, and encounters with gross injustice. Whether due to the widespread occurrence of apparently genuine evil in the long evolutionary history or the specific occurrence of evil in our own lives, belief in a loving God seems in need of justification today more than ever.[65]

Some believe they can evade the problem of evil by suggesting that God does not cause evil. Free creaturely choices gone awry and the general constraints inherent in any finite structure cause evil. But these answers are not enough. Believing that God is not the cause of evil does not solve the problem of evil. Genuinely evil events that produce human and nonhuman suffering demand an answer for why a loving and powerful God fails to prevent such evils.

64. Alfred Lord Tennyson, "In Memoriam" (55–56), 1850.

65. For a summary of the arguments for why evolutionary history intensifies the problem of evil, see Jeffrey P. Schloss, "Neo-Darwinism: Scientific Account and Theological Attributions," in *Back to Darwin: A Richer Account of Evolution*, ed. John B. Cobb Jr. (Grand Rapids: Eerdmans, 2008).

The typical view of divine power is that God has the inherent capacity to prevent evil events single-handedly, should God so choose. The standard answers for why God chooses not to prevent these events—evil is an illusion, evil is required for greater good, evil develops character, evil is a mystery—are ultimately unsatisfactory. Evolution suggests that widespread suffering does not always make the world a better place. Radical creaturely suffering outweighs possible creaturely benefits from learning through suffering. Suffering extends well beyond what seems necessary for the evolution of life. Particular instances of evil—say, the rape of a sister or the invasion of cancer in a son's young life—demand an answer.[66] An adequate account of God's love requires an explanation of genuine evil.

One recent attempt to tackle the problem of evil has gained influence among Christian scholars exploring the interface between science and theology. This theory draws from a short passage in the Christian Scriptures in which the writer speaks of God's self-giving love (Phil. 2:5–8). The word used to describe this divine self-giving is *kenosis* (from the Greek verb *kenoō* in Phil. 2:7). Biblical scholars do not agree about how best to conceive of kenosis, but many interpret it as divine self-limitation for the sake of others.

A collection of essays, *The Work of Love: Creation as Kenosis*, explores what kenosis might contribute to the dialogue between science and theology in general and to solving the problem of evil in particular. Kenosis theory champions divine love while reconceiving God's power. Most of the book's contributors reject divine unilateralism and affirm a crucial role for free creaturely contributions. In its most robust form, kenosis theory avoids the God-of-the-gaps problem created by the natural/supernatural scheme. Kenosis contends that creatures invariably rely on God's creative self-giving for their existence in general and for their ability to love in particular.

John Polkinghorne, the book's editor, adopts kenosis as an affirmation of God's voluntary self-limitation that allows creatures

66. For a powerful exploration of God's love and suffering from a womanist theologian, see Karen Baker-Fletcher, *Dancing with God: The Trinity from a Womanist Perspective* (St. Louis: Chalice Press, 2006). For an accessible exploration of evil and ultimate answer that is similar to my own, see Tyron L. Inbody, *The Transforming God: An Interpretation of Suffering and Evil* (Louisville: Westminster John Knox, 1997).

to enjoy power and freedom. We explored Polkinghorne's view of divine self-limitation briefly in the preceding chapter. The affirmation of divine kenosis as described in the book provides grounds to argue, says Polkinghorne, that "no longer can God be held to be totally and directly responsible for all that happens."[67]

Polkinghorne's notion of divine voluntary self-limitation is, he remarks, "quite different from Process Theology's conception of an external metaphysical constraint upon the power of deity"; this kenotic vision maintains "that nothing imposes conditions on God from the outside."[68] Divine voluntary self-limitation also differs from what Polkinghorne calls "Classical Theology's picture of God." Classical theology envisioned God "in total control" and invulnerable, "such that there is no reciprocal effect of creatures upon the divine nature, of the kind that a truly loving relationship would seem to imply."[69] God calls on creatures to play some role in their own creation. "The kenotic Creator may not overrule creatures, but the continuous Creator must interact with creation."[70] The word "interact" is preferable to "intervene," says Polkinghorne, because the latter carries "connotations of arbitrary interruption."[71] There is an unavoidable cost in God's choosing to interact and not interrupt free creaturely contributions. "Creatures will behave in accordance with their natures," he says, which means that "lions will kill their prey; earthquakes will happen; volcanoes will erupt and rivers flood."[72]

Polkinghorne admits that his scheme does not solve all the problems of theodicy. He believes, however, that it tempers many problems by removing the suspicion that God is incompetent or indifferent. Polkinghorne summarizes his view by saying that God allows

the created other to be and to act, so that, while all that happens is permitted by God's general providence, not all that happens is in accordance with God's will or brought about by divine special providence. Such an understanding is basic to the interpretation of evolutionary history as creation's making of itself. Such an under-

67. Polkinghorne, *Work of Love*, 95.
68. Ibid.
69. Ibid.
70. Ibid., 96.
71. Ibid., 100.
72. Ibid., 95.

standing is also basic to theodicy's disclaimer that God does not will the act of a murderer or the destructive force of an earthquake, but allows both to happen in a world in which divine power is deliberately self-limited to allow causal space for creatures.[73]

God's exercise of love and power emerges from "the interior 'constraints' of the self-consistency of the divine nature."[74] Divine voluntary self-limitation maintains God's total benevolence by qualifying, in a kenotic way, the operation of God's power.

I find the general theory of kenosis helpful. As typically presented, however, it does not provide an adequate solution to the problem of evil. We briefly explored this inadequacy in relation to voluntary divine self-limitation in the last chapter, and Polkinghorne admits that his version of kenosis theodicy is not entirely satisfactory. I argue that his version of kenosis theodicy cannot provide an adequate solution to the problem of evil, because the God whose self-limitation is wholly voluntary in relation to free creatures remains culpable for failing to prevent genuinely evil occurrences. It is not enough to say that God does not cause but merely allows genuine evil to occur. The God who allows genuine evil despite possessing the capacity to stop it remains culpable for failing to prevent the occurrence of genuine evil.

Divine kenosis as understood by Polkinghorne entails that God retains the capacity to withdraw or override the freedom of others should God so choose. The God whose self-limitation involves retaining the capacity to veto creaturely freedom is the God who ought to become un–self-limited, from time to time, to stop the horrors that innocent victims endure. To put it another way: the God capable of restraining creaturely freedom ought to do so occasionally in the name of love. Vetoing the power of evildoers, if such vetoing is possible, is sometimes if not always the loving thing to do.

Polkinghorne is right, however, to be wary of solutions to the problem of evil suggesting that some force outside of or greater than God imposes metaphysical limitations. Versions of process theology

73. Ibid., 102.
74. Ibid., 96. For arguments similar to Polkinghorne's, see William Hasker, *Providence, Evil, and the Openness of God* (London: Routledge, 2004); idem, *The Triumph of God over Evil: Theodicy for a World of Suffering* (Downers Grove, IL: InterVarsity, 2008).

that suppose an external metaphysical constraint or the imposition of outside conditions on God's power ought to be rejected.[75] I do not find satisfying theodicies requiring that external constraints be placed on God. We best solve the problem of evil by rethinking God's own character and relations—what Polkinghorne refers to as the interior constraints of the self-consistency of the divine nature—rather than suggesting that an outside dominating opposition confines God.

The alternative that I suggest agrees with kenosis adherents who say that the three-word sentence "God is love" resides at the heart of the highest revelation of God. Like most Christians, I believe that Jesus Christ best reveals this truth in his life, words, ministry, death, and resurrection. The best of the Christian tradition also confirms the supreme importance of divine love. Some other religious traditions point, in their own ways, to love as crucial for understanding the nature and activity of God.[76] Our own experiences and reasoning capacities suggest that the being whose superior cannot be conceived of would be a being whose primary attribute is love. God's loving actions are expressions of a loving divine nature.

My alternative also agrees with Polkinghorne that creatures possess a measure of freedom. This freedom is a necessary feature in the part each creature plays when contributing to its own coming to be and self-organization. This freedom is God-given in each moment, but this freedom is never unlimited. Freedom always arises in relations and obligations, with restraints and restrictions unique to the agent and circumstances.

We have seen throughout this book that love requires relations with others. Agents cannot express love in absolute isolation; love is inherently relational. Loving actions require intentional sympathetic responses to others with whom the lover possesses relations, and love involves promoting the well-being of those with whom the lover relates. God has revealed this relational love in many ways. Christians typically claim Jesus of Nazareth most profoundly revealed this relational God. God's relational love is revealed in many other ways and in many traditions, and God's omnipresence provides the basis for this widespread witness.

75. It should be noted that not all process theodicies rely on the view that conditions outside God place restraints on God. My criticism pertains only to those that do so rely.

76. See Oord, *Science of Love*, chap. 1.

If love is an essential divine property and love always requires relations, we should conclude that God requires relations with others. To put it succinctly: divine relatedness is an aspect of the divine essence.[77] Just as God did not voluntarily decide various features of God's own nature, God does not voluntarily decide to be relational. To relate to all others is essential to what it means to be God. God does not depend on relations to creatures to exist, of course. God exists necessarily. But the ways in which creatures respond to God affect the moment-by-moment constitution of the divine life.

Some Christian theologians agree that relational love is a necessary aspect of the divine essence, but they argue that God only necessarily loves others in the Trinity. Love for creatures, they claim, is contingent on God's wholly voluntary decision. Love for those in the Trinity is necessary; love for those in the universe is arbitrary.

The hypothesis I offer, by contrast, claims that God necessarily relates to and loves all creatures.[78] God has necessarily related to and loves whatever God creates,[79] and God everlastingly creates, relates, and loves. Those who consider relations within the Godhead a crucial element in an adequate doctrine of God should not regard my hypothesis as a rival view, however. One may or may not argue that God relates necessarily within the Trinity. One can affirm both that God necessarily relates within the Trinity and that God necessarily relates to creatures. The two ideas are not mutually exclusive.

77. See the final chapter of my book *Nature of Love*.

78. This alternative admittedly entails various metaphysical consequences pertaining to divine power and creaturely freedom, but these consequences arise from the divine essence and are not imposed by outside conditions.

79. My hypothesis entails the idea that the world was not created out of absolutely nothing, and *creatio ex nihilo* should be abandoned. It should be abandoned because of its shaky theological, scriptural, historical, scientific, and philosophical grounds. For work related to the inadequacy of *creatio ex nihilo*, see Sjoerd L. Bonting, *Chaos Theology: A Revised Creation Theology* (Ottawa: Novalis, 2002); James Edward Huchingson, *Pandemonium Tremendum: Chaos and Mystery in the Life of God* (Cleveland: Pilgrim Press, 2000); David Ray Griffin, "Creation out of Chaos and the Problem of Evil," in *Encountering Evil: Live Options in Theodicy*, ed. Stephen T. Davis, 2nd ed. (Atlanta: John Knox, 1981); Catherine Keller, *The Face of the Deep: A Theology of Becoming* (New York: Routledge, 2003); Michael E. Lodahl, "Out of Nothing's Womb Produce: Is Next-to-Nothing Enough?—or Is It Too Much?" in *God of Nature and of Grace*, 77–106.

Some theologians mistakenly argue that if God requires relations with the creaturely universe, God would cease existing if the universe were to cease existing. This argument does not follow, however, if God exists necessarily. After all, a being that exists necessarily requires nothing outside itself to exist. I argue that God exists necessarily. I suggest that a scheme supposing that God necessarily and everlastingly relates to some creaturely world or another is preferable to a scheme that claims God's relations to the world are accidental or arbitrary.[80] Only the God who necessarily relates to the world should be said to love the world essentially. The God whose relations with the world are arbitrary should be said to love the world arbitrarily.

I earlier called God the "ideal contributor." God's contributory call entails empowering and inspiring creatures, and God perfectly empowers and inspires. I proposed that all creatures feel God's oscillating and diverse, yet direct, causal call.[81] The notion of kenosis corresponds with the notion that God is the ideal contributor, and therefore this aspect of my solution reflects its kenotic basis. God gives the gift that creatures need to live, love, and have their being.

The notion that God is the ideal contributor also plays an important role in the solution to the problem of evil. I speculate that God provides power and freedom to all creatures capable of self-determination, and God does so each moment of each creature's life.

We might call this divine action "prevenient grace," to use the language common in Wesleyan theology. God acts first (preveniently) to initiate each moment in a creature's life, and God provides the power and freedom that creatures require. All creatures are utterly dependent on God. God provides freedom to each agent, and each agent responds freely to the varied choices that each faces.

---

80. If one were to attack the concept of the social Trinity by claiming that the Trinity would fail to exist if one member were to expire, that person would commit the same conceptual error as the error committed by those who claim that the God who necessarily exists would expire should some world or another expire.

81. Among the better collections of writing on divine action in science are Philip Clayton, *Adventures in the Spirit: God, World, and Divine Action*, ed. Zachary R. Simpson (Minneapolis: Fortress, 2008); Robert John Russell, Nancey Murphy, and Arthur R. Peacocke, eds., *Chaos and Complexity: Scientific Perspectives on Divine Action*, 2nd ed. (Vatican City State: Vatican Observatory Foundation; Berkeley, CA: Center for Theology and the Natural Sciences, 2000).

Theologian Randy Maddox calls divine initiating action that requires creaturely freedom "response-able grace."[82] One may also call it cooperation-empowering grace.

The key to solving the problem of evil is my claim that God's prevenient provision of the power for freedom to every creature is a provision that derives from God's essence. This means that prevenient grace is a necessary, not wholly voluntary or arbitrary, aspect of deity. Because God necessarily provides freedom to all individuals as God essentially relates to them, it makes no sense to suggest that God could fail to provide freedom and power. God's essential relatedness to and omnipresence in creation entails that God cannot withdraw, fail to offer, or override the freedom that God necessarily gives creatures each moment. God's loving gift of freedom derives from God's very nature.

My proposal shares affinities with how Maddox talks about John Wesley's understanding of divine power. He writes:

> Perhaps the best way to capture Wesley's conviction . . . is to say that he construed God's power or sovereignty fundamentally in terms of *empowerment* rather than control or *overpowerment*. This is not to weaken God's power but to determine its character! As Wesley was fond of saying, God works "strongly and sweetly."[83]

I refer to Maddox's characterization of Wesley to suggest that God's inspiring and empowering of others is fundamental to God's nature. To say it another way: gifting others is part of what it means to be God. Deity does not overpower creatures, in the sense of vetoing creaturely freedom. God does not withdraw or fail to offer freedom. God cannot do so, because those acts would violate the love God expresses from God's own essence.

As the ideal contributor, God empowers and invites others to love. God does not coerce others. The word *coerce*, as I use it, refers to complete control over or unilateral determination. To coerce is to determine an event or agent unilaterally. A freedom-giving lover

---

82. Maddox, *Responsible Grace*. Barry L. Callen calls this "loving grace" (see *God as Loving Grace*). John B. Cobb Jr. agrees, titling his book on divine love and creaturely response *Grace and Responsibility: A Wesleyan Theology for Today* (Nashville: Abingdon, 1995).

83. Maddox, *Responsible Grace*, 55.

cannot coerce if that lover's nature is freedom-giving love. God's empowering and inspiring is always persuasive.[84] Words that we might use to describe this persuasive action include *call, lead, lure, woo, appeal, attract, nudge,* and *encourage.* These words suggest that God does not and, I claim, cannot fully control creatures. It is not God's nature to control others entirely.

At this point, my solution to the problem of evil should be apparent. The loving God who essentially relates and necessarily provides freedom to all creatures is not culpable for failing to prevent the evil that free creaturely choices generates. God cannot be culpable, because God essentially and lovingly relates to all creatures by providing power for freedom, as limited as this freedom may be in some less-complex creatures. God could no more choose to cease existing than choose to cease providing freedom to those with whom God lovingly relates. The genuine evil of the world results from debilitating choices that these empowered creatures make or the natural constraints that come with finitude. I submit that this proposal solves the theoretical aspect of the problem of evil.[85]

One might say that my solution to the problem of evil arises from my speculation about the power of divine love. I would agree, as long as we distinguish this solution from some that speak of the power of divine love. Some solutions are of the same type as Polkinghorne's version of kenosis. They claim that God is voluntarily self-limited when providing freedom to creatures. The move I propose provides theologians with a way to overcome the inher-

---

84. Important research into how divine power might best be understood is found in Anna Case-Winters, *God's Power: Traditional Understandings and Contemporary Challenges* (Louisville: Westminster John Knox, 1990).

85. Some distinguish between moral evil and natural evil. Examples of moral evil include murder and incest, whereas natural evils include things such as hurricanes and earthquakes. I postulate, however, that a measure of self-determination extends even to the most fundamental elements of existence. This supposition allows one to generalize that the same explanation for why God does not prevent moral evil applies to why God does not prevent natural evil. God cannot prevent both, because providing power and freedom to others, whether those others are complex or simple, is part and parcel of God's unchanging nature. This view is different from and, I believe, superior to the important work on theodicy and evolution relying on eschatology found in Robert John Russell, *Cosmology: From Alpha to Omega; The Creative Mutual Interaction of Theology and Science* (Minneapolis: Fortress, 2008).

ent weakness of the claim that a self-limited deity fails to become un–self-limited, in the name of love, to prevent genuine evil. It provides a coherent way to claim that God's nature is love, and God loves creatures necessarily. Divine causation lovingly provides the power and freedom necessary for creatures to respond. When creatures respond well to providential divine love, the well-being of the world increases and creatures enjoy abundant life. When creatures respond poorly by using their God-given freedom wrongly, the world's well-being decreases and genuine evils occur.

This vision proffers a God whose essence is love, who necessarily "self-empties" or "self-offers" as a moment-by-moment cause among causes, and who relates with creatures that possess God-given freedom. God's self-emptying is a necessary part of what it means for God to relate to, create, and empower creatures. This self-emptying is an essential property of God and does not entail voluntary self-limitation. The loving God of this kenosis theory is not culpable for failing to prevent genuine evil. One way to identify my alternative is to label it "involuntary divine self-limitation" as opposed to "voluntary divine self-limitation." This label suggests that God is not limited due either to arbitrary divine choice or to external factors. Divine self-limitation is an inherent aspect of God's loving nature.

But perhaps the best label for the proposal I offer is "Essential kenosis" theodicy. Essential kenosis meets Polkinghorne's criterion that nothing imposes conditions on God from the outside. In my scheme, God is self-limited in the sense that external constraints do not impose on God's inability to control others. Instead, this inability derives from God's loving nature. Giving gifts to others, including the power for self-determination, is by definition part of what it means to be a loving and relational God. A gift giver whose essence is love cannot do other than give and receive loving gifts and empower others to give and receive lovingly as well. God is essentially kenotic.[86]

Conclusion

The love, science, and theology symbiosis is most effective when it takes seriously research and hypotheses in both science and

86. See the final chapter of Oord, *Nature of Love.*

theology. Throughout this book, I have addressed central issues in the love research program. My work has been descriptive of what is occurring in the natural and social sciences. My work also has been prescriptive: I offer a definition of love, explore how the love archetypes might best be understood to relate and suggest how we ought to regard love of self in relation to loving others.

In this chapter, I looked at the contribution that theology might make to love research. I offered my own proposal of what a theology of love might look like in light of research in the social and natural sciences. I showed the importance of the parenthetical phrase "including God" found in the definition of love offered in earlier chapters. I explored what role God plays in the creaturely promotion of overall well-being. I concluded with a solution—essential kenosis theodicy—to the theoretical aspect of the most vexing problem that humans face: the problem of evil. Much of my work in this final chapter was prescriptive.

Throughout this book, I have drawn only occasionally from the rich resource of the Christian tradition. As one who self-identifies as Christian and who has been strongly influenced by the Christian tradition, I recognize that my biases have shaped my arguments at least to some degree. I do not apologize for this. My arguments may nonetheless enjoy wide appeal. They may appeal to those who identify closely with Christianity, to those who identify closely with some other theistic tradition, and even to those who do not identify closely with any religious tradition at all. I hope to show in a future publication, however, the strong grounding that the Christian Scriptures and traditions provide for the claims presented in this final chapter. But that project must await another day.

I believe I have shown that a clear definition of love and love research in the natural and social sciences is crucial for constructive work in theology and ethics. A strong definition of love and the diverse scientific research on love and altruism should inform any adequate theology of love. The symbiotic work in science, philosophy, theology, and ethics proves profoundly beneficial for a personal, communal, and global turn to love. And we need a turn to love now more than ever.

Author Index

Subject Index

sacrificial love, 10
Schloss, Jeffrey P., 127–28
science
  compatible with theology, 175–82
  defining, 6–11
  love, science, and theology symbiosis,
    5–6, 29, 139–40
  and postmodernism, 7n11
Scripture, Christian, 35n13, 36nn14–15,
  37
self-deception, 125
self-determination, in love, 17–18,
  129–35
Selfish Gene, The (Dawkins), 121–24
"selfish-gene" theory, 120–24
self-love, 47, 48
self-organization theory, 165
self-realization and affirmation, 41
self-renunciation ethic, 144–51
self-sacrifice, 36, 40–42, 107
Seligman, Martin E. P., 69
sensory organs, 7
sexual activity, 46–47, 48
Shaver, Phillip R., 72–73
Sober, Elliott, 108–9, 119–20
social instincts, 104–5, 106, 114
  See also empathy
*Social Psychology of Prosocial Behavior,
  The* (Dovidio et al.), 79
social science, 8n14
sociobiology, 119
Sociobiology: The New Synthesis (Wilson), 119
*Some Do Care: Contemporary Lives
  of Moral Commitment* (Colby and
  Damon), 94
Sternberg, Robert J., 66, 67
storge, 32n2, 67, 68
string theory, 171–72
sympathetic response
  love as, 19–23

tĕhôm, 164–65
Teilhard de Chardin, Pierre, 138n2
Templeton Foundation, 3
Tennyson, Alfred, 201–2
theocosmocentrism, 192–94

theodicy, 204–5, 210n85
theology
  love, science, and theology symbiosis,
    5–6, 29, 139–40
  relational, 190–92
  scientific research compatible with,
    175–82
  See also creation theology
Theophilus of Antioch, 158
Thomas Aquinas, 25
tit-for-tat altruism. *See* reciprocal
  altruism
Tjeltveit, Alan C., 91
Tooby, John, 112
Trinity, 208n80
Trivers, Robert, 110–11

universe
  big bang theory, 140–41, 152, 169
  causation of, 139–44
  creatio ex nihilo, 152–59, 160, 163–64,
    207n79
  creation from chaos, 160–66
  endless universe theory, 167–72
  kenotic nature of, 145–51
  origin and expansion, 151–59
unlimited love, 4, 198
Unto Others: The Evolution and Psychology of Unselfish Behavior
  (Sober and Wilson), 108

Valentinus, 157
values, 6, 9
variation, biological, 99–100, 116–17
virtues development, 90–96

Waal, Frans de, 106–7
Watson, James, 117
*Ways and Power of Love: Types, Factors, and Techniques of Moral
  Transformation, The* (Sorokin), 2,
  3n3
well-being, overall
  acting for, 198–99
  and *agape,* 43
  and *eros,* 47–48
  and evolutionary theory, 101